INFAMOUS MURDERS

INFAMOUS MURDERS

TREASURE PRESS

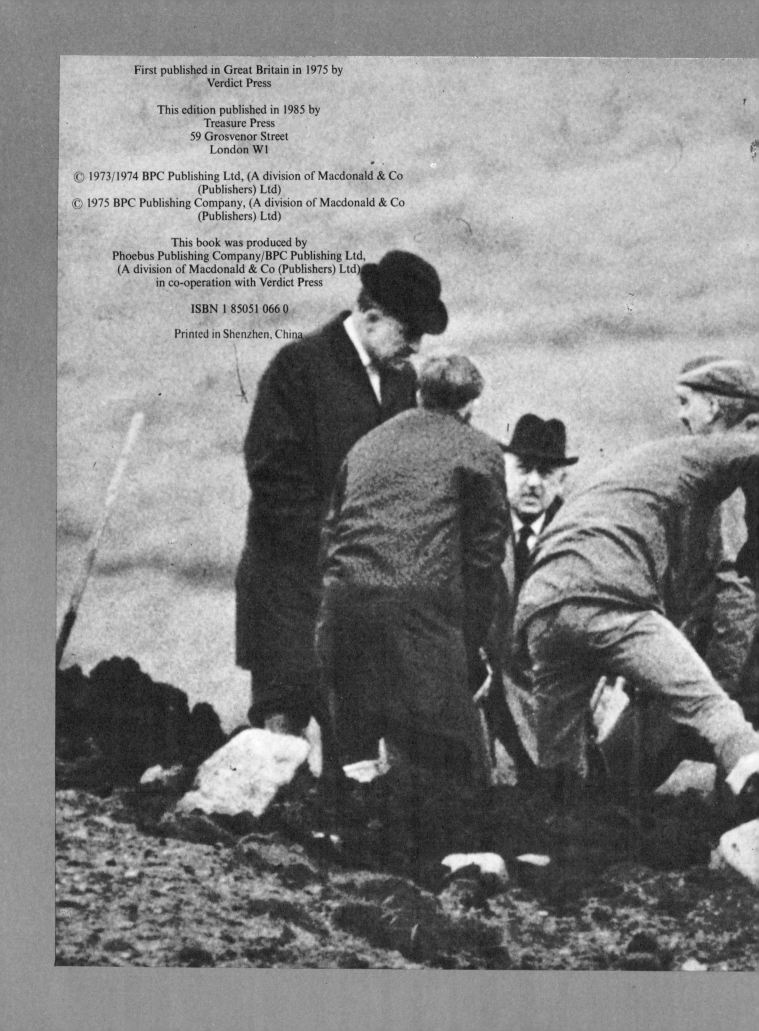

First published in Great Britain in 1975 by
Verdict Press

This edition published in 1985 by
Treasure Press
59 Grosvenor Street
London W1

© 1973/1974 BPC Publishing Ltd, (A division of Macdonald & Co
(Publishers) Ltd)
© 1975 BPC Publishing Company, (A division of Macdonald & Co
(Publishers) Ltd)

This book was produced by
Phoebus Publishing Company/BPC Publishing Ltd,
(A division of Macdonald & Co (Publishers) Ltd)
in co-operation with Verdict Press

ISBN 1 85051 066 0

Printed in Shenzhen, China

CONTENTS

FOREWORD

Ever since Cain slew Abel, the murder of a fellow human being has been regarded, in all societies, as a crime of exceptional horror. Often it was punished by the death penalty, even when capital punishment had been abolished for other offences; the shadow of the gallows in Britain, the guillotine in France, or the electric chair in the United States gave to trials for murder an extraordinary drama.

For what reasons have men—and women too— steeled their hearts and subdued their normal human instincts in order to commit what Shakespeare called 'that bloody sin . . . murder most foul'?

Some have done it from perverted sexual impulses, like Jack the Ripper who cut out his victims' sexual organs; or Neville Heath who flogged his women with a riding whip. Some have done it for money, like Bonnie and Clyde who shot bank clerks as casually as pigeons while they grabbed the cash over the counter; or Raymond Fernandez and his unattractive mistress who swindled lonely women out of their life's savings before disposing of them.

Some have killed to remove an unwanted wife or husband. Some have killed for no apparent reason at all; these provide the most extraordinary cases of all with stories that almost beggar the imagination, like the squalid pair who tortured and killed a little girl before burying her (near some others, it is rumoured) in the Yorkshire moors; or the drug-demented hippies of Charles Manson's 'family', for whom right and wrong had ceased to have any meaning.

Society feels a strong instinct that murderers must be brought to justice, and so a special curiosity attaches to crimes that have remained unsolved. Did Lizzie Borden wield a hatchet to strike down her father and mother? Did William Wallace batter his wife's brains out? They were both cleared in courts of law. The murderers of these victims walked free, and others too; the killers of Marilyn Sheppard and of Elizabeth Short are probably still alive, walking the streets, rubbing shoulders even with some readers of this book.

SEXUAL MURDERS

EAST END SLAUGHTERS

Jack the Ripper

All London was aghast
in the hot summer and autumn of 1888.
A madman was on the loose—
a madman with a knife
and a perverted sense of humour.
And police seemed helpless . . .

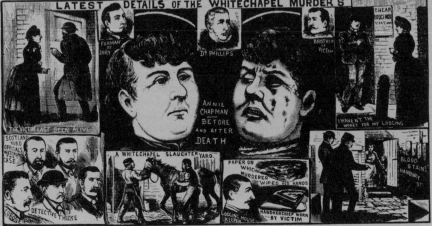

IT WAS lunchtime when the police—Inspector Beck and a young detective named Walter Dew—arrived at the scene of the crime. A light but steady rain was falling, and an inquisitive band of onlookers had gathered outside the entrance of No. 13 Miller's Court, in London's East End. On the inside, in a cramped and squalid room, lay the butchered remains of prostitute Mary Kelly—the sixth and final victim of Jack the Ripper.

The spectators knew of her death, but they didn't yet know the extent and nature of her injuries . . . how she had been cut up as though she were a specimen for dissection . . . how bits of her flesh were hung on picture-nails on the walls . . . how she had been ritually disembowelled . . . how her heart and kidneys had been placed on a table beside her severed breasts . . . how her face had been slashed beyond recognition . . . how her nose and ears had been sliced off and her throat slit.

Bloodbath

As he gazed through a broken window at the bloodbath—"It was more like a slaughterhouse than a room"—Inspector Beck paled, retched, and staggered backwards. "For God's sake, Dew, don't look!" he gasped. But Dew (later to win fame as the officer who arrested Crippen) ignored his superior's warning and took the other's place at the opening. He looked beyond the bread and soft drinks bottles, past the print of "The Fisherman's Widow", and at the naked body.

"What I saw when I pushed back an old coat and peeped through a broken pane of glass into the sordid little room which Kelly called her home," he wrote afterwards, "was too harrowing to be described. It remains with me—and always will remain—as the most gruesome memory of the whole of my police career."

The date was Friday, November 9, 1888, the day of the Lord Mayor's Show, which passed not far away from the building in which Mary was found. While the news of the killing of the 25-year-old whore—who a few hours earlier had still been attractive, her features not yet raddled by disease or drink—spread throughout the crowds, the police decided to break into the room. It had been blocked behind the door by a heavy chest of drawers, and the officers used a pick-axe to gain entrance.

The policemen deduced that the Ripper had spent some two hours cutting the girl up. He had escaped by the window, leaving Mary Kelly—who was pregnant—to be discovered by the first interested person (a rent collector, as it happened). As soon as the detectives had finished their preliminary examination it was the turn of the doctors to make what they could of the corpse.

It took a team of surgeons six hours to

piece the organs and shreds of flesh together. When the body bore some resemblance to that of a dead human being, the photographers moved in—and took pictures of the remains from every side and angle. They even—following a theory popular at the time—photographed Mary Kelly's eyes thinking the image of her murderer would be recorded on them.

Meanwhile, as the dead woman was placed on the public death-cart and taken to Shoreditch Mortuary, news came that the Commissioner of the Metropolitan Police, Sir Charles Warren, had resigned—and that Sir Robert Anderson had taken his place. This was learnt too late to stop Sir Charles's bloodhounds from nosing into the court, baying wildly, excited by the smell of blood.

Four days later, when an inquiry into the killing was held by the Shoreditch coroner, *The Times* put into black and white what many people in the capital were thinking—and some were saying. "When evidence is not to be had, theories abound. Even the most plausible of them do now carry conviction; but enough is not known to justify search being made in certain specific directions. In this, as in the other crimes of the same character, ordinary motives are out of the question.

Bank Holiday Monday

"No hope of plunder could have induced the murderer to kill one who, it is clear, was reduced to such extremity of want that she thought of destroying herself. The body bore the marks of the frenzy and fury which characterized the previous murders. An appetite for blood, a love of carnage for itself, could only explain what has been done. And there are the same indications of dexterity, if not anatomical skill, such as would be possessed only by one accustomed to handling the knife."

The cry for the Ripper's blood was taken up by Queen Victoria, dwelling in gloomy widowhood in Scotland's Balmoral Castle. In a sharp note to the British Prime Minister, the Marquis of Salisbury, she stated: "This new most ghastly murder shows the absolute necessity for some very decided action. All these courts must be lit, and our detectives improved."

Earlier, after receiving a catch-the-Ripper petition signed by some 5000 women of the East End—"we would also beg that Your Majesty will . . . close bad houses within whose walls such wickedness is done and men and women ruined in body and soul"—the Queen had turned her displeasure on the Home Secretary.

"Have the cattleboats and passenger boats been examined?" she demanded. "Has any investigation been made as to the number of single men occupying rooms to themselves? The murderer's

clothes must be saturated with blood and must be kept somewhere. Is there sufficient surveillance at night?"

Although she got no immediate satisfaction from her ministers, she did attract the attention of the Ripper himself. On November 21, in a letter sent to the magistrates at Thames Police Court, the killer—who, according to the postmark, was in Portsmouth—wrote chirpily:

"Dear Boss, It is no use for you to look for me in London because I'm not there. Don't trouble yourself about me until I return, which will not be very long. I like the work too well to leave it alone. Oh, it was a jolly job the last one. I had plenty of time to do it properly in. Ha, ha, ha! The next lot I mean to do with

WINDPIPE SEVERED, Elizabeth Stride, a 45-year-old prostitute, died in Berners Street. The Ripper had apparently been interrupted at his work.

vengeance, cut off their head and arms. You think it is a man with a black moustache. Ha, ha, ha! When I have done another one you can try and catch me again. So goodbye, dear Boss, till I return. Yours, Jack the Ripper."

The man who terrorized the East End of London for three months in the autumn of 1888 made his debut on the night of August 6, the Bank Holiday Monday. At the time the area—a sprawling slum described by the American novelist Jack London as a "Social Abyss . . . [where men] live worse than the beasts, and have less to eat and wear and protect them from the elements than [savages]"—contained the "flotsam of humanity".

Some 15,000 men, women and children were homeless, another 130,000 were in workhouses, and the foggy streets, alleyways, courts and yards were prowled by more than 80,000 prostitutes. These

women—who usually looked some 15 to 20 years older than they were—would go to bed with a man for sixpence, and would accept a penny if it was nearing 3 a.m. and that was all he had.

Such a person was 35-year-old Martha Turner, who on the Monday evening had been drinking with some soldiers in pubs along the riverside in Limehouse. She needed money for a bed for the night, but it is not known whether or not she got it from one of the young men—who belonged to the regiment guarding the Tower of London. What *is* known, however, is that Martha's slashed body (there were 39 knife wounds on it) was found lying on the first landing of George Yard Buildings in Commercial Street early on the Tuesday morning. "Whoever it was," said the examining doctor, "he knew how and where to cut."

Carved to death

The Ripper had struck, and it took him 24 days (a long time by his standards) to strike again. This time the prostitute he chose to carve to death was even less prepossessing than Martha Turner. Mary Ann Nicholls, 42, with five of her front teeth missing, badly needed fourpence for a doss-house bed on the night of August 31. Drunk and wearing what she called a "jolly, new bonnet", she was last seen alive staggering around the vicinity of Bucks Row. She was next seen dead, disembowelled and with her throat hacked across, at 3.45 a.m.

In a report in the *Star* newspaper it was stated that, "No murder was ever more ferociously and more brutally done. The knife, which must have been a large and sharp one, was jabbed into the deceased at the lower part of the abdomen, and then drawn upwards, not once but twice. The first cut veered to the right, slitting up the groin, and passing over the left hip, but the second cut went straight upward, along the centre of the body, and reaching to the breast-bone. Such horrible work could only be the deed of a maniac."

At the inquest on Mrs. Nicholls it was suggested by a medical witness that the murderer was left-handed, and that the wounds were "deftly and . . . skilfully performed". Those who knew the dead woman betrayed no surprise at her savage end. "She was a dissolute character and a drunkard," said her father. But her estranged husband, William Nicholls, a labourer, showed more sympathy when he identified the body. Looking down on the corpse, he said brokenly, "I forgive you for what you did to me, now that I find you like this."

For his third scarlet woman victim the Ripper settled upon 47-year-old Annie Chapman, known to her friends as "Dark Annie". This time there was a gap of

only eight days between killings, and it was late on September 7 when Annie found herself without a client and with nowhere to sleep. Midnight came and went, and at two in the morning she was turned away from her usual doss-house in Dorset Street. The keeper dismissed her with an abrupt, "No money, no bed", and scoffed at her reply: "I haven't got it. I am weak and ill and have been in the infirmary."

She stumbled wearily off to No. 29 Hanbury Street, and passed through a passage leading to the backyard – where fellow prostitutes sometimes conducted their business, and where drunks went to be sick or to sleep it off. It was there – after a dawn cry of "Murder!" – that she was discovered, with her entrails hanging out, near the ground-floor room of a woman who sold cat's meat. The murder had been carried out as viciously and diabolically as before, but this time there was a macabre difference: two new farthings, various other coins, and two brass rings were laid around her feet in the form of a sacrifice.

The wife of a veterinary surgeon who had left her because of her drinking, Mrs. Chapman was regarded as being a rung or two above the other East Enders. The details of her death – "the abdomen had been entirely laid open; the intestines . . . had been lifted out of the body, and placed on the shoulder of the corpse"

EIGHTY-FOUR YEARS ON. The last picture of 29 Hanbury Street before it was demolished in 1972. Here Annie Chapman, victim number three, was murdered.

– were fully given in the medical journal, *The Lancet*. The knife used, it was stated, must have been "at least five inches long", and the Coroner declared: "An unskilled person could not have done this, only someone used to the post-mortem room."

The head, it was revealed, had been almost severed, and a handkerchief tied round the neck to stop it from being "sucked into her throat". The blood must have cascaded like a fountain, and this led *The Times* to ask how the murderer could have made his getaway – going back along the passage through the house – "reeking with blood, and yet . . . he must have walked in broad daylight along streets comparatively well frequented, even at that early hour, without his startling appearance attracting attention".

Public outcry

The newspaper answered its own question by concluding: "He is a man lodging in a comparatively decent house in the district, to which he would be able to retire quickly, and in which, once it was reached, he would be able at his leisure to remove from his person all traces of his hideous crime." Other, less reputable, journals took up the call, and the walls

of the East End suddenly bloomed with vividly coloured hoardings about the "incomparable and elusive" killer.

The satirical magazine *Punch* took serious exception to this, and blustered: "Imagine the effect of these gigantic pictures of violence and assassination by knife . . . on the morbid imaginations of imbalanced minds. These hideous picture-posters are a blot on our civilization, and a disgrace to the drama"; while *The Times* became even more socially conscious and announced that: "London at large is responsible for Whitechapel and its dens of crime. If the luxury and wealth of the west cannot find some means of mitigating the squalor and crime of the east, we shall have to abate our faith in the resources of civilization."

George Bernard Shaw, then a novelist and music critic, joined in the denunciations in a letter to the *Star*. "Less than a year ago the West End Press were literally clamouring for the blood of the people – hounding on Sir Charles Warren to thrash and muzzle the scum who dared to complain they were starving – heaping insult and reckless calumny upon those who interceded for the victims – applauding to the skies the open class bias of the magistrates and judges . . . behaving, in short, as the propertied class always does when the workers . . . show their teeth."

Sir Charles Warren, however, was

9

more generally regarded as being, morally, as villainous as the Ripper. A former military man with experience of handling troops in Egypt, he treated his policemen as if they were perpetually on parade. He had more faith in bloodhounds than detectives, and had two champion dogs — Burgho and Barnaby — specially trained for their duties in Hyde Park. After tracking down innocent strangers and, on one occasion, a plain-clothes officer, the hounds proved their ultimate futility when brought panting to Miller's Court.

"Double Event"

Before that, Sir Charles's deputy, Assistant Commissioner Sir Robert Anderson, displayed his indifference to the murders by taking a month's holiday in Switzerland, and later wrote in his memoirs that: "When the stolid English go in for a scare they take leave of all moderation and common sense. If nonsense were solid, the nonsense that was talked and written about these murders would sink a Dreadnought." And, in a magazine article, he blamed the extreme public interest in the Ripper on the Press.

"At the time," he pontificated, "the sensation-mongers of the newspaper press fostered the belief that life in London was no longer safe, and that no woman ought to venture abroad in the streets after nightfall, and one enterprising journalist went so far as to impersonate the cause of all this terror as 'Jack the Ripper', the name by which he will probably go down in history. But no amount of silly hysteria would alter the fact that these crimes were a cause of danger only to a particular section of a small and definite class of women in a limited district of the East End."

This complacency was soon shattered by the Ripper when he performed his famous "Double Event", which accentuated the words of the Whitechapel Vigilance Committee (formed after the death of Annie Chapman) that: "Finding that, in spite of murders being committed in our midst, the police force is inadequate to discover the author or authors of the late atrocities, we . . . intend offering a substantial reward to anyone, citizen or otherwise, who shall give such information as will be the means of bringing the murderer or murderers to justice."

The Double Event took place within an hour on Sunday morning, September 30.

"I SEND YOU HALF THE KIDNE". Jack sent a piece of the organ to the Chairman of Whitechapel Vigilance Committee. He claimed to have eaten the other half.

The first prostitute to go under the Ripper's knife was 45-year-old Elizabeth Stride a carpenter's wife, nicknamed "Long Liz", who was found by a hawker in an alley off Berners Street with her windpipe cut and her throat still bleeding. The time was shortly after one o'clock, and 45 minutes later the second body was discovered in nearby Mitre Square by Police Constable Watkins — whose beat took him through the area, and who, like every other officer on duty in the East End that autumn, heard and saw nothing suspicious.

Pig-headed dolt

Like Mrs. Stride, 43-year-old Catherine Eddowes had joked at the thought of meeting the Ripper. "He's got other girls to bother about instead of me," she told her friends drunkenly. " 'Sides, the minute I see any man carrying a shiny black bag I'll throw me head back and scream it off!" She was so drunk at eight o'clock on the evening of September 29 that she reeled about, imitating a fire-engine. For this she was arrested and kept in Bishopsgate Police Station until 1 a.m. the next morning. As she was released, she flounced past the duty sergeant, calling out: "Tata, old cock. I'll see you again soon!" The irony of which was lost on the sergeant.

"From hell

Mr Lusk

Sor I send you half the Kidne I took from one women prasarved it for you tother piece I fried and ate it was very nise I may send you the bloody knif that took it out if you only wate a whil longer

Signed Catch me when you can Mishter Lusk"

"Old boss you was rite it was the left Kidny i was goin to hoperate agin close to your spitalfilds just as i was goin to dror mi nife along of er bloomin throte them cusses of coppers spoilt the game but i guess i will be on the job soon and will send you another bit of innerds

jack the ripper

O have you seen the devle with his mikerscope and scalpul a lookin at a kidney with a slide cocked up"

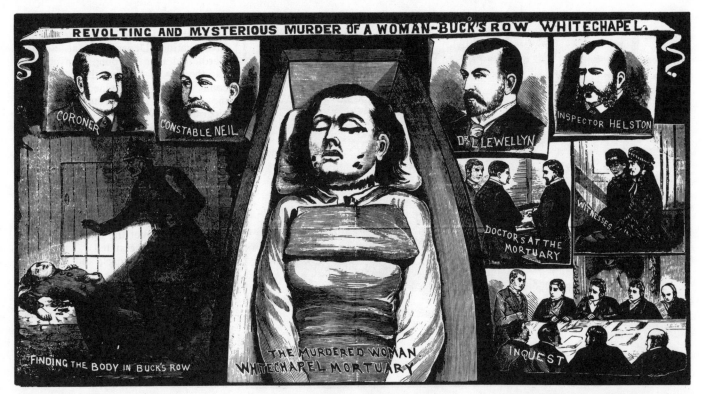

REVOLTING AND MYSTERIOUS MURDER OF A WOMAN-BUCK'S ROW WHITECHAPEL.

CORONER

CONSTABLE NEIL

DR. L. LEWELLYN

INSPECTOR HELSTON

DOCTORS AT THE MORTUARY

WITNESSES

FINDING THE BODY IN BUCK'S ROW

THE MURDERED WOMAN. WHITECHAPEL MORTUARY

INQUEST

AN ARTIST'S grisly impression of Mary Ann Nicholls in the mortuary (above). Broadsheets kept the East Enders informed. But in fact there was no capture.

She spent the next 30 minutes walking from the police station to Mitre Square—where presumably she met the murderer, and where he ripped her open "like a pig for the market" according to P.C. Watkins. "I have been in the force a long while," he told newsmen later, "but I never saw such a sight." For once the excess of blood proved too much—or too embarrassing—for the killer. He stopped to wash his hands in a public sink, and then (so the police reasoned) chalked on a doorway the ambiguous message that: "The Juwes are not the men to be blamed for nothing."

The writing of the "Juwes" slogan (Jews?—or some masonic reference?) could have provided the most fruitful clue yet—but for the intervention of Sir Charles Warren. He descended on the scene (without dogs, for once) and ordered the words to be rubbed out before they could be photographed. His explanation for this was the lame one that the sentence could have caused "religious trouble", and that there were not the men available to deal with a "racial riot".

Sir Charles's action was even more extraordinary as the crime had taken place in the City of London, over which he had no jurisdiction. This brought him into conflict with the Commissioner of City Police, Major Henry Smith, who privately recorded that Warren was "a dolt, a sheer, pig-headed dolt". In an attempt

TWO MORE HORRIBLE

MURDERS

IN THE EAST-END.

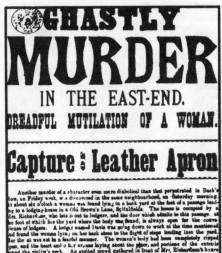

to bring the Ripper, or those sheltering him, out into the open, the police next released a letter which the murderer had sent to the Central News Agency two days before the Double Event. It read:

Ghoulish missive

"I am down on whores and I shan't quit ripping them till I do get buckled. Grand work, the last job was. I gave the lady [Annie Chapman] no time to squeal. How can they catch me now? I love my work and want to start again. You will soon hear of me and my funny little games . . . The next job I do I shall clip the lady's ears off and send to the police officers just for jolly . . . Keep this letter back till I do a bit more work, then give it out straight. My knife is nice and sharp. I want to get to work right away if I get

GHASTLY

MURDER

IN THE EAST-END.
DREADFUL MUTILATION OF A WOMAN.

Capture of Leather Apron

Another murder of a character even more diabolical than that perpetrated in Buck's Row, on Friday week, was discovered in the same neighbourhood, on Saturday morning. At about six o'clock a woman was found lying in a back yard at the foot of a passage leading to a lodging-house in Old Brown's Lane, Spitalfields. The house is occupied by a Mrs. Richardson, who lets it out to lodgers, and the door which admits to this passage, at the foot of which lies the yard where the body was found, is always open for the convenience of lodgers. A lodger named Davis was going down to work at the time mentioned, and found the woman lying on her back close to the flight of steps leading into the yard. Her throat was cut in a fearful manner. The woman's body had been completely ripped open, and the heart and other organs laying about the place, and portions of the entrails round the victim's neck. An excited crowd gathered in front of Mrs. Richardson's house.

a chance. Good luck. Yours truly, Jack the Ripper."

The letter was considered to be genuine, as on Sunday, September 30, just a few hours after the double murder, the police received a postcard referring to the killings. They had not yet been officially announced, yet the writer of the card said:

"I was not codding, dear old Boss, when I gave you the tip. You'll hear about Saucy Jack's work tomorrow. Double event this time. Number one squealed a bit. Couldn't finish straight off. Had not time to get ears for police. Thanks for keeping last letter back till I got to work again. Jack the Ripper."

A few days later he followed this with a typically ghoulish missive. It was a cardboard box sent to George Lusk, Chairman of the Whitechapel Vigilance

authenticity of the letters was Sir Melville Macnaghten (later Chief of the Criminal Investigation Department at Scotland Yard, and then a young man about to join the Force). "I have always thought I could discern the stained forefinger of the journalist," he wrote in his autobiography, *Days Of My Years*. ". . . Whoever did pen the gruesome stuff, I am certain that it was not the mad miscreant who had committed the murders."

Suicide?

Even so, Sir Melville did not decry the fear that pervaded the entire city. "No one who was living in London that autumn will forget the terror created by these murders," he stated. ". . . I can recall the foggy evenings, and hear again the raucous cries of the newspaper boys: 'Another horrible murder, murder, mutilation, Whitechapel.' Such was the burden of their ghastly song . . . no servant-maid

BUCKS ROW just prior to demolition in 1972. Renamed Durward Street, the site of Mary Nicholls's killing was a tourist spot for over 80 years.

13 MILLERS COURT (above) where Mary Kelly, the Ripper's last victim, was mutilated almost beyond recognition. Another splash on Jack (right).

Committee, and it contained a kidney taken from the body of Catherine Eddowes. Also enclosed was a note headed, "From Hell". It said, "Mr. Lusk. Sir I send you half the Kidne I took from one woman prasarved it for you, tother piece I fried and ate it was very nice. I may send you the bloody knif that took it out if you only wate a whil longer. Signed Catch me when you can Mister Lusk."

It was followed by two more letters from another port — Liverpool, this time — suggesting that the maniac was a sailor, or was planning to leave the country by ship. One person who doubted the

deemed her life safe if she ventured out to post a letter after ten o'clock at night."

The terror – and the killings – came to an end with the cutting up of Mary Kelly in Miller's Court on November 9. By then various theories had been put forward as to the Ripper's identity – he was a mad surgeon, a mad policeman, a mad lodging-house keeper, even a mad midwife, Jill the Ripper.

Since that time many suggestions as to Jack the Ripper's real identity have been put forward. One author gives him the name of "Dr. Stanley", described as a distinguished surgeon seeking to revenge himself

WAS THIS JACK THE RIPPER?
Montague John Druitt committed suicide. After his death the murders stopped. Many experts believe he was responsible.

on the prostitute who had given his son V.D. Another startling theory is that he was the Duke of Clarence, heir to the throne of England; or a friend of the Duke's called James Stephen, the son of a High Court judge. One author suggests that he was an East End ritual Jewish slaughterman. Other candidates are a Dr. Alexander Pedachenko or a Pole named Severin Klosowski, unqualified doctor's assistants in the Russian

army, who were associated with the Russian revolutionaries living in London's East End.

Perhaps the most probable theory is that put forward by Daniel Farson, who identifies the Ripper as Montague John Druitt, a gifted athlete at school, an Oxford graduate, but a failed barrister who had access to his cousin's surgery in The Minories and who committed suicide less than a month after the last killing. There is evidence that the police and his own family had some suspicion of his frightful activities, and that he drowned himself when he suddenly realized that he was insane.

AN OFFICER AND A GENTLEMAN

Neville Heath

A tall, handsome young Air Force hero Neville Heath . . . to women his easy charm was utterly fatal. Neville Heath was more than a fraud . . . he was a suave sex-maniac, one of the most violently depraved men the world has known . . .

Rodney Shackell

LUNCHTIME had come and gone, yet there was still no sign of life from Room No. 4 at the Pembridge Court Hotel in Notting Hill, London. The maid responsible for the room, eager to get on with her cleaning and tidying, was understandably irritated. She peeped through the keyhole. The room was in darkness and there was nothing to be seen. She knocked at the door again. Still there was no answer.

Perhaps she should inform someone. She sought out Mrs. Alice Wyatt, who helped her father-in-law to run the 19-bedroomed hotel, and explained the situation. Mrs. Wyatt looked at the clock. It was 2 p.m. She thought it was time to investigate. She let herself into the bedroom with her pass key and drew back the curtains. In one of the single beds, the sheets and blankets pulled up around her neck, lay a young, dark-haired woman. It was hardly necessary to move the bedclothes to establish that she was dead. The red bloodstains all over the second bed told their own story.

The police arrived within minutes. Beneath the bedclothes they found a badly mutilated body. The dead woman's nipples had been practically bitten off. There were 17 weals, apparently made by the plaited thong of a whip with a metal tip, across her back, chest, stomach, and face. Her ankles were bound together with a handkerchief and she had bled from the vagina. It was clear that her face had been washed, but there were still traces of blood on her cheeks and in her nostrils. The blood on the second bed suggested that she had been killed there and her body moved after death — while interlacing markings on the pillowcase pointed to a bloodstained whip having lain there.

Female companion

The victim's body was removed to Hammersmith Mortuary where Dr. Keith Simpson, the pathologist, carried out a post-mortem. He found the woman had died from suffocation, probably caused by a gag or by having her face pressed into a pillow.

Meantime, the police had started the hunt for the killer. The trail did not prove difficult to follow. The woman's body was found on Friday, June 21, 1946. Room No. 4 had been let the previous Sunday to a man with a female companion (not the dead woman), who had signed the register "Mr. and Mrs. N. G. C. Heath", giving an address in Hampshire.

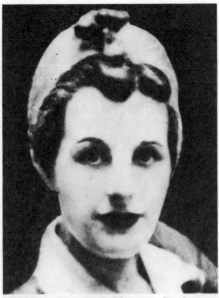

VICTIM: Film extra Margery Gardner liked the "bohemian" life. At the Panama Club, she drank and danced her way to a dreadful death with debonair Heath.

Within hours, Superintendent Thomas Barratt, who was in charge of the case, had established that Mr. N. G. C. Heath was Neville George Clevely Heath, a handsome, 29-year-old former officer, six feet tall and the possessor of a criminal record, although not for violence. The police had also uncovered the identity of the dead woman. She was 32-year-old Mrs. Margery Gardner, occasionally a film extra, separated from her husband and fond of the gay, bohemian life.

On the night before the killing, she drank and danced with Heath at the Panama Club in South Kensington. Around midnight they left the club together, hailed a cruising taxicab and directed it to the Pembridge Court Hotel. Harry Harter, the cabdriver, remembered the journey well. "I picked them up in the Old Brompton Road and put them down about 50 yards from the Pembridge Court Hotel," he told detectives. "The man asked me how much the fare was. I said it was 1s. 9d. and he gave me 2s. 2d. Then they walked towards the hotel. He put his arm round the woman's waist and I saw them enter the hotel gate."

The police were well pleased with their progress. It was beginning to look as if an arrest was merely a matter of days. It was decided to release Heath's name and description to the newspapers as a man who, in the cautious legal phrase, the police would like "to assist them with their inquiries". At this point, however, the police faced a dilemma. They had collected four photographs of Heath from his home in Merton Hall Road, Wimbledon. Should these photographs be published along with Heath's name and description. It seemed on the one hand that identification would prove a critical issue in Heath's trial if, as expected, he proved to be the murderer, and widespread publication of his likeness might easily prejudice the chances of a conviction. If, on the other hand, Heath's suave and easy charm masked a sex maniac, he might easily kill again unless he were captured quickly. In the end the decision was taken not to release the photographs. As a result, another woman was to die.

Name and description

While his name and description was being flashed to police stations and newspapers all over the country, Heath was in the Sussex seaside resort of Worthing. He had travelled down to the South Coast on the day Margery Gardner's mutilated body was found, and booked in under his own name at the Ocean Hotel. The purpose of his visit was to look up yet another of the many women in his life,

"FIANCÉE" Yvonne Symonds (right): "Yvonne, there's been a nasty murder in London . . . in the room where we stayed last weekend." Police soon pinpointed Heath, but by this time he was staying in Bournemouth under an assumed name.

A RAKE'S PROGRESS...THAT ENDED IN MULTIPLE MURDER

Police pieced together details of Heath's extraordinary career of crime and service in the armed forces, during which, in the course of ten years, he managed to get himself commissioned and dishonourably discharged on three occasions. In outline, his dossier reads:

February 1936. Obtained short-service commission in R.A.F.

August 1937. Court-martialled for being absent without leave for nearly five months. Other charges included escaping while under arrest and "borrowing" a non-commissioned officer's car without permission. Sentenced to be cashiered. Commuted subsequently to dismissal.

November 1937. Placed on probation on charges of fraudulently obtaining credit at a Nottingham hotel and attempting to obtain a car by false pretences. Eight other offences, including posing as "Lord Dudley", taken into account.

July 1938. Sentenced to three years' Borstal treatment for housebreaking and stealing jewellery worth £51 from a friend, and for obtaining clothing worth £27 by means of a forged bankers' order. Ten other offences taken into account.

September 1939. Released from Hollesley Bay Colony because of the outbreak of the war.

October 1939. Enlisted in Royal Army Service Corps.

March 1940. Commissioned and posted to the Middle East.

July 1941. Placed under arrest after a dispute with a brigadier. Went absent without leave. Court-martialled for these offences and for obtaining a second pay-book by making a false statement; making a false statement to his commanding officer, enabling him to be absent from his unit; and on five charges relating to dishonoured cheques. Sentenced to be cashiered.

November 1941. Absconded from the troopship that was bringing him to England when it docked at Durban in South Africa. Went to Johannesburg where he passed himself off as a Captain Selway, M.C., of the Argyll and Sutherland Highlanders.

December 1941. Enlisted in South African Air Force under the name of Armstrong. Commissioned.

May 1944. Seconded to Royal Air Force. Shot down on the Dutch-German border while piloting a Mitchell bomber.

August 1945. Court-martialled and dismissed the service in South Africa on six charges, three of conduct prejudicial to good order and military discipline and three of wearing military decorations without authority.

February 1946. Arrived back in Britain.

April 1946. Fined at Wimbledon Magistrates' Court in South London for wearing a military uniform and decorations to which he was not entitled.

Yvonne Symonds, whom he had met at a dance in Chelsea the previous Saturday. After the dance he took her to the Panama Club. "Let's find a hotel and sleep together," Heath suggested. His new companion refused.

Heath spent the whole of the next day with her. He was at his most debonair and charming. Yvonne Symonds found him fascinating. When he proposed, she gladly accepted—although she had known him for only a few hours. Once again Heath suggested: "Let's spend the night together." This time she agreed, and she was the "Mrs. N. G. C. Heath" who had occupied Room No. 4 at the Pembridge Court Hotel the previous Sunday night. Heath phoned her several times in the course of the week. Now, down in Worthing, he phoned again and arranged to take her out to lunch on the Saturday.

Utmost courtliness

By then the news of Margery Gardner's killing was out, and, in the course of the meal, Heath suddenly said: "Yvonne, there's been a nasty murder in London. Have you read about it in the papers?" Miss Symonds said she hadn't. "I'll tell you all about it later," Heath promised. He returned to the subject that night when he took her to dine and dance at the Blue Peter Club in Angmering. "That murder I mentioned," he said. "It took place in the room we stayed in last weekend. I knew the girl. She was with some man who had nowhere to stay so I gave him the key to the room and went and slept somewhere else. The police—an Inspector (it should have been Superintendent) Barratt—got on to me and took me round to the room. I saw the body. It was a pretty gruesome sight."

Miss Symonds did not doubt Heath's story for a moment. This, after all, was the man who had swept her off her feet, who, in their brief time together, had always treated her with the utmost courtliness and consideration. How had the girl died? "A poker was stuck up her," replied Heath bluntly. "I think that's what killed her—although Inspector Barratt seems to believe she might have been suffocated."

Miss Symonds was horrified. "What sort of person could commit a brutal crime like that?" she asked.

"A sex maniac, I suppose," shrugged Heath.

He took her home safely at the end of the evening and chastely kissed her goodnight. She was to speak to him only once again. That was the following morning after she and her parents had read Sunday newspaper accounts of the murder and a renewed appeal by the police—the first one had been published on the Saturday—for Heath to come forward. Miss Symonds immediately rang

Inside the image: **HEATH'S ROOM** · **BUILDER'S LADDER HERE**

"A LITTLE DECEPTION": After savagely murdering Doreen Marshall, Heath returned to his hotel room by way of a fire escape and a ladder.

her fiancé at the hotel where he was staying.

"My parents are very worried about the story in the papers," she told him.

Heath remained the cool man-of-the-world. "I thought they would be," he said laconically. Then he added: "I've got a car and I'm driving back to London to sort things out. I'll probably give you a ring this evening." But he did not ring. Nor did he return to London. Instead he caught a train to Bournemouth where he booked into the Tollard Royal Hotel, using the improbable name of Group-Captain Rupert Brooke — Brooke being the brilliant young English poet who died in Greece in the First World War.

Until now, Heath had acted in a careless, almost reckless, manner for a killer who, presumably, did not want to be caught. Margery Gardner had been found in a room rented to him, and, in describing the murder to Yvonne Symonds, he had revealed an intimate knowledge of the crime. His claim that "Inspector" Barratt had taken him to the scene was quite untrue and would not withstand investigation if Miss Symonds talked. Before leaving Worthing, Heath therefore took his first positive step to try to point the

finger of suspicion away from him. He wrote to "Chief Inspector" Barratt. The letter arrived on the police officer's desk at New Scotland Yard on the Monday morning. It read:

"Sir, I feel it to be my duty to inform you of certain facts in connection with the death of Mrs. Gardner at Notting Hill Gate. I booked in at the hotel last Sunday, but not with Mrs. Gardner, whom I met for the first time during the week. I had drinks with her on Friday evening, and whilst I was with her she met an acquaintance with whom she was obliged to sleep. The reasons, as I understand them, were mainly financial.

Invidious position

"It was then that Mrs. Gardner asked if she could use my hotel room until two o'clock and intimated that, if I returned after that, I might spend the remainder of the night with her. I gave her my keys and told her to leave the hotel door open. It must have been almost 3 a.m. when I returned to the hotel and found her in the condition of which you are aware. I realised I was in an invidious position, and rather than notify the police I packed my belongings and left.

"Since then I have been in several minds whether to come forward or not, but in view of the circumstances I have been afraid to. I can give you a descrip-

tion of the man. He was aged approximately 30, dark hair (black), with a small moustache. Height about 5ft. 9ins., slim build. His name was Jack and I gathered that he was a friend of Mrs. Gardner's of some long standing.

"The personal column of the *Daily Telegraph* will find me, but at the moment I have assumed another name. I should like to come forward and help, but I cannot face the music of a fraud charge which will obviously be preferred against me if I should do so. I have the instrument with which Mrs. Gardner was beaten and am forwarding this to you today. You will find my fingerprints on it, but you should also find others as well. N. G. C. Heath."

The parcel containing the instrument never arrived, and for the next 13 days — from Sunday, June 23, until Saturday, July 6 — Heath lived what was apparently the life of a carefree holidaymaker in Bournemouth. The guests, and the staff, at the Tollard Royal Hotel found him pleasant and amusing company. His entire wardrobe seemed to consist of grey flannel trousers and a mustard-coloured sports jacket, and during most of his stay he appeared to have no cash, putting all his drinks on the bill, but nobody was particularly concerned. The man they knew as Group-Captain Rupert Brooke was obviously an officer and a gentleman.

It was also established that, while in South Africa, Heath was married in 1942 and had a son. His wife had divorced him in October 1945, on the grounds of desertion.

Within a couple of days of Heath's arrival in Bournemouth, every police force in the country, including the local one, had a copy of his photograph as a wanted man. The decision not to release pictures to the newspapers was adhered to, however, even as the days passed, producing nothing but the inevitable crop of frustrating false leads as to Heath's whereabouts. With each 24 hours that passed, death came a day nearer to 21-year-old Doreen Marshall.

Doreen Marshall was a pert and pretty ex-Wren (the Women's Royal Naval Service), the daughter of a company director, living in Middlesex. After being demobilized she suffered a severe attack of influenza, and her father decided that a few days by the sea would help to put her on her feet again. He packed her off to Bournemouth where she booked in at the Norfolk Hotel.

It is not exactly clear how her path crossed with Heath's. His own account, written later, said: "On Wednesday, July 3, during the morning, I was seated on the promenade on Westcliff when I saw two young ladies walking along the front. One of these two was a casual acquaintance whom I had met at a dance at the Pavilion during the latter half of the preceding week (her Christian name was Peggy but I was unaware of her surname). Although I was not formally introduced to the other I gathered that her name was "Doo" or something similar. The girl Peggy left after about half-an-hour and I walked along the front with the other girl whom I now know to be Miss Marshall. I invited her to have tea with me in the afternoon and she accepted.

Smilingly agreed

In the course of tea at the Tollard Royal Hotel that afternoon, Heath asked: "Would you care to join me for dinner tonight?" Miss Marshall smilingly agreed. After dinner they sat in the hotel lounge until shortly after midnight. Other guests noted that Heath seemed to be slightly drunk and, as the evening wore on, his companion appeared unhappy. At one point she begged one of the men present to order her a taxi. Soon afterwards, Heath cancelled it and said: "My guest has decided to walk home." He left the hotel with Miss Marshall about 12.15 a.m.

"I'll be back in about half-an-hour," he told the porter.

"A quarter-of-an-hour," snapped Miss Marshall.

Nobody saw her alive again. As for

Heath, it was never established at what time he returned to the hotel. He regained his room by climbing a ladder and getting in through a window. It was, he explained later, "a little deception" on his friend the night porter. The mystified porter confessed subsequently that at 4.30 a.m. he had peeped into Heath's bedroom to see if he was there. The guest was fast asleep.

Thursday passed apparently normally. So did most of Friday. Then the manager of the Tollard Royal Hotel, Ivor Relf, received a phone call from the manager of the Norfolk Hotel. "One of our guests appears to be missing," he said, "and we believe she dined at your place on Wednesday." He added that the missing guest, Miss Marshall, had come from Pinner, outside London.

Suave demeanour

Heath, in the meantime, showed no signs of agitation or excitement. The only changes in him—both significant, it was to turn out—was that he now seemed to have money in his pockets and had taken to wearing a silk scarf to hide a couple of scratches on his neck. There was nothing else about the demeanour of Group-Captain Rupert Brooke to arouse suspicion, and it was not until the Saturday morning that Mr. Relf got around to mentioning the phone call from the Norfolk Hotel.

Heath, playing it as coolly as ever, laughed off the notion that the missing woman might have been his dinner guest. "I believe she came from Pinner," said Mr. Relf. "I have known that lady for a long while, and she certainly doesn't come from Pinner," replied Heath airily.

But he was now to take a step as extraordinary as his decision to write to Superintendent Barratt. He telephoned the police and asked if they had a photograph of the missing woman. The officer in charge of the case was out and Heath said he would ring again later. He phoned for a second time at 3.30 and, on hearing that the police did have a photograph of Miss Marshall, offered to come round a couple of hours later to have a look at it and see if he could be of any help.

He can hardly have suspected it, but the step he took through the door of the police station was to be his last as a free man. Heath identified himself as Brooke, but he was almost immediately recognised from the photographs circulated to police stations throughout the country as the man wanted for questioning about the death of Margery Gardner. Heath still insisted that he was Brooke. However at

VICTIM: "Miss Marshall did not wish me to accompany her." Not far from the beach, police with bloodhounds searched for the body of Doreen Marshall in wooded Branksome Chine.

POLICE GAZETTE

PUBLISHED BY AUTHORITY.

NEW SERIES.   TUESDAY, JUNE 25, 1946.   No. 147, VOL. XXXIII.

Manuscript for publication should be addressed " THE COMMISSIONER OF POLICE, NEW SCOTLAND YARD. S.W.1." with " C.R.O. (P.G.) " in top left corner.

HAROLD SCOTT
The Commissioner of Police of the Metropolis.

Special Notice

MURDER

M.P. (FH).—It is desired to trace the after-described for interview respecting the death of **MARGERY GARDNER**, during the night of 20th-21st inst.—**NEVILLE GEORGE CLEVELY HEATH**, alias **ARMSTRONG, BLYTH, DENVERS** and **GRAHAM**, C.R.O. No. 28142-37, b. 1917, 5ft. 11½in., c. fresh, e. blue, believed small fair moustache, h. and eyebrows fair, square face, broad forehead and nose, firm chin, good teeth, military gait ; dress, lt. grey d.b. suit with pin stripe, dk. brown trilby, brown suede shoes, cream shirt with collar attached or fawn and white check **sports jacket** and grey flannel trousers.   Nat. Reg. No. CNP/2147191.

Has recent conviction for posing as Lt.-Col. of South African Air Force.   A pilot and believed to possess an " A " licence, has stated his intention of going abroad and may endeavour to secure passage on ship or plane as passenger or pilot.   May stay at hotels accompanied by woman.

Enquiries are also requested to trace the owner of gent's white handkerchief with brown check border, bearing " L. Kearns " in black ink on hem and stitched with large " K " in blue cotton in centre.

9.45 that evening, Detective-Inspector George Gates told him: "I am satisfied that you are Neville George Clevely Heath and I am going to detain you pending the arrival of officers of the Metropolitan police."

"Oh, all right," murmured Heath, not, it seemed, particularly concerned.

Now the evidence began to pile up on all sides. Heath, who had gone to the police station without a coat, apparently believing that he would not be there long, asked if his sports jacket could be brought from the hotel. In a pocket the police found a cloakroom ticket issued at Bournemouth West station on the Sunday Heath arrived in the town. The ticket led the police to a suitcase which, on being opened, was found to contain a blood-stained scarf and a leather riding-whip with a plaited thong. The tip had worn away, exposing the metal underneath.

Artificial pearl

Detectives also found in the sports jacket the return half of a London-Bournemouth rail ticket, subsequently proved to have been the one issued to Miss Marshall, and an artificial pearl. In a drawer in Heath's hotel room was a soiled, blood-stained handkerchief, tightly knotted, with human hairs adhering to it. It was established also that, in the previous 36 hours, Heath had pawned a ring belonging to Miss Marshall for £5 and a fob watch for £3. But where was Miss Marshall herself?

A statement written by Heath after he was detained at Bournemouth hinted that she had probably left the town. After

HEATH'S TRIAL caused a sensation. If the police photograph (opposite) had been issued to the public, the second murder could have been avoided.

walking out of the hotel in the early hours of Thursday morning, it continued, they had "sat on a seat near the hotel overlooking the sea. We must have talked for at least an hour, probably longer, and then we walked down the slope towards the Pavilion. Miss Marshall did not wish me to accompany her but I insisted on doing so—at least some of the way. I left her at the Pier and watched her cross the road and enter the gardens. Before leaving her I asked her if she would come round the following day, but she said she would be busy for the next few days, but would telephone me on Sunday if she could manage it. I have not seen her to speak to since then although I thought I saw her entering Bobby's Ltd., on Thursday morning."

The body of Doreen Marshall was discovered in Branksome Chine on the Monday, two days later. It was the circling flies that led a passer-by, who had heard about a missing woman, to her. Her body

had been dragged into some rhododendron bushes. She was naked except for her left shoe, but she was covered with her own clothing—underwear, a black frock and a yellow swagger coat—and some boughs of fir trees. Twenty-seven artificial pearls, which came from her broken necklace and matched the one found in Heath's pocket, lay nearby. Her powder compact and stockings were some distance away and her empty handbag was found at the bottom of the chine.

Like Margery Gardner, she had been savagely mutilated. Her throat had been cut, causing her death. In places the wound was three-quarters-of-an-inch deep. Before that, her hands had been pinioned, but there were cuts on them suggesting that she had tried to fight off an assailant with a knife.

Question of sanity

Heath was charged with both murders, but his trial, which opened at the Central Criminal Court on September 24, dealt only with the murder of Margery Gardner. The horrifying details of Doreen Marshall's death came out in evidence, however. It was quickly clear that the real question was not whether Heath had killed the two women but whether he was sane. The defence did not bother to put him into the witness-box. They pinned all their hopes for cheating the gallows on insanity, and the debate about whether Heath was or was not in his right senses proved the only interesting part of the short, three-day trial.

At the end, however, the jury took only 59 minutes to find him guilty. He was sentenced on September 26 and executed on October 26. To the very last he remained the debonair playboy, completely in control of himself, ordering a grey, pin-striped suit, grey socks, grey shirt and polka-dot blue tie for his trial, asking for his diaries and address books to be destroyed once the verdict was known: "I have caused enough trouble in this world already without causing more."

He refused to see any members of his family, but the day before he hanged he wrote two letters to his mother. The first said: "My only regret at leaving the world is that I have been so damned unworthy of you both." In the second he wrote: "I shall probably stay up reading tonight because I'd like to see the dawn again. So much in my memory is associated with the dawn—early morning patrols and coming home from nightclubs. Well, it wasn't really a bad life while it lasted . . . Please don't mourn my going—I should hate it —and don't wear black."

It was said that his last wish to the governor of the prison was for a whisky. Then, on reflection, he added: "In the circumstances, you might make that a double!"

DEATH THROUGH THE PORTHOLE

Gay Gibson

She was attractive, passionate and travelled alone. Not surprisingly, Steward James Camb desired her and saw nothing wrong with a little shipboard flirtation. But did that include attempting to rape her and then pushing her into a shark-infested ocean . . . ?

WHEN stocky, 31-year-old James Camb appeared at the Assize Court of Winchester Castle accused of murdering a woman passenger on board the vessel where he worked as a steward, the scene was an unusual one.

For one thing, the court on that morning of March 18, 1948, was unable to sit in the usual chamber because of a subsidence in one of the castle walls. It had to make do with temporary accommodation formed by plywood partitions.

The bizarre appearance of the makeshift court was heightened by a large array of exhibits which had been introduced by the prosecution. They included a cabin bed, pillows, sheets and towels, a bell push, a porthole mounted on a wooden frame, and a collection of miscellaneous objects ranging from women's cosmetics to a female contraceptive appliance.

The trial judge, Mr. Justice Hilbery, was accompanied on the bench by the High Sheriff and his chaplain. The prosecution was led by Mr. G. D. Roberts, K.C., a former international rugby footballer who was known affectionately throughout the legal profession as "Khaki Roberts", a nickname he had received after an early appearance on the rugger field. Mr. J. D. Casswell, K.C., another athletic barrister who had represented Oxford three times in the Long Jump, led for the defence. Both men were leading counsel on the Western Circuit and well matched in forensic skill as well as athletic prowess.

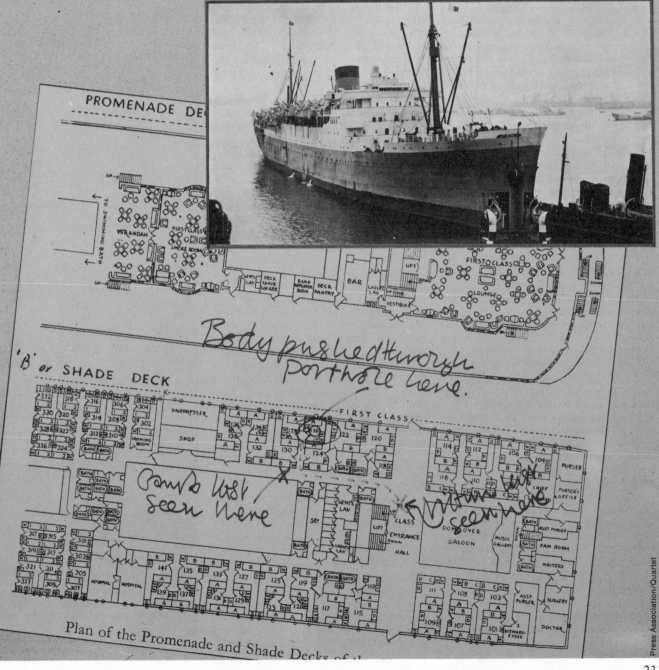

Plan of the Promenade and Shade Decks of the

23

When the prisoner was asked to plead to the indictment by the Clerk of the Court, he answered "Not guilty, sir" in a clear and confident voice. His confident and even jaunty demeanour throughout the four days of the trial contrasted strongly with the story he was to tell of losing his head and becoming panic-stricken on the night of October 18, the year before. As a result of his actions on that night, James Camb was charged with murdering a young actress named Eileen Isabella Ronnie Gibson, professionally known as Gay Gibson, on the high seas in the Union Castle liner *Durban Castle*. The accused steward was married with one daughter, though he was said to be inclined to promiscuous behaviour with other women.

Mortal remains

In opening the case for the prosecution, "Khaki" Roberts drew the attention of the jury to two peculiar features of the case. The first was that a crime committed on a British ship anywhere in the world—and this one was stated to have occurred about 90 miles off the West African coast, when the *Durban Castle* was sailing through a shark-infested sea—is subject to the jurisdiction of the British courts. Secondly, Gay Gibson's mortal remains had never been recovered. "There is no body here, no *corpus delicti* as the lawyers say," observed the prosecutor, adding that though this was unusual it was by no means unprecedented. According to the prosecution, the ship's steward had disposed of her body by pushing it through her cabin porthole, either after he had strangled her or after he had overcome her resistance when she was still alive.

Mr. Roberts went on to outline the dead woman's background and the events leading up to her disappearance from the *Durban Castle* on her homeward bound voyage to Southampton. Although born in India, where her father was a businessman, she had been educated in England and had served during the war in the Auxiliary Territorial Service (A.T.S.); she had later transferred to a theatrical touring company of service personnel known as "Stars in Battledress", since she had always hankered for a career on the stage. Early in 1947, she and her mother left England for South Africa to join her father, who was then employed near Durban. Feeling that there was more scope for her as an actress in Johannesburg, she went there shortly after her twenty-first birthday, and happened to meet an actor-producer named Henry Gilbert. Gilbert was so impressed by her performance in a radio show that he immediately cast her as leading lady in *The Man with a Load of Mischief*. In this she played opposite Eric Boon, ex-lightweight British boxing champion.

Unfortunately the successful run of this play was unexpectedly terminated by the discovery that the theatre did not comply with existing fire regulations, and before the producer could arrange for it to go on at another theatre Gay Gibson decided to return to England and try her fortune on the West End stage. It was with this end in view that she hopefully embarked on the *Durban Castle* at Capetown on October 10, 1947, in the prosecution's words, "to all appearances a healthy girl, bright and cheerful, and looking forward to continuing her theatrical career here."

Miss Gibson occupied Cabin 126 on B deck on the port side of the ship. There was not a great deal of activity among the passengers, since the ship was less than half full, and the days were uneventful and rather boring. Gay Gibson usually had her meals in the saloon with a Mr. Hopwood, an official of the Union Castle line, and a Wing-Commander Bray, and she would go to bed about 11.30, when Mr. Hopwood made a habit of seeing her to the door of her cabin where he would bid her goodnight.

From the outset of the voyage James Camb, who was the promenade deck steward, took an interest in Miss Gibson and when they were a few days out from Capetown, he suddenly asked Miss Field, Gay Gibson's cabin stewardess, if she knew that Miss Gibson was three months pregnant, adding that Miss Gibson had told him so herself. The stewardess replied that if true it was a dangerous thing to say, and the conversation finished.

Too hot

About five in the evening of October 17, Miss Field saw Camb near Miss Gibson's cabin, and suspecting that he might be going there she told him that if he did so she would report it, since the deck steward's duties were confined to the promenade deck and the gallery leading off it, and he was not permitted to go to any of the passengers' cabins. About two hours later the stewardess saw Gay Gibson dressed in a black evening gown and silver shoes, ready for the dinner and the dance which was to take place afterwards. She seemed happy and cheerful.

As usual she sat at the same table as Mr. Hopwood and Wing-Commander Bray, and later she danced with the Wing-Commander and two other passengers. She had two or three drinks in the course of the evening and smoked very little. About eleven o'clock there was some talk of having a swim in the ship's pool, since it was a hot night, and Gay Gibson left the others, saying she was going to her cabin to look for a swim suit. Half an hour later she returned, saying she could not find it. She remained for some time with the other two, leaning over the ship's rail and chatting until

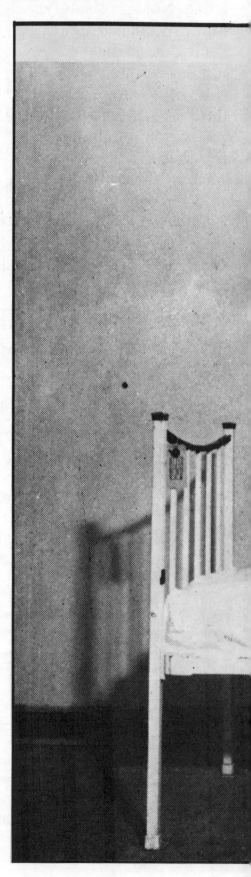

SCENE of the crime was Gay Gibson's cabin pictured (right) as it was on the murder night and (below) as set up in court showing the fatal porthole . . .

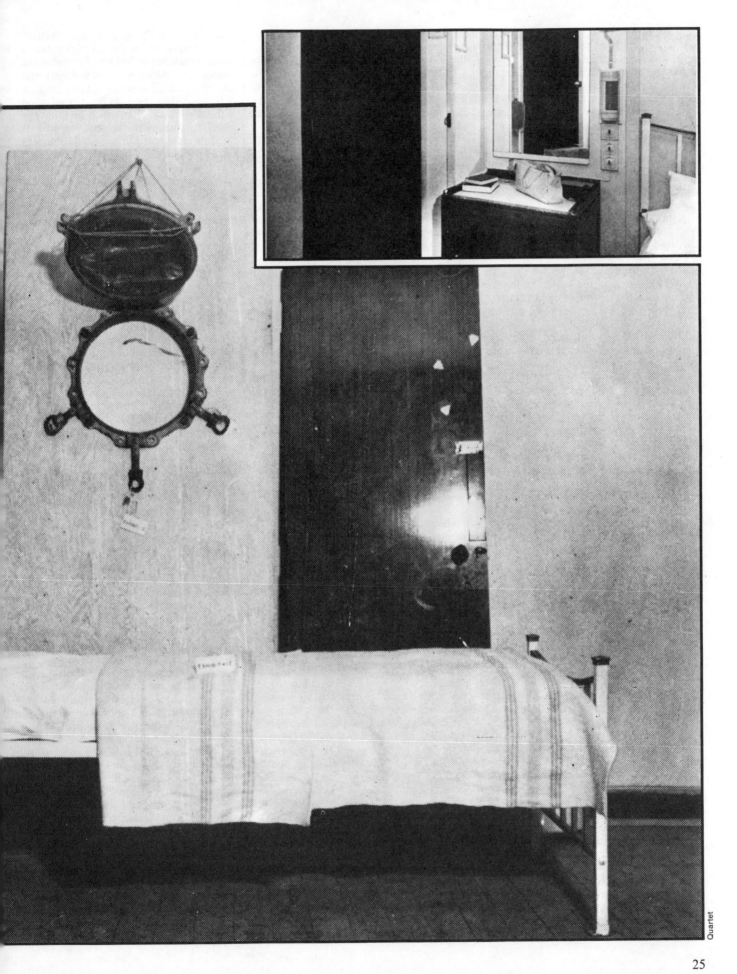

12.40 a.m., when Mr. Hopwood escorted her to her cabin as usual and said goodnight to her for the last time.

Several curious things occurred in the course of the evening and night hours. During the time that Gay Gibson left her two table companions to look for her swim suit, the ship's senior nightwatchman, James Murray, observed her and Camb talking together in the long gallery which led off the promenade deck. He overheard the deck steward say, "I have a bone to pick with you, and a big one at that." He was unable to hear any more.

Later it appeared that after Hopwood had said goodnight to her, she did not go to bed immediately, since about one o'clock the boatswain's mate, whose name was Conway, saw her on the after end of the deck on the port side, leaning against the rail and smoking a cigarette. She was still wearing her black evening dress and silver shoes.

Conway was in charge of a working party engaged in washing down the promenade deck and told her that she would get wet if she stayed where she was. She thanked him and said she had found it "too hot down below". That was the last time he saw her. It was indeed a fine, hot night, as one might expect in the tropics. The bow wave was curling back and hitting the ship's sides, while the steady roar of the dynamos came from the engine room behind the bridge.

A few minutes before 3 a.m. Murray, the nightwatchman, who was sitting with his assistant, Frederick Steer, in the first class galley on A deck, heard a cabin bell ring above his head. It was the nightwatchman's duty to answer any of the cabin bells, which at that time were all switched through to the galley. Accordingly Steer made his way to B deck, where the indicator showed that the bell had been rung in Cabin 126. On reaching this cabin he saw that two lights were showing outside, green and red, indicating that both the steward and the stewardess had been rung for. This struck Steer as odd, since normally a passenger would ring for either one or the other.

Man's face

The light was on in the cabin and shone through the grille in the door. Steer knocked and tried to enter. The door was opened a few inches and then suddenly shut in his face, but not before the nightwatchman was able to see a man's face, right hand and body, clad in a sleeveless singlet and dark trousers held up by a belt. It was Camb, the deck steward. As he shut the door, Camb said, "It's all right!"

Steer immediately returned to the galley to report to Murray and together they went back to Cabin 126. The lights were still on, but no sound came from within. After listening for some minutes and hear-

ing nothing. Murray went up to the bridge and reported the matter to the officer of the watch. But not wishing to get a fellow member of the crew into trouble he did not tell the officer that it was Camb whom his mate had seen. The officer dismissed him, saying that the morals of the passengers were their own affair.

At about 7.30 the same morning, Miss Field, the stewardess, went to Cabin 126 and receiving no answer to her knock, tried the door. It was open, which she considered unusual, since she knew that Miss Gibson was in the habit of locking her cabin at night and unlocking it when the stewardess called her in the morning. At first she did not attach much importance to the fact that the cabin was empty, since she thought that Miss Gibson might have gone to the bathroom. She noticed, however, that the bed was rather more disarranged than usual, and she also noted that there were one or two stains on the sheet and pillow case.

Vast expanse

When Miss Gibson did not return, the stewardess became anxious and eventually reported her absence to the Captain, whose name was Patey. After the ship had been thoroughly searched without result, the Captain concluded that she must have gone overboard and ordered the ship to reverse course, at the same time alerting all other ships in the neighbourhood by radio. But Captain Patey soon realized that a search for a missing passenger in such a vast expanse of shark-infested sea was hopeless, and he ordered the ship to resume her normal course.

Soon afterwards Steer told the Captain that it was Camb whom he had seen in Cabin 126. The Captain then sent for the deck steward and told him that he was suspected of having been there. Camb at once denied it, and said that he had not been near any passenger cabin since he had gone to bed at 12.45. Next day Camb agreed to submit to a medical examination, since Captain Patey told him that it was in his own interests to do so. He was accordingly seen by the ship's surgeon, Dr. Griffiths, who found scratches on his shoulders and wrists. Camb explained them away by saying that they were self-inflicted, since he had felt itchy due to the heat some days previously and had scratched himself.

Meanwhile the police in Southampton were informed by ship's radio of what had happened, and in the circumstances Camb was held for questioning when the *Durban Castle* docked. At first the steward repeated his previous denial to Captain Patey that he knew nothing about Gay Gibson's disappearance. But on being further questioned he made a statement to the effect that he had been in her cabin, sexual intercourse had taken

place between them with her consent, and that while still in the act of copulation she had clutched at him and foamed at the mouth, after which she was suddenly still and he could not hear her heart beating.

He had then tried artificial respiration without success, after which he lifted her body to the porthole and pushed it through. He was fairly certain she was dead, but he felt "terribly frightened". Camb was told that he would be detained and was then charged with murder. "I did not think it would be as serious as this," he told another police officer who came to his cell to arrange for his finger prints and photograph to be taken. "I can't understand why the officer of the watch did not hear something. It was the hell of a splash when she hit the water. She struggled. I had my hands around her neck, and when I was trying to get them away she scratched me. I panicked and threw her out of the porthole."

However, the inference which the prosecuting counsel invited the jury to draw was that Miss Gibson objected to the prisoner's advances. and she pressed both bells for outside help. She scratched the prisoner and then for his self-preservation he strangled her. Alternatively Mr. Roberts suggested to the jury that they might think that in order to destroy the evidence of rape or attempted rape which might be proved against him, Camb had thrown her out of the porthole.

Unused appliance

The most significant exhibits put in by the prosecution were the two sheets on the bed in Cabin 126, which revealed traces of human blood belonging to Group "O". These smears also showed traces of saliva and lipstick. Camb's blood group was "A", so that it would appear that the blood came from the body of Gay Gibson. In addition, a contraceptive appliance was found in a suitcase in the cabin which belonged to the dead woman. It was unused and its existence was to throw doubts on Camb's story that there had been sexual intercourse with consent.

Captain Patey and various members of the ship's company, including boatswain's mate Conway, the nightwatchmen Murray and Steer, and Gay Gibson's stewardess Miss Field, as well as her table companion Mr. Hopwood, all confirmed their recollections of Miss Gibson during the time she was on board the *Durban Castle*.

Dr. Griffiths and other medical witnesses also testified, but Griffiths was the only one to see Camb within a few hours of Gay Gibson's disappearance, when the scratches on his body were still fresh,

ASSAULTING women passengers was a regular pattern of behaviour for James Camb, but with Gay Gibson (inset) he went too far.

whereas the rest of the medical experts had to depend on photographs taken a week later after the scratches had healed.

Dr. Donald Teare, the well-known pathologist, testified for the prosecution as well. While agreeing that the bloodstains on the bedclothes were consistent with strangulation, he would have expected that there would also have been traces of urine. In fact, he was unaware that an examination conducted by another expert witness, Dr. Frederick Hocking, who was to be called for the defence, showed that urine had in fact been passed by Miss Gibson "as a terminal act", although this had not been revealed by the police laboratory findings which Dr. Teare was bound to accept. The doctor who had examined Gay Gibson on her release from the A.T.S., gave evidence that her general physical condition was good.

Business proposition

Since the defence was that the prisoner was a welcome visitor to Gay Gibson's cabin and that her death was due to natural causes during the performance of the sexual act with him, it was inevitable that Camb's counsel should seek to prove in cross-examination that she was a young woman of easy morals. It is never pleasant to have to attack the character of a dead person, particularly when she is a girl, and Mr. Casswell's tactics brought a dignified protest as a reaction.

The suggestion that Gay Gibson was not averse to jumping into bed with casual male acquaintances was also indignantly denied by her mother, who was also called by the prosecution and would hear nothing against her child. She was one of the finest types of English womanhood, said Mrs. Gibson, physically, mentally and morally. "My daughter was not pregnant," she declared with emphasis.

"Did you know your daughter was going about with several men in Johannesburg?" Mr. Casswell asked her.

This Mrs. Gibson again denied. "She told me everything and I know she was not interested in men only in her career."

"Can you explain the contraceptive which was found in her cabin?"

The witness brushed this question aside. "You know university students and others often carry them about with them," she said. "That is nothing to go by."

While denying that her daughter had misconducted herself with several men whose names were put to her, Mrs. Gibson admitted that a man named Charles Sventonski had paid her passage to England and had given her £500. "It was a business proposition," the witness explained. "He was ready to back her in her career as a business proposition."

"You say you see nothing wrong in your daughter accepting £500 from a man she had only known for a short time?"

"She said she would very soon pay him back. She was a hard-working conscientious girl, and she was hoping to become successful in her career."

Mr. Casswell then opened the defence and called the prisoner to the witness box. He appeared calm and self-possessed, showing no visible signs of emotion either when his counsel took him through his story, or later when subjected to a most probing cross-examination by the prosecutor. He confirmed that the second or third day out of Capetown Gay Gibson ordered a drink and they fell into conversation. She told him that she was in love with a man named Charles in Johannesburg and thought she might be going to have a baby, though it was too soon to tell yet.

Camb later brought afternoon tea to her cabin and she gave him a standing order for a supper tray to be left outside her cabin at night. He explained the words he had been overheard using, "I have a bone to pick with you, and a big one at that", as referring to the fact that she had not used her supper tray the night before or her tea tray that day.

About eleven o'clock that evening he had followed her down to her cabin after

WITNESSES for the defence (from left to right) Mike Abel, Dr. Ina Schoub and Henry Gilbert. Their evidence was used in an effort to attack Gay's morals.

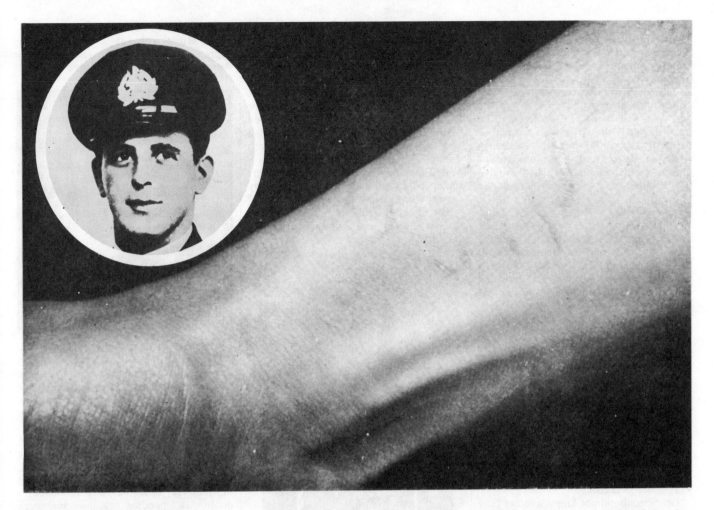

TELL-TALE scratches on Camb's arm (above) were photographed one week after the murder when the ship docked at Southampton. They had noticeably healed.

he had overheard her saying that she was going to look for a swim suit. A glass of rum had been left on her supper tray and Camb, according to his story, said he had a good mind to bring down a drink later and join her. She replied something like, "Please yourself—it's up to you." In fact, he did join her in her cabin shortly before 1 a.m. She was lying on the bed in a dressing gown but wore no pyjamas underneath and was naked when she took it off later and Camb got into bed with her.

"What happened after that?"

"There was a certain amount of preliminary love play, and then sexual intercourse took place."

"When sexual intercourse took place, what were your relative positions?"

"I was lying on top of Miss Gibson. I was face down."

"What happened in the end?"

"She suddenly heaved under me as though she was gasping for breath."

"What happened to her body?"

"It stiffened for a fraction of a second and then relaxed completely limp."

"What did you do when her body showed these symptoms?" counsel asked.

"I immediately got off the bed," the witness answered. "She was completely relaxed as though she was in a dead faint. One eye was just slightly open. Her mouth was a little open too. There was a faint line of bubbles, which I assumed to be froth, just on the edges of the lips. It was a muddy colour and appeared to be slightly blood-flecked."

According to his story, the prisoner then tried to revive her and when she remained senseless he lost his head and put her out of the porthole. When Steer had tapped on the door, he admitted saying, "All right." But he could not account for the pressing of the bells. Nor would he admit that he had received any injuries from Miss Gibson. He also denied having made the statement to the police about her struggling and the body going into the water with "the hell of a splash".

"Would you describe yourself as a truthful man?" was the first question put to him in cross-examination by Mr. Roberts. It was a deadly one.

"I think so, sir."

"You do," counsel went on. "You were the last person to see Miss Gibson alive?"

"Yes."

"You put her through the porthole at three o'clock on the morning of October 18?"

"Yes."

"Did you for the next eight days make untrue statements with regard to that, on at least six occasions?"

"I did that, yes," Camb admitted. "I was thinking only of myself."

"Self-preservation," commented the prosecutor. "Did you intend to persist in that untrue denial on your part?"

"I think I did."

"Did you intend to take that secret with you to your grave?"

"I would say yes."

"No matter what unhappiness or misery was caused to her relations or anyone else?"

"By that time I had already entangled myself into lies."

"When did you decide to alter your story?"

"In the police headquarters."

"Why?" Counsel rapped sharply.

"I realized by then that I was definitely incriminated by the witness Steer," replied Camb. He went on to agree with the prosecutor that he had told an untrue story until he felt that that story would not save him.

"Don't you call that curious conduct for a truthful person?"

"I should say it was beastly conduct," was the witness's candid if callous reply. His behaviour in the witness box did not impress either judge or jury in his favour.

The defence called a number of witnesses from South Africa, including Henry Gilbert, the actor-producer, and his wife Ina, who was a medical doctor, and an actor named Mike Abel, who had played with Gay Gibson in the theatre there, to testify to the fact that she suffered from a variety of complaints, including asthma, which might have caused or contributed to her death.

Abel swore that she had had five fainting fits during the time that he knew her, and that on one occasion her lips had gone blue. She was also said to be hysterical and neurotic. Dr. Ina Schoub, Gilbert's wife, had not examined her professionally, she said, but she stated in evidence that Gay Gibson had discussed sex with her rather intimately. "She told me that she had had sexual experience and that she was expecting a period within the next week." Later, when her period was overdue, Dr. Schoub said she had asked her whether she had used a contraceptive during her sexual experience. "She looked very blankly at me," the witness went on. "She didn't seem to know anything about it, and asked me to explain things to her. I told her about it, and advised that she should be fitted with a Dutch cap."

Fortunate accident

Dr. Schoub did not know whether Gay Gibson had taken her advice. She added that the contraceptive appliance found in her belongings was "not quite the same thing" as a Dutch cap, which "should be fitted by a doctor".

The last two defence witnesses were pathologists, Dr. Frederick Hocking and Professor James Webster. Their testimony was to the effect that in their opinion Gay Gibson's death might have occurred in the way Camb had described. But Dr. Hocking also testified that he had examined the top sheet on the bed in Gay Gibson's cabin and that this examination revealed the presence of dried urine—not noticed by the government pathologists—in which were some cells of the type which line the external female sex organs. He agreed, as did Professor Webster, that in cases of strangulation it was a common feature for the bladder to discharge its contents.

These admissions, though made by defence witnesses, in fact greatly strengthened the case for the prosecution, since the presence of urine contradicted Camb's story that at the moment of the girl's death his body was on top of hers, as obviously in that event the urine would have been ejected over him. The virtually irresistible inference was that he was not in contact with that part of the girl's body at all, but was at the head of the bed, gripping her throat to prevent any further attempt on her part to summon aid.

And that was what the jury decided had happened; it took them only three-quarters of an hour, after a fair but unfavourable summing up by Mr. Justice Hilbery, to find the prisoner guilty. Asked by the Clerk of the Court whether he had anything to say why judgment of death should not be passed upon him, he repeated that he was not guilty. The judge sentenced James Camb to be hanged by the neck until he was dead.

The Court of Criminal Appeal held that there was no ground for interfering in the

GAY'S LIFE . . . She was an ambitious young actress with a thirst for life. Her expression (below left) is hard and determined. Below: Gay at work on stage.

case and dismissed Camb's appeal. Nevertheless he escaped the gallows as the result of a fortunate accident for him. While the appeal was pending, the House of Commons, on a free vote, added a new clause to the Criminal Justice Bill then before Parliament, suspending the death penalty for five years and substituting life imprisonment for murder. Although the House of Lords subsequently rejected it, the Home Secretary decided that during the interval while the issue remained in doubt all pending capital sentences should be commuted to life imprisonment. Camb was one of those to benefit.

It subsequently transpired—and this could not be put in evidence at the trial—that Camb had assaulted other women passengers on three different occasions on the *Durban Castle*. Once he entered a woman's cabin and made advances to her, which she had only been able to repel after a struggle. He did this again without success in the case of another female passenger. Finally he tried to strangle a woman passenger in a shelter on deck where tools were kept; she lost consciousness and eventually recovered to find Camb standing over her.

Again, none of these women had dared to report the matter.

James Camb was released from prison on licence in September 1959. He changed his surname to Clarke and got a job as a head waiter. In May 1967 he was convicted of indecently assaulting a girl of 13 and somewhat surprisingly was put on probation for two years. Sometime after that he went to Scotland where he again obtained employment as head waiter.

Here he was charged with sexual misbehaviour with three schoolgirls, as a result of which his licence was revoked and he was returned to jail to continue his life sentence.

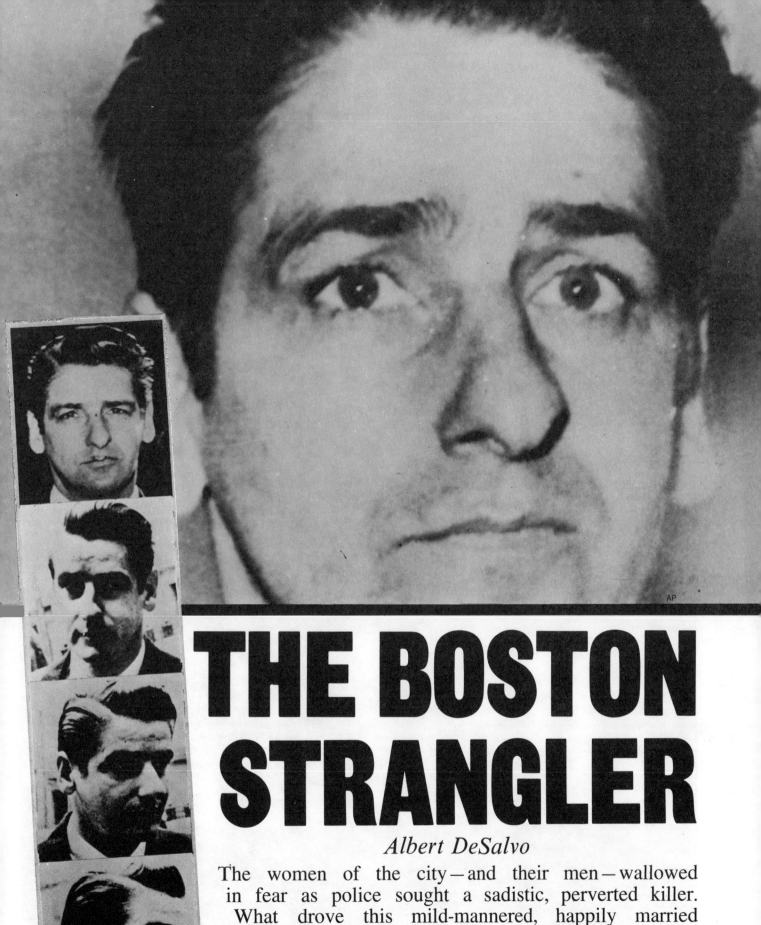

THE BOSTON STRANGLER

Albert DeSalvo

The women of the city—and their men—wallowed in fear as police sought a sadistic, perverted killer. What drove this mild-mannered, happily married man to perpetrate one sexual atrocity after another? Unfortunately the answer was to die with him. . . .

31

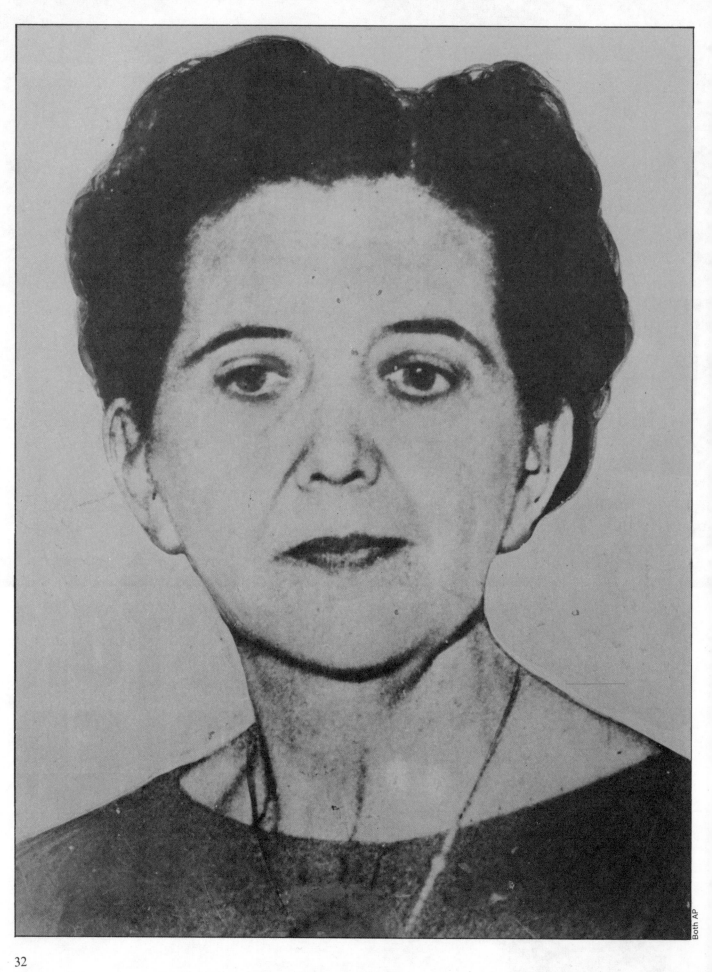

32

JUST before eight o'clock on the evening of June 14, 1962, 25-year-old Juris Slesers, a bespectacled research engineer with the Massachusetts Institute of Technology, climbed the three flights of stairs to his mother's apartment at 77, Gainsborough Street, in the Back Bay district of Boston.

He was anxious to be on time to drive his 55-year-old mother, Mrs. Anna Slesers, to a service at the nearby Latvian Church. Mrs. Slesers, divorced 20 years earlier, was herself a Latvian who had fled from the Soviet occupation of her country.

Juris knocked at the door and waited. From inside the small apartment there was no sound of movement. He knocked again, and when there was still no response, he hammered on the door. He was rapidly becoming anxious.

It seemed strange that she should either be sleeping or have gone out when she was expecting him to call. In the end Juris decided that he could wait no longer. Summoning his full strength, he took a short run at the door and burst it open.

All was dark inside the apartment, and Juris walked into a chair which—in a manner alien to his mother's usual tidiness—had been left in the middle of the narrow hallway. He looked first into the living-room and then the bedroom. Finding no sign of his mother, he returned to the hallway and strode through it towards the kitchen and bathroom.

Clumsily shaped bow

His mother was there, between those two rooms, lying on her back, her blue housecoat flung open and revealing her total nakedness and her legs spread wide. A blue cord, belonging to the housecoat, was knotted tightly around her neck and fastened beneath her chin in a clumsily shaped bow. Juris could see at a glance that she was dead. He stared around wildly for a moment, taking in the fact that the bath was half full of water, and that rubbish from a wastebin had been spread on the kitchen floor. Then he called the police.

. Within minutes detectives and a doctor were at the apartment—but there was not much for them to go on. Apart from the strewing of the contents of the wastebin there were a few other signs of disturbance—drawers had been opened and rummaged through. But there was no evidence of a serious attempt at robbery. Mrs. Slesers had been sexually assaulted, and the officers' initial conclusion was that an intruder had somehow entered the apartment intent upon committing a

A DIVORCEE, Anna Slesers
(far left), was his first victim; only
six months later the wire services
were reporting the Strangler's eighth.

robbery. However, finding a scantily dressed woman who looked much younger than her years, he had been overcome by sexual desire. The intruder had then strangled the woman merely, perhaps, to ensure her silence.

No other leads presented themselves, and the death of Mrs. Slesers was listed, for the time being, as another unsolved murder. But then, on Saturday, June 30, there occurred another series of events that started a new line of police action. Mrs. Nina Nichols, a 68-year-old widow, returned to her apartment on Boston's Commonwealth Avenue after a three-day visit to out-of-town friends. She immediately telephoned her sister, Mrs. Marguerite Steadman, at whose house she was due for dinner within an hour.

The two women chatted for a few minutes, Mrs. Nichols assuring her sister that she would be on time for the meal. Suddenly she broke off the conversation, saying: "Excuse me, Marguerite, there's my door buzzer. I'll call you right back." She did not do so, the dinner hour of six o'clock passed, and Mrs. Nichols failed to arrive at the Steadmans' home.

Two nylon stockings

By 7.30 Mr. Steadman, concerned at his wife's anxiety, rang the janitor at the Commonwealth Avenue apartment building and asked him if Mrs. Nichols had left. No, the janitor said, her car was still parked by the building. At Mr. Steadman's request, he agreed to go up to the apartment and investigate.

Receiving no answer to his knock, the janitor let himself in with his pass-key. He saw at once, from the clothes and other items strewn around the floor, that the apartment had been ransacked. Then, as he looked towards the open bedroom door, he saw the naked body of Mrs. Nichols lying near the bed. Her housecoat had been pulled up above her waist and two nylon stockings had been tied very tightly around her neck.

Even in the few fearful moments in which he stared at the horrifying sight the janitor could see that the end of the stockings had been drawn together in the shape of a crude bow.

It was this strangely brutal "trademark" that immediately made the police associate this killing with that of Mrs. Slesers—and there were other similarities. Like Mrs. Slesers, Mrs. Nichols had been sexually assaulted; when detectives carefully searched the apartment they found that, although its contents had been disturbed, nothing of value had been taken.

Among several easily-disposable items

BOASTFULNESS and contrition mingled in DeSalvo's attitude. The psychiatrists would call him a "completely uncontrolled" schizophrenic.

of value left untouched was a $300 camera. The inference appeared to be that the killer had wanted only to give the *impression* that the motive was robbery—while his real intention was murder-with-sex. The man whom they must seek, the police concluded, was not a thief but someone distinctly more frightening—a sex maniac.

But the pattern was arranging itself even more swiftly and alarmingly than the police yet realized. Two days later, on Monday, July 2, two elderly women living in an apartment house in Lynn, Massachusetts, north of Boston, reported that their neighbour, 65-year-old Helen Blake, had not been seen since the previous Saturday. They had opened Miss Blake's apartment door with a pass-key, they told the police, but on noticing signs of disorder they had been too afraid to look further.

Detectives went at once to the apartment and found Helen Blake lying face downwards on her bed, dead. Her pajama top had been pushed up to her shoulders, leaving her, otherwise, completely naked. She had been sexually attacked and strangled with a nylon stocking. Apparently after death, her brassiere had been bound around her neck. The brassiere straps had been knotted under her chin in the form of a large bow.

There was now no doubt in detectives' minds that they were facing a crisis. Boston Police Commissioner McNamara ordered the cancellation of all police leave, and circulated a warning to women—especially those living alone—to lock their doors, admit no strangers, and report any prowlers. All listed sex offenders in and around Boston were picked up for questioning. Discreet inquiries were made about patients who had been discharged from nearby mental institutions.

Revoltingly obscene

But, as hard as they worked, the police could find no direct clue to the killer. More than a month passed without a report of another similar murder. There were some in Boston who began to hope that the death plague had passed. Then, on August 21, a widow of 75, named Ida Irga, was found strangled in her apartment in Boston's West End. A pillow case was tied bitingly deep around her neck, and she, too, had been the victim of sexual assault.

In her case, however, the murderer had added some appalling touches to his handiwork. He had placed two chairs widely apart and tied a leg of the body to each chair. The result was that the first person to open the apartment door—and that happened to be the 13-year-old son of the building's caretaker—would be confronted with a revoltingly obscene sight.

What baffled the police more than

anything else was that in all these cases the murderer seemed to have been willingly admitted to the victims' homes. There was no evidence of break-ins, therefore the murderer must have adopted a plausible play-acting role that would secure him entrance.

Perhaps he passed himself off as a gas or electricity employee? Perhaps, indeed, he *was* such an employee whose mind had given way? The questions were endless, the answers few. And the shadowy figure—who had by now become known as The Boston Strangler—continued to be received into women's homes and to kill them.

More women were to die at the Strangler's hands between August 1962 and January 1964—until the final total was 13. Four of the prey were in their twenties; the youngest was 19 and the eldest 85. One victim, 23-year-old Joann Graff, was strangled on November 23, 1963, with her nylon stockings left knotted in a bow. This at a time when she, like the rest of America, was stunned by the shock of the previous day's assassination of President John F. Kennedy.

There were suspects who were interrogated, and there were men who, for a variety of reasons, "confessed" to being the Strangler. But when the murders ceased in January 1964 it seemed that

the real killer might never be traced. Then, on October 27, 1964, a report to the police from a young housewife in Cambridge, Massachusetts, dramatically changed the situation.

She said that at 9.30 a.m. she was dozing in bed, after seeing her teacher-husband off to work, when a man suddenly appeared at the door. He was of medium build, dressed in green slacks, and with his eyes shrouded by large green sunglasses. As the young wife gave a startled gasp he said: "Don't worry, I'm a detective," and came slowly towards her. "You leave this room at once!" the girl shouted. But the man leapt forward, pinned her to the bed and waved a knife in front of her eyes. "Not a sound or I'll kill you," he commanded.

Kissed and fondled

Swiftly, he gagged her with her underwear. He tied her to the bed, spread-eagled, with her ankles to the foot of the bedstead, her wrists to its head, and then kissed and fondled her body. She lay writhing and petrified until, to her unbelieving relief, he abruptly ceased and loosened her bonds sufficiently for her to slip from them.

Rising from the bed, he ordered: "You be quiet for ten minutes." Then, in what seemed like an embarrassed after-

the Strangler

began making because he had so much time on his hands.

They sold in the prison gift shop for £3 to £8. Immediately after his death, visitors to the jail rushed to snap them up.

De Salvo was once involved in drug trafficking in the prison, but there was no information yet to link this with his death.

Walpole State Jail in Massachusetts is one of the toughest in the U.S. There have been riots and a dozen murders in the past year.

George Nasser, De Salvo's friend and former cellmate, was jailed for two vicious killings.

But the Strangler himself was serving a life sentence for armed robbery and sex offences.

...he confessed to ...men in the early ...tried for ...nce.

then turned him
...ed him with the

...d been beaten up
...recently argued
...other inmates,

...y is that the
...d because other
...trying to cut
...his lucrative

THE BEST EPITAPH for DeSalvo came from F. Lee Bailey, his attorney: a "vegetable walking around in a human body".

thought, he added: "I'm sorry." The next instant he fled from the bedroom and the apartment.

The moment she was free, the girl frantically rang the police. When the detectives arrived she gave them so detailed a description of the intruder that, from it, a police artist made a meticulously accurate sketch. One detective recognized the sketched face immediately. "This," he said, "looks like the Measuring Man", and went straight to offenders' records.

In the records was a full account of the Measuring Man—who, in 1960, had assaulted women by calling upon them, posing as an artist's agent, and taking their personal measurements as a prelude to supposed employment as models. The intimacies he sought in using his tape measure led to his arrest and 11 months in jail. He had been released in April 1962; his name was Albert H. DeSalvo.

The police telephoned maintenance man DeSalvo, invited him to talk to them, and on November 3 he presented himself at police headquarters in Cambridge. He vehemently denied attacking the young housewife. But she, watching

Picture by Mark Sennet

De Salvo—13 women died at his hands

through a window of the interrogation room, identified him instantly. To the police it appeared to be no more than a routine matter—although, as a precaution, DeSalvo's photograph was teletyped to neighbouring states. The response was astonishing.

From surrounding police forces there poured in messages saying that the photograph had been identified by scores of women as that of a man who had sexually assaulted them. To many detectives he was known as the "Green Man" because so many women had described

their assailant as wearing green slacks.

When DeSalvo's 30-year-old wife later visited her husband at police headquarters, detectives felt that she suspected him of extreme forms of sexual indulgence. She urged him: "Al, tell them everything; don't hold anything back."

"I've committed more than four hundred breaks, all in this area, and there's a couple of rapes you don't know about," he said, in tones that suggested a mixture of contrition and boastfulness. He pointed out Cambridge apartments to police which he had entered by using a small strip of polyethylene to slip the locks.

Daily Express

DeSalvo, held and awaiting trial on "Green Man" rape charges, was sent to the Boston State Hospital at Bridgewater for observation. There he was found to be "potentially suicidal and quite clearly overtly schizophrenic", and not competent to stand trial. In Cambridge on February 4, 1965, Judge Edward A. Pecce accepted that recommendation and ordered DeSalvo to be committed to Bridgewater, because of mental illness, "until further orders of the court".

So, at 34, Albert DeSalvo, broad-shouldered and husky, disappeared for a time from public view. There was still no evidence that he was the Boston Strangler. Finally, however, he began to talk to those he trusted—such as Assistant Attorney General John S. Bottomley.

He recalled his fateful meeting with Anna Slesers, his first murder victim. It was pure chance, he said, that led him to her apartment building. He climbed the stairs, knocked at the door, and, fatally for her, Mrs. Slesers opened it. "I was sent to do some work in your apartment," he said. She, all trusting, let him in. He described how he killed her, but gave no reason for doing so.

Two bottles of milk

He recounted his visit to 65-year-old Helen Blake. Once again he gained admittance by telling his potential victim that he had to do some work in her apartment. Miss Blake was puzzled. "This is the first I've heard about it," she said—but she accepted his further explanation that, "I'm supposed to check all the windows for leaks and I'm going to do some interior painting." Helpfully, he carried in two bottles of milk standing outside her door.

As she got on with her housework, they chatted casually. Then, without warning, he clutched hold of her. "I grabbed my hand right behind her neck," he said. "She was a heavy-set, big-breasted woman. We were standing near the bed. She went down right away, passed right out." Under her housecoat she had been wearing pajamas and he pulled those off. "She was unconscious," he went on. "I got on top. I had intercourse . . . I think I put a bra around her neck, and a nylon stocking, too."

His encounter with Nina Nichols was equally haphazard, he declared. He wandered around her apartment building, ringing door bells but receiving no answer until he rang one, "and I see the name Nina Nichols over it". Mrs. Nichols answered and was given the inevitable story about checking the apartment. However, she was hesitant. She wanted to know who had sent him. The building superintendent, he replied. Still she was uncertain. Boldly, DeSalvo took a chance and told her: "Look, you can call him

up." This offer satisfied Mrs. Nichols, and she let him in.

As in the previous killings, he suddenly grabbed at his victim and "she fell back with me on the bed, on top of me". Mrs. Nichols fainted, so he rolled her on to the floor and had intercourse with her before trying to strangle her with a belt he found lying nearby. When the belt broke he took a stocking and knotted it tightly three times around her neck.

He was asked to demonstrate the type of knot he tied. He did so, using his own shoelaces. The listening and watching investigators exchanged glances: the knot DeSalvo tied was in the form of a crude bow—the Strangler's bow.

Between two chairs

Mrs. Ida Irga died in much the same way—but DeSalvo could give no reason for leaving her bound, with her legs yawning between two chairs. "I just did it," was the only explanation he could offer. It was pointed out to him that Mrs. Irga was 75, and could not fairly be counted as a sexually attractive woman. DeSalvo reacted with impatience.

"Attractiveness had nothing to do with it," he snapped. "When this certain time comes on me, it's a very immediate thing. When I get this feeling, instead of going to work I make an excuse to my boss. I start driving and I start building this image up, and that's why I find myself not knowing where I'm going."

Sophie Clark, however, was a desirable, Negro student of 20, found murdered by the Strangler on December 5, 1962. She had been gagged, three stockings had been twisted with enormous force around her neck, and she had been raped and left with her legs forced widely apart. But Sophie had not been such an easy victim as the elder women dispatched by the Strangler—for there were signs in the room of a struggle.

DeSalvo recalled that she had not wanted to let him in because her roommates were out. Once more, his glib tongue proved persuasive. He pretended to know her room-mates and talked fast about modelling and how Sophie Clark could earn $20-$30 an hour. He asked her to turn around—"to let me see how you're built"—and as she did so he threw her on to the settee. She fainted and he had intercourse. Later, as she revived, she began to fight back, and it was then that he killed her.

Yes, said DeSalvo, almost dreamily, he remembered the date of that adventure very well indeed. It was his wedding anniversary.

One victim, Patricia Bissette—who was 23 and who died among her Christmas decorations in her apartment on Boston's Park Drive on December 31, 1962—won a kind of post-mortem sympathy

from DeSalvo. She was so trustful that she made him coffee and chatted as if they were old friends. "She talked to me like a man, treated me like a man," he said, sadly. All the same he forced his lust on her, and she died like the others. He made one special concession to the corpse of this girl: he covered it, respectfully, with a bathrobe.

He worried aloud about his reason for killing a girl who had evoked in him a spark of decent, human feeling. "I don't know," he mused, "whether I did this for the sex act or out of hate for her—not her in particular, but a woman. After seeing her body, naturally the sex act came in. But I did not enjoy it. There was no thrill at all. . . . She did me no harm, and yet I did it. Why to her?"

The Strangler's last victim, Mary Sullivan, 19, who died on January 4, 1964, suffered the most savagely at his hands. Her body was found not only strangled, but mutilated by the use of a broomstick handle and with other atrocities committed upon it. DeSalvo acknowledged the sickening handiwork as his—but protested that it seemed, somehow, to have been done by someone who was himself and yet, at the same time, was someone else.

"I'm realizing that these things are true, and that these things that I did do, that I have read about in books, that other people do, that I didn't think or realize I would ever do these things," he pleaded.

Lack of evidence

The stories that he told, the confessions he dictated, the sketches he made of some of the victims' homes, pointed to the fact that Albert DeSalvo was, indeed, the Boston Strangler. That somewhere, in the darkness of his mind, were unknown forces that had driven him to kill so mercilessly and so pointlessly. But, because of lack of supporting evidence, the law felt unable to accept his word. Accordingly, he was not charged with being the Strangler or with committing the Strangler's crimes.

Instead, he was eventually tried for other crimes, pre-dating the Strangler period: crimes of armed robbery, assault and sex offences against four women fortunate enough to have lived to identify him. In 1967 he was sentenced to life imprisonment. However, as it happened, he had only six more years to live.

On November 26, 1973, the 42-year-old criminal was found in his prison cell in Walpole State Prison, Massachusetts, dead from 16 stab wounds. The best epitaph on Albert DeSalvo came from his attorney, F. Lee Bailey, who stated that his client was insane, a schizophrenic, "a completely uncontrolled vegetable walking around in a human body".

THEY KILLED FOR MONEY

THE BRIDES IN THE BATH

George Smith

The notorious bigamist who preyed on lonely, unsuspecting women.
He married them, took their money . . . then he drowned them.

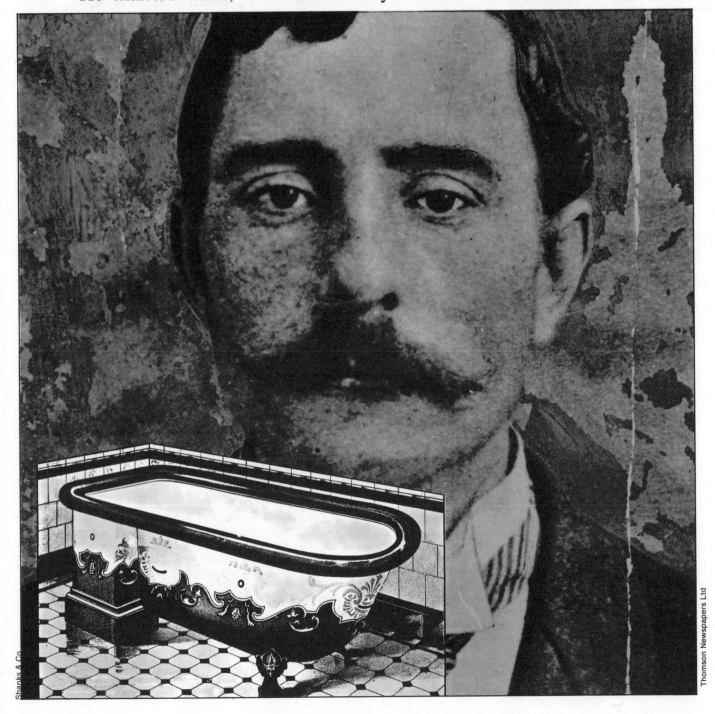

FOR NINE days during the summer of 1915 the attention of the British public was temporarily diverted from the bloody trench warfare in France to an amazing murder trial which took place in London's Central Criminal Court, the Old Bailey. The accused whom the police brought into the dock on June 22, 1915, was a 43-year-old criminal adventurer charged under his real name of George Joseph Smith—although he had employed a number of aliases in the course of his unsavoury sexual and criminal career.

As a youngster he had been sent to a reformatory and later went to prison twice for stealing. From an early age, in spite of a certain talent for drawing and playing the piano, he was the despair of his respectable mother—who prophesied with remarkable accuracy that he would die with his boots on. He had tried his hand at a variety of occupations: gymnasium instructor in the army, music hall songwriter, baker, junk shop owner, and finally dealer in antiques.

Lonely women

However, his principal occupation was preying upon lonely and unsuspecting women who, unfortunately for them, found him most attractive. It was one of these women, Bessie Mundy—whom he had "married" bigamously as Henry Williams in 1910—that he was tried for murdering two years later. She died while taking a bath at the lodgings where they lived together in Herne Bay, on the English south coast.

The presiding judge at the trial was the great commercial lawyer Mr. Justice Scrutton. The prosecution was led by the senior prosecuting counsel Mr. (later Sir) Archibald Bodkin, afterwards Director of Public Prosecutions. Smith was defended by Sir Edward Marshall Hall, the most popular and successful criminal advocate of his day and then at the height of his powers. As Smith had no money, Marshall Hall provided his services for £3 5s. 6d.—the maximum fee allowed defence counsel by the Poor Prisoners' Defence Act.

After Smith had formally pleaded not guilty, Mr. Bodkin began his opening speech for the prosecution. In outlining the prisoner's career to the jury, the prosecutor drew particular attention to the fact that the accused—under the assumed name of George Oliver Love—had married Caroline Beatrice Thornhill at Leicester in 1898. A year or two later she left him, but she remained his legal wife and was alive at the time of the trial. In 1908, Smith met a young woman named Edith Pegler in Bristol and "married" her under his own name. They lived together from time to time, and though he would leave her for long periods, he always returned to her in the end. In fact he had

done so after the death of Bessie Mundy.

On August 26, 1910, the prisoner went through a ceremony of marriage, posing as Henry Williams, with 31-year-old Beatrice ("Bessie") Constance Annie Mundy in Weymouth Registry Office. She had a small fortune of £2,500 left by her late father, who had been a bank manager. She could not touch the capital sum, which was held in trust for her, but she was paid £8 a month from the trust, which she allowed to accumulate.

By September 1910 the accumulated balance amounted to £138, and this Smith obtained by applying for it to the trust solicitor in his "wife's" name. As soon as he received it, he made off, leaving her without a penny. He subsequently wrote to her explaining that his health had become "terribly impaired" as the result of an "infectious disease" which he claimed she had given him, and that a long cure was necessary before he could return.

Meanwhile, Bessie went to live in lodgings with a friend in Weston-super-Mare. There, by an extraordinary coincidence, while walking along the esplanade one day in March 1912, she spotted her errant "husband". Instead of running away or calling the police, she spoke to him and again fell completely under his charm. She immediately left her lodgings to spend the night with him, not even taking her nightdress. The reunited couple then moved together to lodgings in Herne Bay.

There was no bath in the new house, but Smith bought one secondhand and installed it in an empty room in the lodgings. This was on July 6, 1912. Next day they both made wills, the unfortunate Bessie appointing her "husband" sole executor and legatee. Four days later the couple called on a local doctor named French. Smith said that his wife had shown signs of epilepsy—although the lady described herself as being perfectly well except for occasional headaches.

Completely submerged

On the morning of July 13, Dr. French received a note from Smith: "Do come at once. I am afraid my wife is dead." When the doctor arrived at the lodgings, he found that this was so, the woman's body being completely submerged in the bath water. In one hand she clutched a piece of soap.

At the coroner's inquest, Dr. French stated that in his opinion the woman drowned as the result of a fit of epilepsy in the bath. In these circumstances it was not surprising that the jury returned a verdict of death by misadventure—"the cause of death being that while taking a bath she had an epileptic seizure causing her to fall back into the water and be drowned".

The dead woman's estate was proved at £2,571, and under the terms of her will

her "husband" inherited all of it. He first invested the proceeds in house property, and after selling out at a considerable loss, used the £1,300 that was left to buy an annuity which brought him an income of £76 a year. Clearly George Joseph Smith had an expectation of a long life.

"This case is of a very grave character," said the prosecutor after he had told the jury how Bessie Mundy had died, "and one to which you will give the most earnest attention in the interests not only of the prisoner, but also of the public." Counsel paused dramatically for a few moments. He then turned to the judge and said that he had an important point of law concerning the admissibility of certain evidence to put to him. Mr. Justice Scrutton accordingly directed the jury to retire while it was being argued.

Virtually doomed

This was a move which Marshall Hall had feared, since he knew from the documents in his brief that there was evidence that his client had "married" two other women, that the two had likewise died in their baths, and that they had previously both executed wills making the prisoner sole beneficiary. Hall realized that if once this evidence was admitted his client was virtually doomed.

Mr. Bodkin's point was that the prosecution was entitled to call evidence of any character tending to prove that this was a case of killing by deliberate design and not by accident—and that the accused in causing the death of Bessie Mundy was operating a "system". In reply Marshall Hall submitted that evidence of "system" was only admissible where it was necessary for the defence to set up a denial of intent. It was not necessary in this case, he said, since as yet the prosecution had not put forward sufficient evidence to displace the primary presumption of innocence in the prisoner.

It was a gallant effort on the lawyer's part, but it proved of no avail. The judge ruled that such evidence *was* admissible. However, he warned the jury that they must not use it to infer that the prisoner was a man of bad character and infamous acts, but only to help them to decide whether Miss Mundy's death was the result of an accident or had been deliberately engineered by Smith.

The prosecutor then proceeded to outline the facts of the two additional murders for which he suggested that the prisoner was responsible. In 1913 Smith had bigamously married a buxom young nurse named Alice Burnham whom he had seen praying in a Wesleyan-Methodist chapel in Southsea. Her father, a fruitgrower in Buckinghamshire, had been keeping a sum of £104 for her, and when Smith wrote to Mr. Burnham demanding that it should be handed over, Mr. Burnham

MUSTACHIOED MURDERER George Joseph Smith (right) was a skilful seducer. Women found him irresistible and gave up not only themselves but their money in response to his charm. He drowned three of his wives in the bath. Below, the two who escaped: Caroline Thornhill (top), Edith Pegler.

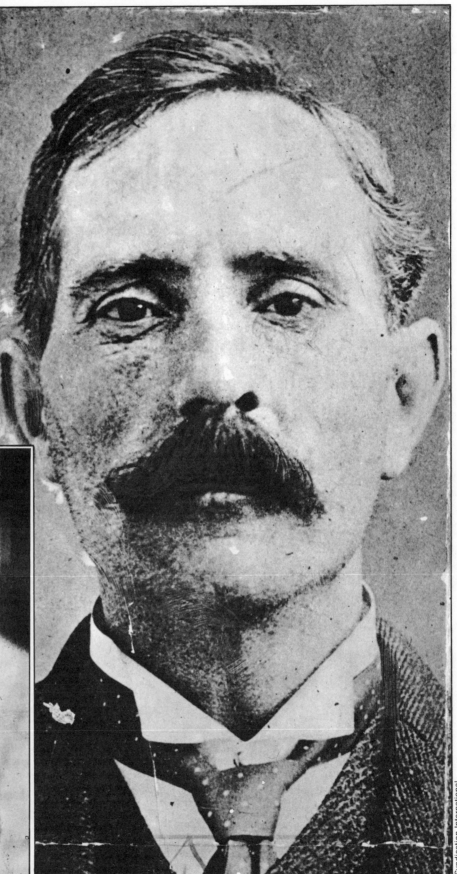

FIRST VICTIM . . . . Bessie Mundy pictured with Smith after their "marriage". Two years later she lay in her grave (right). At the inquest the jury gave a verdict of "misadventure". Smith's luck did not last.

BUXOM BRIDE number four, Alice Burnham. Smith collected £500 insurance.

replied in a letter in which he asked some questions about his son-in-law's family background. To his letter he received the following astonishing postcard:

Sir, — In answer to your application regarding my parentage, my mother was a bus-horse, my father a cab-driver, my sister a roughrider over the Arctic regions. My brothers were all gallant sailors on a steam-roller. This is the only information I can give to those who are not entitled to ask such questions contained in the letter I received on the 24th inst.

Your despised son-in-law,
G. SMITH

In the end Smith got Alice Burnham's £104 through a solicitor. He also saw to it that she took out an insurance policy of £500 on her life, as well as making a will leaving everything she had to him. Together they visited Blackpool and stayed in lodgings — where the landlady saw water coming through the ceiling one evening when Alice was taking a bath. She was afterwards found drowned in the bath. Much to the landlady's surprise, Mr. Smith had the body put in a plain deal coffin and given a pauper's funeral. "When they are dead, they are done with," he remarked callously. The coroner's jury brought in a verdict of accidental death.

Insurance money

Shortly afterwards Smith received the £500 insurance money on Alice Burnham's life, which he prudently handed back to the insurance company in order to increase his annuity by some £30 a year. He spent Christmas with one of his former "wives", Edith Pegler, and her family in Bristol, saying he had just returned from a profitable antique dealing visit to Spain.

About a year later, under the name of John Lloyd, he contracted another bigamous marriage, this time in Highgate to a clergyman's daughter named Margaret Lofty. She was the most highly born as well as the most short-lived of his brides. She likewise made a will the day after their "marriage", and later the same evening the sound of splashing was heard coming from the bathroom, followed by the slapping of wet hands on flesh, and finally a sigh.

A short while later the landlady heard the mournful strains of the hymn "Nearer my God to Thee" being played on the harmonium in the Lloyds' sitting-room. Then she heard the slamming of the front door. Before long the male lodger returned and knocked at the landlady's door. He asked about the key which she had given him, but which he had forgotten, and added: "I have bought some tomatoes for Mrs. Lloyd's supper."

A third coroner's jury exonerated Mr. Lloyd, who showed great emotion. "We were only married on Thursday," he said. Being a Friday evening the incident attracted the attention of the national press, and on the following Sunday the *News of the World* headlined the story of a "Bride's Tragic Fate on Day after Wedding".

Under observation

Among those who read the story was the late Alice Burnham's father, and also another landlady who later turned Mr. Lloyd away when he came to engage lodgings. He could not provide a satisfactory reference after he had been shown the bath which he had complained was very small—although as an afterthought he murmured: "I daresay it is large enough for someone to lie in." Both the landlady and Mr. Burnham got in touch with the police, and as a result Mr. Lloyd was kept under observation. He was arrested on February 1, 1915, when about to enter a solicitor's office in Shepherd's Bush, London, with a view to proving the late Margaret Lofty's will.

He was first charged with causing a false entry to be made at his bigamous marriage to his third victim. Then after he had been identified by Mr. Burnham, he was remanded in custody for further police inquiries. Two months later he was charged with the murder of Bessie Mundy, Alice Burnham, and Margaret Lofty—although he was only indicted for killing the first named.

"In each case you get the simulated marriage," said Mr. Bodkin in concluding his speech to the jury. "In each case all the ready money the woman had is realised. In each case the woman made a will in the prisoner's favour. In each case the property could only be got at through the woman's death . . . In each case there were inquiries about the bathroom. In each case the prisoner is the first to discover the death. In each case the prisoner is the person in immediate association with each woman before her death. In each case the bathroom doors are either unfastenable or unfastened . . . In each case there is the immediate disappearance of the prisoner."

The only one of Smith's "brides" to testify was Edith Pegler, the only one whom he loved enough neither to desert, to rob, nor to kill. On the whole, she said, the prisoner had been kind to her. But she added a curious fact when she stated that Smith had once warned her of the danger of baths to women. "I should advise you to be careful about these things," she stated he had told her, "as it is known that women often lose their lives through weak hearts and fainting in a bath." While she was giving her evidence, the prisoner showed some signs of distress.

When a police inspector took the stand, Smith lost all control. "He is a scoundrel!" he shouted as he jumped up from his seat in the dock. "He ought to be in this dock. He will be one day!"

"Sit down," said the judge. "You are doing yourself no good." But the prisoner refused to be pacified and he banged his fist on the ledge in front of him, his face white with fury. "I don't care tuppence what you say," he roared back at Mr. Justice Scrutton, "you can't sentence me to death. I have done no murder!"

The police inspector described how he had induced a woman friend, who was a strong swimmer, to don a bathing costume and subject herself to an experiment in one of the baths, which had been filled with water. The inspector pulled up her legs at the narrow end so that her head fell under water. She immediately lost consciousness and there was considerable difficulty in bringing her round.

This testimony was corroborated by the celebrated pathologist Sir Bernard Spilsbury, who was called for the prosecution after the three baths had been brought into court as exhibits. "If a woman of the stature of Miss Mundy was in the bath in which she died," said Sir Bernard, "the first onset of an epileptic fit would stiffen and extend the body. In view of her height, 5 feet 7 inches, and the length of the bath, 5 feet, I do not think her head would be submerged during that stage of the fit . . .

Limp body

"After the seizure has passed the state of the body is that of relaxation. The body would probably be limp and unconscious. Bearing in mind the length of the body and the size of the bath, I do not think she would be likely to be immersed during the state of relaxation . . . Dr. French has described the legs straight out from the hips and the feet up against the end of the bath, out of the water. I cannot give any explanation of how a woman—assuming she had had an epileptic seizure—could get into that position by herself. *If the feet at the narrow end were lifted out of the water, that might allow the trunk and head to slide down the bath.*"

Defence counsel could do little with this formidable witness in cross-examination. However, Marshall Hall tried his best, as always. He endeavoured to get the witness to say that clutching a piece of soap lent support to the theory of epilepsy.

"It is not impossible," was as far as Spilsbury would go, "not very likely," he concluded cautiously.

When the case for the prosecution was closed—no less than 112 witnesses had been called and 264 incriminating exhibits put in—Marshall Hall rose and announced briefly: "I do not call any evidence." This gave him the last word

ONE DAY was all Margaret Lofty (above) lasted—just enough time to sign her will in Smith's favour. Opposite, Smith listens calmly to the overwhelming evidence presented against him. But he frequently interrupted the trial with passionate outbursts. Far right, Sir Archibald Bodkin, prosecuting counsel (top) and the famous Sir Edward Marshall Hall who used all his celebrated verbal skill in a vain attempt to get Smith acquitted of the ghastly charges.

with the jury, and again he exerted all his great rhetorical skill with the scanty material at his disposal.

The gist of his defence argument was that no act of violence had been proven, and that it would have been impossible for his client to have killed Bessie Mundy without leaving marks of violence and evidence of a struggle. "If you tried to drown a kitten, it would scratch you, and do you think a woman would not scratch?"

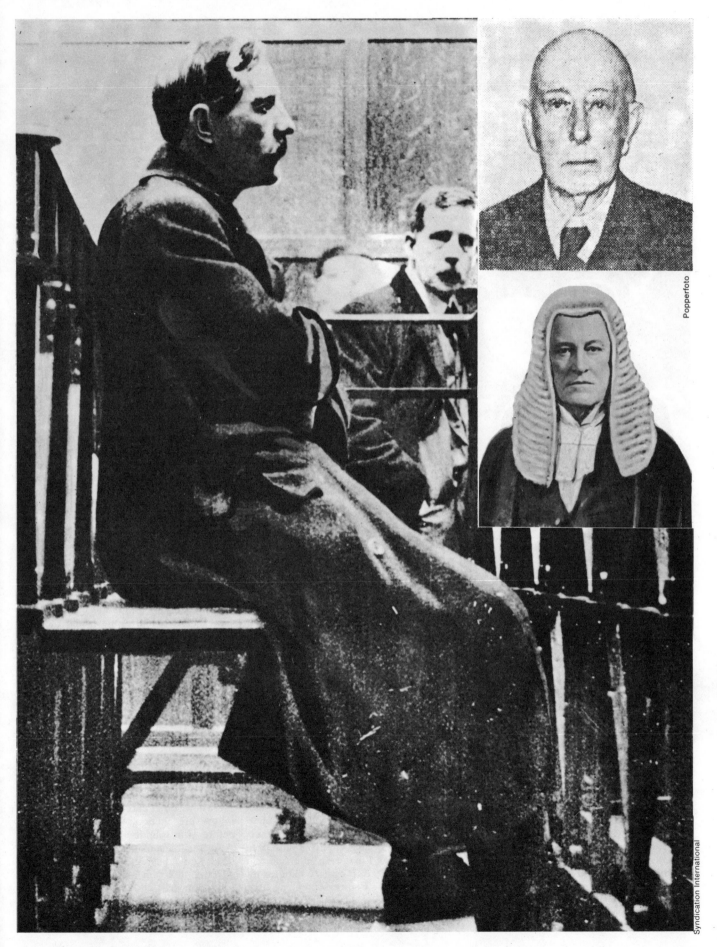

Syndication International

Popperfoto

WATERTIGHT EVIDENCE ... Home Office pathologist Sir Bernard Spilsbury arrives at the Old Bailey clutching vital evidence. It was his testimony which tied up the case against Smith. The whole trial was a fascinating and lurid diversion for Londoners accustomed to a diet of gloomy war news. Above, crowds jostle and push at the doors of the Old Bailey on the last day of the trial in tense anticipation of the verdict being pronounced.

As evidence of Smith's humanity he stressed the mutual affection between the prisoner and Edith Pegler, adding that the crimes of which Smith had been accused were outside the orbit of sane humanity.

Most dramatic moment

"Let me with all the solemnity I can," he besought the jury, "and with all the power of conviction I can put into words say to you: be fair to yourselves, be fair to the prisoner, be just to justice itself before you decide the fate of this man by saying that this terrible accusation against him has been proved."

Mr. Justice Scrutton summed up largely against the prisoner, as he was obliged by the evidence to do. With great effect he compared the knocking at the landlady's door by Smith—shortly after Margaret Lofty had died—to the knocking at the gate just after the murder of Duncan in *Macbeth*—"The most dramatic moment in English poetry," the judge called it.

"You may as well hang me at once, the way you are going on," the prisoner shouted from the dock. "It is a disgrace to a Christian country, that is. I am not a murderer, though I may be a bit peculiar."

It took the jury only twenty minutes to find Smith guilty. Before sentencing him to death by hanging, Mr. Justice Scrutton observed sternly: "Judges sometimes use this occasion to warn the public against

the repetition of such crimes—they sometimes use such occasions to exhort the prisoner to repentance. I propose to take neither of these courses. I do not believe there is another man in England who needs to be warned against the commission of such a crime, and I think that exhortation to repentance would be wasted on you."

An appeal was lodged challenging the evidence of the other murders, but the Court of Criminal Appeal held that this evidence of "system" had been rightly admitted, and the appeal was dismissed. The Home Secretary refused a reprieve and the law took its course.

Holy Communion

Smith protested his innocence to the last. On the morning of his execution in Maidstone Prison, in Kent, he partook of Holy Communion. To the prison chaplain who administered the sacrament he said: "I beg of you to believe me when I say I am innocent. No one else does, except my wife. I don't care now. I shall soon be in the presence of God, and I declare before Him I am innocent."

As the hangman put the cap over his head and adjusted the noose, he again declared, "I am innocent." Then the trap-door fell and the pinioned figure disappeared into the pit below the scaffold. George Joseph Smith died like his three lonely-hearts brides—by suffocation.

BLUEBEARD

Henri Landru

He loved 283 women . . . and killed ten of them. In a country famed for its lovers, he was the most famous. His name was Landru, but they called him Bluebeard . . .

THROUGHOUT the morning of December 7, 1921, a curious crowd of spectators gathered outside the Court of Assize in the Palais de Justice at Versailles. The entrance was guarded by police and troops, who turned away almost everyone who tried to gain admission to the small and shabby courtroom, since there was only accommodation for a handful of people inside apart from the court officials and lawyers concerned with the trial. It was a case which had already attracted world-wide interest, since the accused man was said to have had relations of one sort or another with no less than 283 women and to have murdered ten of them, having previously seduced them and persuaded them to hand over their money and property to him for safekeeping or invest-ment.

Enormous indictment

Punctually at one o'clock in the after-noon President Gilbert in red robes and gold-braided hat took his place on the bench accompanied by two assessors. The uniformed soldiers on duty in their steel helmets presented arms smartly and the usher rang his bell calling every-one in court to order. Immediately below the judicial bench was a table containing the grim exhibits in the case, pieces of charred clothing and human bones. At a sign from the President, a little door at the side of the courtroom opened and the prisoner appeared, escorted by three gendarmes, two of whom stood on either side of him and one behind as he stepped into the appointed place in court which served as a dock. A tall red-bearded figure, he looked a rather weary old man, al-though in truth he was only 52. His com-plexion wore the familiar prison pallor, since he had been in custody for more than two years.

The President's first duty was to estab-lish the prisoner's identity. "Your name is Landru?" he asked the man on whom every eye in court was firmly fixed. "Henri Désiré, son of Alexandre Julien and Henriette Floré Landru? You were born in Paris on 12 April 1869, and your last residence was 76 Rue de Roche-chouart?"

"Yes," Landru quietly replied.

The Clerk of the Court thereupon rose to his feet and proceeded to read the indictment, a document of enormous length, which it took the Clerk three hours to do and which occupied the great-er part of the first day of the trial. It was an extraordinary story of forgery, swind-ling, seduction and multiple murder. For the most part Landru listened to this appalling account with an air of apparent unconcern, his bearded face bent forward between his shoulders. Only once did he look up and scowl in the course of the lengthy recitation of his misdeeds. That was when the Clerk uttered the phrase, "exploitation of women". An audible titter ran round the courtroom at the mention of the 283 women with whom Landru was stated to have had "relations".

Landru's usual technique was the fam-iliar one of the matrimonial advertise-ment. A typical example of this "come into my parlour" technique appeared in *Le Journal,* a Paris morning newspaper, on May 11, 1915:

Widower with two children, aged forty-three, with comfortable income, affectionate, serious, and moving in good society, desires to meet widow with a view to matrimony.

Among the women who replied to this advertisement was a 44-year-old widow named Madame Anna Colomb, who gave full particulars of her family and fortune, discreetly giving her age as 29. In due course she received a letter from a Mon-sieur Cruchet, who described himself as a director of a factory in Montmartre. At the meeting which followed Cruchet told Anna Colomb that he was a war refugee, an engineer from Rocroi, who had left everything before the advancing Ger-mans and had come to Paris to build up his business afresh.

He added that he had a car, a little apartment in town and a modest house, the Villa Ermitage, at Gambais, near the forest of Rambouillet, not far from Paris. He now wished to marry and settle down, he said. The result was that Madame Colomb found Monsieur Cruchet most attractive and loved him "because he is a real gentleman and says such beautiful things to me".

Wife and children

After a while, however, Landru's ardour for the lady began to cool. The truth was that he had several other affairs on hand since there had been many replies to his advertisement and he could not spare all the time that the infatuated Anna Colomb demanded. However, they eventually came together again, she gave up her own apartment and went to live with her lover in his flat in the Rue Chateaudun, while she gave him her furniture to put into store. She also visited the villa at Gambais where Landru was known as Monsieur Fremyet.

Elsewhere and with other women he had different aliases: Petit, Dupont, Diard and Guillet. He had another villa at Vernouillet on the river Seine near Paris. He also had a second apartment in Paris, 76 Rue de Rochechouart, not to mention a wife and four children who lived at Clichy, where he ran a garage.

SURROUNDED BY WOMEN right to the end . . . Henri 'Bluebeard' Landru, some of his victims, and the ground where their remains were buried after burning.

Mme. COLOMB

Mme. LABORDE LINE

Mme. BUISSON.

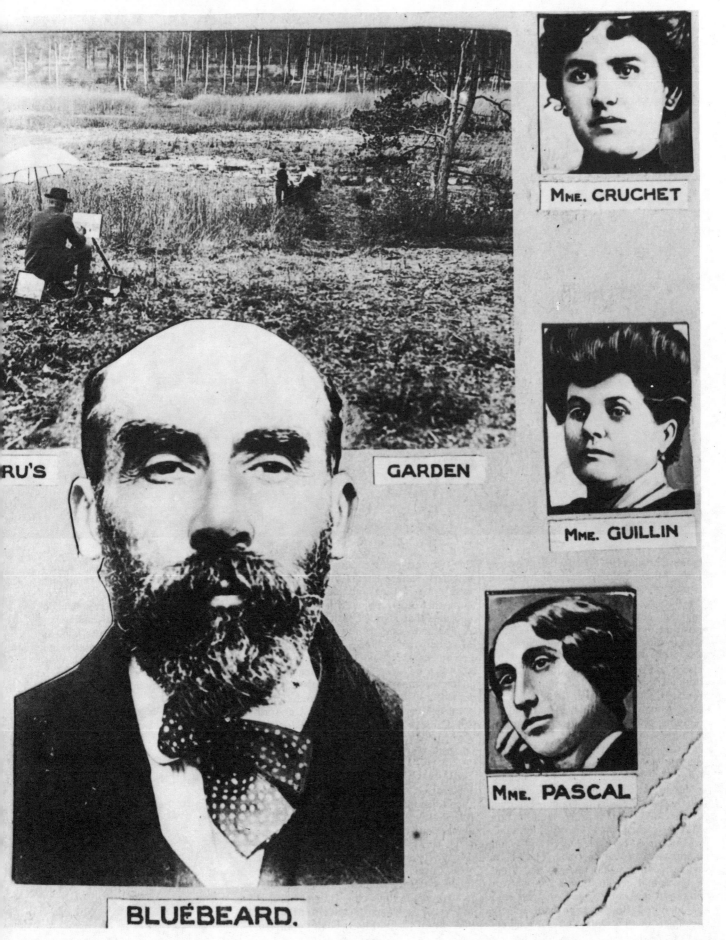

RU'S GARDEN

Mme. CRUCHET

Mme. GUILLIN

Mme. PASCAL

BLUÉBEARD.

On Christmas Eve 1916, the court was told, Mme. Colomb invited her sister Mme. Pelat to Gambais to meet her lover. M. Fremyet ingratiated himself by saying that he would soon regularise their position by marrying his mistress, after which they would be moving to Nice. That was the last Mme. Pelat saw of her sister and M. Fremyet. After writing to both of them at Gambais and receiving no reply, she addressed a letter to the local Mayor, asking him if he could tell her where M. Fremyet was and how to get into touch with him.

It so happened that not long before this the Mayor had received a similar request from a certain Mlle. Lacoste about her sister Mme. Celestine Buisson, who had also visited the villa in Gambais and had disappeared. On making inquiries the Mayor learned that the Villa Ermitage was occupied by a M. Dupont, of whom there was likewise no trace. The Mayor suggested that Mlle. Lacoste and Mme. Pelat should get into touch with one another. In due course they met and compared notes. Both women had seen the occupier of the villa and they agreed

that Cruchet-Fremyet and Dupont were singularly alike. Meanwhile the police were investigating another disappearance, that of a genuine Mme. Cruchet. It appeared that Jeanne Cruchet and her son André had gone to live with a certain M. Diard in his house at Vernouillet in December 1914 and had not been seen or heard of since. After making further inquiries, the police were satisfied that Cruchet, Fremyet, Dupont and Diard were one and the same person. On April 10, 1919, a warrant was issued for the arrest of the individual whose identity corresponded with any of these aliases.

Unmistakable figure

Next day, the court was told, Mlle. Lacoste happened to be walking along the Rue de Rivoli when she suddenly saw the unmistakable figure of the man she recognized as M. Dupont. He had a smartly-dressed young woman on his arm and Mlle. Lacoste saw them enter a shop. She followed them inside where she heard the man order a white china dinner service to be sent to his apartment. After the two had left the shop Mlle. Lacoste continued

"THE WOMEN never reproached me . . . perhaps some of them will turn up for the trial." The only people who turned up for Bluebeard's trial were a string of witnesses testifying that the missing women had last been seen with him. As the accused man gave evidence, the judge had to suppress laughter in court. When Bluebeard finally faced the guillotine, his humour could only be described as deadpan.

to follow them but eventually lost them in the crowd. She thereupon went to the nearest police station and reported her suspicions. On following up this clue, the police learned that the dinner service had been ordered by M. Lucien Guillet, an engineer, of 76 Rue de Rochechouart.

The following morning Landru was arrested in his apartment and told he would be charged with murder. He protested that he was Lucien Guillet, born at Rocroi, in 1874, and seemed shocked that he should be accused of a capital crime. He was then searched and the police discovered a black loose-leaved note-book in his pocket which he made an unsuccessful attempt to dispose of by throwing it out of the window.

Meticulous account

The note-book revealed that Landru kept a meticulous account of his daily expenses. For instance, on the day he invited Anna Colomb to Gambais, he had recorded one return ticket and one single ticket to the local station, similarly with Celestine Buisson. The note-book also showed that the replies to his matrimonial advertisements had been carefully classified and information had been filed about their fortunes, children, relations and so on. The names were briefly marked under the following heads:

1. To be answered *poste restante*.
2. Without money.
3. Without furniture.
4. No reply.
5. To be answered to initials *poste restante*.
6. Possible fortune.
7. To be further investigated.

The first police searches of the Villa Ermitage and the house at Vernouillet revealed nothing of importance, but later a stove was discovered in which Landru was alleged to have burnt the bodies of his victims after he had cut them up.

Afterwards 295 bone fragments of human bodies were discovered. These were believed to belong to three corpses; there was also a miscellaneous collection of women's clothing, buttons, and trinkets of various kinds.

Besides the Mesdames Buisson, Colomb and Cruchet and the latter's 18-year-old son, seven more women whom Landru knew were stated to have disappeared without trace. Their names were given to the court as Mme. Thérèse Laborde-Line, widow, aged 47, and a native of Buenos Aires, whom Landru called 'Brésil'; Mme. Desirée Guillin, a widow, aged 59, formerly a governess, who had inherited 22,000 francs which Landru drew out of her bank account with a forged signature, having also sold her furniture; Andreé Babelay, a servant girl, aged 19, whom Landru met in the Metro; Mme. Louise Jaume, a married woman, aged 38, who was separated from her husband, and whose money and furniture Landru appropriated after he had taken her to Gambais; Mme. Anne-Marie Pascal, a divorceé, aged 33, and a struggling dressmaker of easy morals, whose furniture and personal belongings were found in Landru's garage; and Mme. Marie-Thérèse Marchadier, a prostitute turned brothel-keeper, who gave up her establishment and went with Landru to Gambais, after parting with her furniture.

All the names with accompanying particulars appeared in the sinister black note-book which Landru had tried to hide from the police when he was arrested.

On the second day of the trial, President Gilbert examined the prisoner on his past record. "You have received seven sentences for fraud, Landru," he remarked. "Your parents were honest and decent folk. Your father was for a long time a fireman in the Vulcain Ironworks. Your mother worked at home as a dressmaker. After her death, your father who had retired to the Dordogne, came to Paris to see you but found you were in prison. He was so upset by your conduct that in 1912 he committed suicide in the Bois de Boulogne."

As the prisoner did not dispute these facts, the judge went on: "You were a clever boy at school and earned high praise from your teachers. On leaving school you were admitted as a subdeacon to a religious establishment?"

"Only for a short time," Landru added.

"Perhaps it was there," said the judge, "that you learned that unctuous manner which has been one of your chief methods of seduction, and which has helped you to capture the trust and affections of so many woman."

President Gilbert paused, but the prisoner remained silent. "Then," continued the judge, "you took up more profane occupations. Not far from you there lived your cousin Mme Remy, who had a young daughter."

"She had two," Landru interrupted.

"Very well. One of them became your mistress, and you had a daughter born in 1891. Two years later you regularized the position, married her and acknowledged the child. In all you had four children?" Landru nodded his agreement.

"You had a lot of different jobs," said the judge. "Clerk in an architect's office,

TRIAL BY PRESIDENT

PROCEDURE in French criminal trials differs from that in other national courts in several important respects. For one thing, the presiding judge, who sits with two legally qualified assessors and is called the President, takes a much more prominent part in the proceedings than, say, his British counterpart, whose function broadly speaking is limited to seeing that the rules of evidence and the rights of the accused are observed, to summing up the evidence to the jury, and in the event of the jury returning a verdict of guilty to passing sentence.

On the other hand, the President of a French assize court has the full record of the case in front of him which he has read, and he interrogates the prisoner on every detail of the charges during the proceedings. The basis of his interrogation is the dossier which has been compiled by the pre-trial investigating magistrate known as the *juge d'instruction*; this is usually the result of prolonged questioning by this official while the prisoner is in custody.

In French courts the whole of the prisoner's past criminal record forms an essential part of the indictment and is read out at the beginning of the trial. This also contrasts with British courts, where a witness of fact is only permitted to testify to matters of which he has direct and personal knowledge, but in France hearsay evidence is admissible—i.e. witnesses may repeat what they have been told by others.

Finally, in France the President of the Court must consult with the two assessors and take into account their views on the punishment due.

agent, toy salesman and so on. In fact you had no definite, stable occupation."

"Which proves how inadequate were the inquiries which were made about me," Landru again broke in. "The police are often inefficient."

"Yet," said the judge, "when the magistrate confronted you with this information you had nothing to say?"

Flattered conceit

The prisoner threw up his hands as if amazed at such official stupidity. "It was not my business to guide the police," he exclaimed. "Have they not been accusing me for the past three years of deeds which the women who disappeared never for one moment reproached me with?"

These words produced some laughter among the onlookers in court which the judge suppressed by calling for silence. "It is you," he emphasised his words by pointing a finger at the prisoner, "it is you who have made it impossible for these women to complain. That is as clear as anything."

Asked to explain to the jury why the names of so many women were in his note-book, at first he was evasive. Finally when pressed by the judge, he said: *"Eh bien! Voila!* It is the list of a business man, who entered the names of his clients with whom he did business." He had bought these women's furniture from them to help them during the war, he explained, intending to sell it back to them when the German armies had been driven out of France.

"Why then recruit your clients by means of matrimonial advertisements?" the judge asked.

"Just a little business ruse, very innocent," Landru replied. "It flattered their conceit," The prisoner let his gaze wander in the direction of the jury, as if to say what a clever answer he had given. But they did not look at all convinced. Then he turned again to the judge and said: "You say that some of these women have not been found. Perhaps they will turn up during the trial." However, none of them did so.

During the succeeding days a string of relatives of the ten women who had vanished came forward to testify to the occasions when they had last seen the women in question, usually in Landru's company. Others testified having seen dense smoke coming out of the chimneys of the houses which Landru had occupied at Gambais and Vernouillet, accompanied by a most offensive stench. Indeed one of the neighbours complained about it to the police at Vernouillet. This was at a critical stage of the First World War, and though the police did call at the house they eventually dropped the matter as they had more serious matters to think about at that time than malodorous smoke from a domestic chimney – particularly when Landru assured them that he had only been burning some refuse. There were also stories of portions of putrified human flesh being recovered from a lake near Gambais by fishermen.

One witness who attracted particular attention was the pretty young woman who had been with Landru when he went shopping in the Rue de Rivola, and as events fortunately turned out for her was "the one that got away". She gave her name as Fernande Segret, her age as 29,

"BE BRAVE? But I *am* brave," replied Bluebeard, refusing confession or Mass, rum or cigarettes. The execution was to be a public one, in the square outside . . .

Le Petit Journal
illustré

HEBDOMADAIRE
61, rue Lafayette, Paris

PRIX : 0 fr. 30
5 Mars 1922

Avant l'heure suprême

Dans sa cellule de la prison de Versailles, la veille même de son exécution, Landru, parfaitement calme et toujours méthodique, a passé des heures à compulser ses dossiers — Espérait-il y trouver un dernier moyen de retarder la minute fatale... ou bien pensait-il au sort mystérieux de ses fiancées ?

THE FINAL HOURS: Did Bluebeard hope for a last-minute stay of execution? Cool as ever, he achieved the celebrity of a star at his trial.

and her occupation as "lyric artist". She described how she had become engaged to Landru whom she knew as Roger Guillet, how her mother had described him as an imposter and an adventurer, and how despite this warning she had insisted on going to live with him as his mistress. She was deeply in love with him, she said, and wished to marry him.

Rather disappointed

"I went to Gambais seven or eight times," said the love hungry Fernande Segret. "The villa was not what you would call well furnished. In one room there were some guns and cartridges which he knew well how to use."

"Do you know what means your fiancé had?" the judge asked her. "How did you live?"

"Landru told me his garage brought in a good deal, enough for our needs. I went there one day, and was rather disappoint-

ed, as there was only one apprentice working in the place, for he had told me he had a considerable business there."

Asked if they ever had any quarrels, pretty Mademoiselle Segret replied that they had two she remembered in particular. One was when a letter came for him addressed in another name. The other was when she began to look through some of his papers in their flat in the Rue de Rochechouart and he flew into a great rage. "I promised not to do it again," she added, "but I showed my astonishment since all my correspondence was read by him."

There was "a delicate point" he wished to clear up, said the judge to this witness. She had told the examining magistrate that in her sexual relations with the accused she had found him extremely passionate but at the same time quite normal.

"Is that right?"

"Oh, yes!" replied Mademoiselle Segret. "Very normal." What President Gilbert was trying to ascertain was whether Landru was a sadist and pervert. Apparently he was not, though the medical evidence pointed to his being a

dangerous psychopath, though well aware of what he was doing.

In his speech to the court, the chief prosecutor declared: "I demand the extreme punishment—death for Landru, the murderer of Vernouillet and Gambais. He is entirely responsible for his deeds. The doctors have certified this, and the ability which he has shown here is proof of his sanity. He had no pity on his victims. Why then should you have pity on him?"

It took the jury an hour and a half to find Landru guilty on all charges except two. Only in respect of those of defrauding the domestic servant Andreé Babelay of her property (she had virtually none) was he acquitted.

Mercy recommendation

Prompted by Landru's defence counsel, the jury surprisingly added a recommendation to mercy, calling upon the President of the Republic to reprieve the condemned man. However, the judge sentenced him to death by the guillotine, to be carried out publicly in front of the prison where he was confined.

"Be brave!" one of the officials said when they came to fetch him, as was customary, between five and six o'clock in the morning. "I *am* brave," replied Landru. Asked if he would make his confession to the priest and hear Mass, he exclaimed, "Never on your life!" "Anyhow," he added, "I cannot think of keeping these gentlemen waiting." He also refused the usual offer of a glass of rum and a cigarette.

As he was led out into the prison yard, he shivered a little in the cold early morning air, since he was wearing thin trousers and an open-necked shirt. Then the prison gates were flung open and for a minute or two he faced a cordon of troops holding back the spectators who had gathered in front of the guillotine which had been erected in the square outside the prison.

In a matter of seconds the executioner and his assistant strapped him face downwards on the platform of the guillotine.

Curious tailpiece

The Landru story has a curious tailpiece. More than sixty years later a film entitled *Landru,* scripted by the best-selling novelist Françoise Sagan, was made and publicly shown. Fernande Segret, whom everyone thought was dead as she had not been heard of for years—in fact she had been working as a governess in the Lebanon—suddenly turned up and sued the film company for 200,000 francs damages. She got 10,000. She then retired to an old people's home in Normandy where she eventually drowned herself, saying she was tired of people pointing to her as "the woman in the Landru case".

THE BANK ROBBERS
Bonnie and Clyde

Bonnie and Clyde ranged through the mid-West. They brought bloodshed to the towns they descended on.

TIME, aided by the Hollywood film cameras, has given Bonnie and Clyde an aura of glamour. As many myths surround them as surround Robin Hood. The legend of Bonnie and Clyde projects them as underdogs and social protesters, fighting for their rights at the time of the great American Depression.

The truth is that they were a couple of small-time crooks who robbed purely for personal gain, and murdered either to avoid capture or out of the hatred of the police common to most low-grade criminals. Public Enemy Number One, John Dillinger, voiced the view of top gangsters when he heard of their death. "They were kill-crazy punks and clodhoppers, bad news to decent bank robbers," he said. "They gave us a bad name."

Great passions

Clyde Chestnut Barrow, sixth of the eight children of a poor Texas farmer, was born on March 24, 1909. He was irascible, quick-tempered, and a latent homosexual with two great passions in life—guns and automobiles. He also had a strong streak of sadism. Childhood friends and neighbours say he enjoyed wringing a chicken's neck almost to the point of death, then watching its agony, or breaking a bird's wings and laughing at its attempts to fly.

Bonnie, the girl who would one day grow into a tough, cigar-smoking killer and nymphomaniac, was 18 months younger than Clyde and a cut above him socially. She was the daughter of a bricklayer who died when she was four. Her family, devout Baptists, then moved to Cement City, near Dallas, Texas. Clyde was already living in West Dallas, where his father had settled down to the slightly more lucrative job of running a filling station after giving up his farm.

MERCILESS killers incapable of any feeling of remorse, Bonnie Parker and Clyde Barrow nevertheless managed to capture the public imagination. Bonnie was under 5 feet tall but as tough and ruthless as her partner.

How the couple actually met is, like the number of murders and robberies they committed, a matter of conjecture. The most likely theory is that their paths crossed when a mutual friend in West Dallas broke an arm and Bonnie went to look after her. That is the way that Bonnie's mother, Mrs. Parker, told it. The time was January, 1930. Clyde was nearly 21, Bonnie just past her nineteenth birthday.

Clyde fell at once for the petite (under 5 ft. tall), fair-haired girl with the bright blue eyes and impudent red mouth, Bonnie fell for him, too, despite his "snake eyes" and somewhat effeminate looks.

The night after Bonnie arrived back in Cement City from looking after her friend, Clyde turned up as well and stayed so late that Mrs. Parker let him sleep on a couch in the living-room. "I was glad," she explained later, "that she had become interested in another man and stopped grieving over Roy."

Criminal activities

Roy was Roy Thornton, a childhood sweetheart Bonnie had married when only 16. Mother-in-law trouble had caused the break-up of the marriage. To both Bonnie and Clyde, the most important people in the world would always be their mothers. Even at the height of their career of terror, with the police of several states hunting them, they were always slipping home to see Ma.

Clyde was still asleep on the couch on the morning after that first visit when the police came for him. He was wanted on seven charges of car theft and burglary. He faced the prospect of 14 years in prison. But, after pleading guilty to three of the offences, he was let off with a light sentence of two years' jail.

Bonnie had hysterics when Clyde was taken away. "It was such a shock to learn the truth about him," said her mother. But Clyde had never made any secret of his criminal activities, and Bonnie was merely suffering from rage and frustration at having the new man in her life forcibly removed from her.

It didn't take her long, however, to set him free again. The girl who, according to her mother, "had never been mixed up with crime or criminals before in her whole life", calmly smuggled a gun to Clyde in jail. He broke out with two other prisoners, only to be recaptured a few days later after robbing a railway office at Middletown, Ohio, at gunpoint. Now he was sentenced to the full term of 14 years.

"It was his experiences in prison that changed Clyde," asserted his sister. "Before that he was wild but loving. Prison made him hardened and bitter."

Certainly life in a Texas prison of the period was no picnic. Convicts had to work all day in the hot cotton fields, and

BROTHER Buck Barrow— also a member of the gang— poses with the tools of his trade: car and weapons.

were beaten if they slacked or complained. At night they had to run all the way back to the jail, herded by warders on horseback. Again they were beaten if they lagged behind.

First murder

It was a common practice for prisoners to sever their heel tendons to make themselves unfit for work. Clyde went even further. He persuaded a fellow-convict to chop two of the toes off his left foot with an axe.

He was still on crutches when, in February 1932, he was released under a general parole granted by the woman governor of Texas, "Ma" Ferguson. Mrs. Parker was not exactly pleased to see him. "Please try to go straight from now on for Bonnie's sake," she pleaded when he appeared at her home.

"I'll try," Clyde promised. "But," he added realistically, "it won't be easy. Nobody will give me a job, and the cops will be after me every time there's an unsolved robbery."

He made one attempt at an ordinary job. The husband of one of his sister's friends was working with a construction company in Massachusetts, and promised to get him fixed up. But Massachusetts

was on the other side of the country, farther than he had ever been away from home before.

He stood the "isolation" for a fortnight. Then, homesick and lonely, and still in fear of the police, he returned to West Dallas. "If I've got to hide from the law all my life," he explained, "I want to be where I can slip back sometimes and see my folks."

Three days later, Bonnie left home. She told her mother: "I've got a job demonstrating cosmetics at a store in Houston." It was a lie. She had gone off with Clyde to start the campaign of stick-ups and murders that would—even if Dillinger was unimpressed—earn "The Barrow gang" the accolade of Public Enemies No. 1 in the south-west of the United States for the next two years.

This was March, 1932. The Barrow gang's first murder was committed on April 17, when they gunned down a jeweller named John W. Bucher in Hillsboro, Texas, and got away with $40. Clyde later claimed that two confederates—whom he refused to name—had done the shooting, and he had merely driven the get-away car.

Bonnie was in jail at the time, having been picked up for questioning about a stolen car. She was released after three months without being charged. In the meantime, Clyde, a new associate named Ray Hamilton, and two other unidentified companions, had shot and killed Sheriff Maxwell and Deputy-Sheriff Moore in the little town of Atoka, Oklahoma.

The shooting took place outside a dancehall. One account says that Clyde and his friends had been drinking heavily. When one of them took out a bottle of whisky and started drinking from it, Maxwell, who was keeping watch on the dancehall with his deputy, said: "Cut that out. We don't permit that kind of thing here."

It was a reasonable request with Prohibition still in force. The guns barked at once, however. Moore, shot through the head and heart, died instantly, and Maxwell slumped to the pavement, fatally wounded.

With Bonnie out of jail, Clyde and

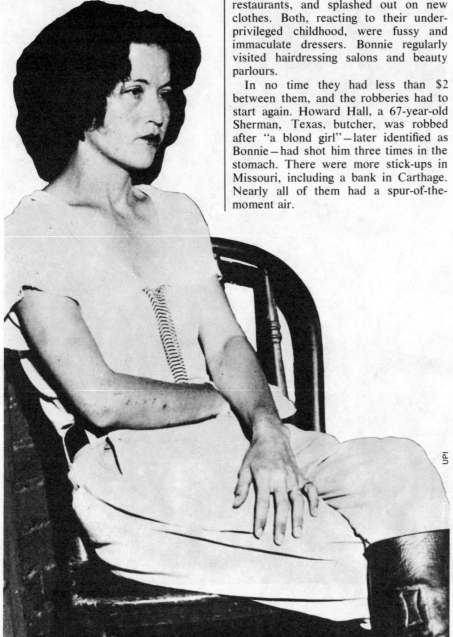

Hamilton, with an unknown number of helpers, held up a large filling station at Grand Prairie, Texas, and escaped with $3500. It was the gang's biggest haul to date. There was no shooting: in view of the gang's growing trigger-happy reputation, nobody on the outside wanted to be a hero.

The mob celebrated their success by driving Hamilton up to Michigan to visit his father. For Hamilton it proved an unhappy trip. He drank too much and talked too much, with the result that he was arrested, taken back to Texas, and sentenced to 263 years in jail after being convicted of a string of robberies – plus the Hillsboro murder, in which he hadn't, in fact, been involved.

Insatiable desire

Meanwhile, Bonnie and Clyde were enjoying a leisurely motoring tour of Michigan, Kansas, and Missouri – which took up most of September and October. They stayed at good hotels, patronized good restaurants, and splashed out on new clothes. Both, reacting to their under-privileged childhood, were fussy and immaculate dressers. Bonnie regularly visited hairdressing salons and beauty parlours.

In no time they had less than $2 between them, and the robberies had to start again. Howard Hall, a 67-year-old Sherman, Texas, butcher, was robbed after "a blond girl" – later identified as Bonnie – had shot him three times in the stomach. There were more stick-ups in Missouri, including a bank in Carthage. Nearly all of them had a spur-of-the-moment air.

The "take" from the Carthage bank was a miserable $80. A disappointed Bonnie and Clyde set out to improve their finances by robbing a second bank – only to find on arriving there that it had closed down four days earlier.

The next murder in which they were involved had a similarly casual aura. They had been joined by William Daniel Jones, a 16-year-old boy who had grown up in the same West Dallas semi-slum as Clyde, and hero-worshipped him. According to one account, Clyde allowed Jones to join the gang only because – with Hamilton in jail – he needed help in coping with Bonnie's insatiable desire for sex.

Whatever the reason, while the three of them were trying to steal a car in Temple, Texas, Doyle Johnson, the son of the car's owner, was shot dead. As Bonnie said later: "Johnson grabbed Jones by the wrist and Jones shot him. Clyde was furious at Jones for making a murder case out of it."

The date was December 5, 1932. Police believed that it was, in fact, Clyde who had fired the shot. There wasn't any doubt about his next killing, however. On January 6 the following year, he shot and killed Deputy Sheriff Malcolm Davis after he and Bonnie had accidentally walked into a trap at Dallas, Texas, set for another bank robber, Odell Chandless.

It is impossible to list the number of robberies and killings the couple committed between January 1933 and May 1934 – when they were to die in a bullet-riddled car. Stick-ups had become their way of making a living; murder the automatic reflex when they were in danger.

Hunted animals

That their career lasted so long was partly the result of the ineptitude of the police of several States, partly the fact that the same police were facing an unprecedented crime wave arising out of the Depression.

But there were several "almost caughts". In March 1933, Bonnie, Clyde and Jones hid out in a rented apartment in Joplin, Missouri. They were joined by Clyde's brother, Buck, and his sister-in-law, Blanche. The neighbourhood was too respectable. One nervous resident reported to the police that the occupants were "darting in and out of the living quarters like frightened animals".

The police sent two squad cars to investigate. In the resulting shoot-out, the gang escaped, although both Clyde and Jones had minor bullet wounds. But two policemen were shot dead, and another seriously injured.

WIFE'S DUTY is to stay with her husband! This was the argument used by Blanche (left), Buck Barrow's wife, to defend her life-style!

In the next month the fugitives were reported in half-a-dozen places in Louisiana, Oklahoma, Minnesota, and Iowa. In each place there was a robbery. The whole of the south-west went in terror of them—but the heat was on.

It was no longer safe for them to stay in tourist camps, let alone rent an apartment. They were forced to sleep in the cars they stole. When one car broke down, they stole another.

But their greatest concern was to keep themselves clean and tidy. They would leave their laundry in some small country town, and come back a few days later to collect it. The two men used barbers in the same towns to get a shave, one waiting in the car outside to sound a warning signal.

It appeared that, for a time at least, they bore crooks' luck. "It can't be long now before they get us," Bonnie reasoned on one occasion. "I want to see my mother once more before I die." But it would be nearly a year before she and Clyde said their final and bloody goodbye.

RIDDLED with bullet holes, the last car driven by Bonnie and Clyde (right and far right) finally comes to a stop. For two years the couple had robbed and murdered almost at will until the fatal ambush on the Gibsland road. The band of officers responsible for mowing down the number one public enemies are pictured below. Strangely, the public mourned.

In the meantime, Clyde, driving their car at 70 m.p.h., failed to notice that a bridge over a gorge near Wellington, Texas, had collapsed. The automobile plunged to the bottom, turning over twice in mid-air, throwing Clyde clear but pinning Bonnie underneath. Then it caught fire.

Near death

"Shoot me if you can't get me clear," she pleaded with Clyde, after he had rescued Jones and their precious armoury of machine guns and revolvers. With the aid of a farmer, Stener Pritchard, and one of his hands—who had seen the accident—the badly-burned Bonnie was finally freed. The Pritchards gave them sanctuary, but quickly became suspicious about their house guests and tipped off the police. Bonnie, Clyde and Jones escaped at gunpoint.

After linking up with brother Buck and his wife, Blanche, they risked booking into a double cabin in a tourist camp near Fort Smith, Arkansas. Bonnie was delirious and near death. Clyde put the story about that she had been injured by the explosion of an oil stove while they were camping. However, even with every lawman in the territory looking for them, they managed to persuade a doctor to treat her who, when she refused to go to hospital, arranged for a nurse to tend her.

That all took money. Accordingly the gang robbed a nearby bank and two Piggly-Wiggly stores. In the process, they shot dead Henry Humphrey, a newly-elected marshal, and made their getaway in his car. During July they drove through Iowa, staging a new stick-up whenever money was running low, and finally fetched up at a tourist camp near Platte City, Missouri.

But there was little rest now. The way they sneaked in and out, and kept the curtains of their two cabins drawn, soon caused new suspicions. Police surrounded the cabins and they had to shoot their way free. The terrible trio—as they could be called—escaped unhurt. Buck, however, suffered three bullet wounds in the head—one bullet going through one temple and out the other, while Blanche was temporarily blinded by splinters of glass from a shattered window.

Chicken dinners

They were in a desperate way. Hungry and thirsty, with Buck dying and both Bonnie and Blanche in agony and in need of medical attention and drugs. One of them went to buy five take-away chicken dinners, while the rest made camp in thick woods near a river at Dexter, Iowa. With the whole territory buzzing with talk of the Barrow gang, the sale of the chicken dinners was enough to bring a posse of some 200 police down on them.

Buck was shot again in the hip, shoulder, and back. Police found Blanche crouched over him, sobbing: "Don't die, Daddy, don't die." Buck and Blanche had been unlucky. Buck had just been paroled from prison, and had resolved to go straight until he became involved in the Joplin shoot-out. Blanche had stuck with him out of love.

Six days after the Dexter Park ambush, a delirious Buck died in hospital. Blanche was not at his side. She was in prison awaiting the trial that would bring her a 10-year sentence. Meantime, the Bonnie and Clyde saga still wasn't over. They and Jones escaped through the fusillade of bullets, waded the river, and were soon on their journey to nowhere again in yet another stolen car.

Jones had a slight head wound, Clyde had been shot four times in one arm. When the wounds had healed, Jones left them and Bonnie and Clyde made their way back to Dallas. They spent most of October, November, December and January there, sleeping in a succession of stolen automobiles, meeting their families at secret rendezvous in the country, and setting out to rob stores and petrol stations in the surrounding territory.

Two blondes

It was largely through Bonnie that they managed to escape detention. She had the bright idea of getting a blond wig for Clyde and dressing him up as a woman. "The police are looking for a man and a blonde, not two blondes," she pointed out. Her ruse worked.

On January 16, 1934, they departed from their normal pattern of crime by freeing Ray Hamilton from his 263 years in Huntsville Prison. Bonnie drove the getaway car, while Clyde hid automatics in bushes near the field where the prisoners were working, and also covered the escape with a machine-gun. One warder was shot dead and, in addition to Hamilton, four other convicts got away.

Hamilton promptly embarked upon a series of bank raids. Despite his denials, Clyde was alleged to be in on them. In fact, he and Bonnie were blamed for practically every crime committed anywhere in the south-west.

On Sunday, April 1, Bonnie, Clyde and Henry Methvin—one of the convicts who had escaped from Huntsville with Hamilton—were trapped by two highway patrolmen in Grapevine, near Dallas. They opened up with machine-guns, killing both officers. Five days later, near Miami, Oklahoma, Clyde shot dead another policeman, Constable Cal Campbell, who had gone to investigate a report that "a Ford with a girl and two men in it is stuck in a ditch".

By now, however, the police of Texas, Oklahoma, Louisiana, Arkansas and Kansas were determined to get the gang. It was generally supposed that it was Henry Methvin's father, Ivan, who put the finger on them in the hope of doing a deal with the police that would allow his son to go free.

Admiring strangers

On the morning of May 23, 1934, six officers waited in bushes by the side of a road eight miles from Gibsland, Louisiana. Shortly after nine o'clock, Bonnie and Clyde appeared in a Ford V-8 sedan. The police guns chattered. In all, 167 shots were fired. At least fifty of these struck Bonnie and Clyde between them, and they died almost immediately. Said one of the policemen: "We just shot the hell out of them, that's all . . . they were just a smear of wet rags."

The couple were taken home to Dallas for burial. Already the legend had started to grow. Many of the flowers for their funerals came from admiring strangers, to whom they were a folk hero and heroine. Onlookers snatched the roses, peonies, and gladioli from the coffins for souvenirs. The crush was so bad at the cemetery that Clyde's sister couldn't get within 40 feet of the gravesides.

Clyde was 25, Bonnie 23, when their saga ended in the way Bonnie had predicted in her poem, *The Story of Bonnie and Clyde*:

Some day they'll go down together,
They'll bury them side by side,
To a few it'll be grief—to the law a
 relief—
But it's death to Bonnie and Clyde.

WET RAGS . . . That was how one of the officers who took part in the ambush described the dead bodies of Clyde (above) and Bonnie (below). It was the end that both knew awaited them and the beginning of the legend that was to come.

THE ACID BATH BLOOD-DRINKER

George Haigh

Totally emotionless killers are rarer than is generally supposed. But John George Haigh was more than this: he also drank the blood of his victims . . .

TO THE permanent residents, and especially the elderly ladies, at the genteel Onslow Court Hotel, in London's South Kensington, Mr. John George Haigh was the epitome of charm and well-bred good manners. At meal times he never failed to acknowledge his fellow guests with a warm smile and the hint of a formal bow as he threaded his way between the separate tables to his own reserved corner of the dining room. In the eyes of the widowed ladies, comfortably, if sometimes tediously, counting off the days in quiet seclusion, he was something of a favourite handsome nephew.

One of these widows, a Mrs. Durand-Deacon, was already enjoying a growing friendship with the 39-year-old, and apparently successful, self-employed engineer. They occupied adjoining tables and, as a result of mutual confidence, Haigh already knew a good deal about her. Olive Henrietta Helen Olivia Robarts Durand-Deacon was 69, a well-preserved, well-dressed, buxom woman, who was a devoted Christian Scientist and whose late husband—a colonel in the Gloucestershire Regiment—had left her a legacy of some £40,000.

She was not the sort of person who could spend her final years in total idleness. To amuse herself, and add to her invested capital, she had made some paper designs of artificial fingernails which, she hoped, could be manufactured in plastic. To her delight, the kindly Mr. Haigh suggested that he might be able to help, and they could choose the materials at his factory at Crawley, in Sussex.

Elaborate preparations

On the afternoon of Friday, February 18, 1949, Haigh drove Mrs. Durand-Deacon the 30 miles south to Crawley in his Alvis car, and at around four o'clock they were seen together in the George Hotel. From the hotel they went to a small factory in Leopold Road, Crawley—a factory that Haigh did not own, as he had said, but where he was allowed the use of a storeroom for his "experimental engineering" work.

There in the factory he had made elaborate preparations for Mrs. Durand-Deacon's visit. He had bought a carboy of sulphuric acid and a 45-gallon drum specially lined to hold corrosive chemicals. He had laid out, on a bench, a stirrup pump, of the type used for firefighting during the days of the German air raids on Britain, gloves, and a rubber apron.

It was strange equipment to assemble for what was supposed to be a discussion about artificial fingernails. But, whatever Mrs. Durand-Deacon might have thought, that was not the purpose for which Haigh had brought her to the deserted workshop.

As the elderly widow turned her back to him to search in her handbag for her

paper designs, Haigh slipped a revolver from his coat pocket and killed her with a single shot through the nape of the neck. Stooping beside the body he took a knife, made an incision in an artery, gathered a few inches of the still-coursing blood in a glass, and drank it at a gulp.

Haigh then began the real work for which he had lured his victim to the factory. He stripped the body and carefully placed on one side the widow's Persian lamb coat, rings, necklace, ear-rings, and a cruciform, which had hung around the neck. That done, he moved to the second part of his plan, in which he had the benefit of previous experience: the disposal of the body by dissolving it in acid.

His own later description of the operation illustrated the workmanlike way in which this 10-stone murderer put his 15-stone victim into an acid bath.

He took an anticorrosive drum, or barrel, as he called it, laid it down lengthwise on the floor "and with a minimum of effort pushed the head and shoulders in. I then tipped the barrel up by placing my feet on the forward edge and grasping the top of the barrel with my gloved hands. By throwing my weight backwards the barrel containing the body rocked to a vertical position fairly easily and I found I could raise a 15-stone body easily.

"You may think that a 40-gallon drum standing only four feet high would be too

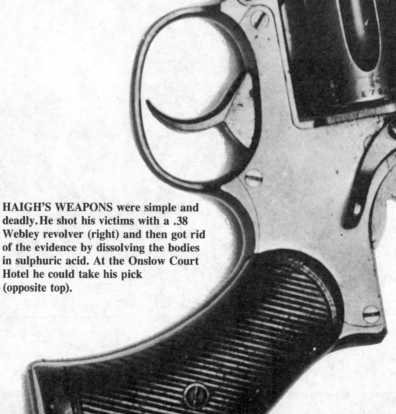

HAIGH'S WEAPONS were simple and deadly. He shot his victims with a .38 Webley revolver (right) and then got rid of the evidence by dissolving the bodies in sulphuric acid. At the Onslow Court Hotel he could take his pick (opposite top).

small for such a body," Haigh went on, "but my experiments showed that as the drum tipped, the body slumped down to the shoulders and the legs disappeared below the surface of the drum."

Having stowed the body neatly in the drum, Haigh poured in the sulphuric acid ("the question of getting the right amount was only learned by experience," he loftily explained) and then added more to make up the correct solution by pumping it in with the stirrup pump. When that was done, he had to wait until, slowly, the acid destroyed every trace of the body.

Tired after his efforts, however, Haigh left the workshop, slipped into his car, and drove to Ye Olde Ancient Priors Restaurant, in Crawley. There he ordered a pot of tea and poached eggs on toast, which he consumed with relish while exchanging good-natured banter with Mr. Outram, the proprietor.

Since this was the beginning of a weekend, during which the small factory would be closed, Haigh left the body in its dreadful bath and returned to the Onslow Court Hotel. There, at breakfast the following morning, Mrs. Durand-Deacon's absence was noticed by some of the other guests —and particularly by a Mrs. Constance Lane who was a close friend of hers.

To Haigh's alarm, it transpired that Mrs. Lane had known of his proposed visit to Crawley with Mrs. Durand-Deacon. While he had been fetching his car, the previous afternoon, the two women had met in the hotel lounge and Mrs. Durand-Deacon had told her friend about her imminent "business trip".

For Haigh it was a devastating piece of information. The masterstroke in his plan had been his expectation that Mrs. Durand-Deacon would want to keep the promising deal over the artificial fingernails a "company secret". Furthermore, at his suggestion, they had met for the start of their journey to Crawley not outside the hotel, but by the entrance to a large London store, some little distance away in Victoria Street. His subtle plan had now been undermined by Mrs. Lane's knowledge, and Haigh knew he would be involved in the questions following Mrs. Durand-Deacon's disappearance.

Little profit

With his nagging fears locked within him, he spent a busy Saturday putting into practice the purpose for which he had murdered the avaricious widow. In the course of a journey which took him to South London, Surrey, and Sussex, he disposed of Mrs. Durand-Deacon's jewellery for around £150. Her Persian lamb coat—which was blood-stained and not yet ready to realize its secondhand purchase price of £50—he left for cleaning at a shop in Reigate. But, since Haigh had pressing debts—including £350 to a bookmaker—which he could no longer avoid paying, his total "gain" was a reduction of his bank overdraft to £78.

Death had brought the blood-drinking criminal little financial profit. By the next day it seemed certain that it would bring him catastrophic personal loss. For Mrs. Lane, now thoroughly disturbed by her friend's failure to return, insisted that she and Haigh should go to the police and make out a missing person report. Haigh had no choice but to agree, attempting outwardly to express a "correct" measure of solicitude and concern.

The report he made, at Chelsea Police Station, appeared plausible enough. He had arrived at the Army and Navy Stores in Victoria Street, on Friday at 2.30, to keep his prearranged appointment with Mrs. Durand-Deacon. When, an hour later, she had failed to arrive he assumed her plans had changed and drove down to Crawley alone. He was thanked for his assistance and returned with Mrs. Lane to the Onslow Court Hotel—still a free man and still not under official suspicion.

But the last grains of sand in his criminal hourglass were flowing fast, and Woman Police-Sergeant Alexandra Maude Lambourne helped to speed them on their

CORROSIVE

ICI. AP

Daily Mirror

FRI
MAR. 4
1949

FORWARD WITH THE PEOPLE

ONE PENNY

No. 14,095

Registered at G.P.O. as a Newspaper.

VAMPIRE— A MAN HELD

THE Vampire Killer will never strike again. He is safely behind bars, powerless to lure victims to a hideous death.

This is the assurance which the *Daily Mirror* can give today. It is the considered conclusion of the finest detective brains in the country.

The full tally of the Vampire's crimes is still not known.

It may take squads of police many weeks yet to piece together full details of the murderer and his ghastly practices.

So far five murders are attributed to him. They are:—

Dr. Archibald Henderson;
Mrs. Rosalie Mercy Henderson, his wife;
Mr Donald McSwan;
Mrs. Amy McSwan, his wife; and
Mr. Donald John McSwan, their son.

The police believe that Donald McSwan, junior, was the first of the Vampire's victims—in 1945—followed two months later by his parents.

Dr. and Mrs. Henderson are known to have disappeared in February of last year.

Held captive for a month?

Mrs. Rosalie Henders

Advertiser's Announcement

Made to sign alibi notes, says brother

AFTER killing Dr. Henderson, the Vampire is believed to have kept Mrs. Henderson alive for at least a month writing letters—and signing typewritten letters—to relatives and friends.

When the Vampire thought himself safe, Rosalie Mercy Henderson followed her husband to a ghastly death.

This theory is held by her brother, Mr. Arnold Henry Burlin, 35, hotelier, of Arnfield-road, Withington, Manchester.

"I am convinced," he told the *Daily Mirror* last night, "that my sister was kept under duress for at least a month ... she was shot and her body disposed of ... I believe she was made to write letters ..."

No. 79—room of horror

In tins, bags and little barrels, detectives bring specimens from 79, back-basement of Gloucester-road, London, S.W. in which the McSwans are believed to have been slain. Police digging found false teeth in the floor.

3 thirsty Russ rush the bar

THREE of the eight Russian repatriation officials by American troops broke from the building la Ignoring calls to halt and the glare of searchlight hind the building and tried to start up a car. An back into the building

The officials have authorities to return said last night.

Gas and water se off. The phones ha being allowed in.

One of the Rus terday asked the guards for r "We are cut off world," he said.

He was giv *Stars and Stri* Army newspap

According radio the R officer has t can Supreme that Russia will allow American search in the for American su

His booby trap tripped the wrong man

The wrong man — a motorist—fell into the trap which Alfred Hatcher, 26, admitted he had set one night for his rival in love.

Reg Moore, 34

Hatcher had tied a piece of twine across the road, Russia said £2 was said £2 when he was fined £2 Edith Scott, 16, had last thought Hatcher meet was meet

Reduced P of FRY Choco

As f all Fry's choco price or increased in Quality unchanged.

FRY'S NEW
Sandwich Assort
Silver Lining Asso
Crunchie
Chocolate Cre
Sandwich Bi
Quality ¼lb.

FRY'S

SCREAMING headlines appeared in the *Daily Mirror* after Haigh's detention in prison. But his case was *sub judice*—and the editor got three months. The vampire (right) was convicted, anyway.

way. She was sent to the hotel to gather additional information about the missing widow; but, unlike the elderly guests at Onslow Court, she did not succumb to Haigh's glib tongue and superficial charm. On the contrary, her combination of police experience and feminine intuition aroused a vague but nevertheless persistent feeling of suspicion.

After talking to Haigh she returned to Chelsea Police Station and wrote a report to Divisional Detective-Inspector Shelley Symes in which she said: "Apart from the fact that I do not like the man Haigh, with his mannerisms, I have a sense that he is 'wrong' and that there may be a case behind the whole business."

Symes respected her judgment sufficiently to ask Scotland Yard's Criminal Record Office to check on whether there was, in the British police phrase, "anything known" about John George Haigh. Within a few hours he learned that something *was* "known", and that Haigh had served three prison sentences—two for fraud and one for theft.

Notorious asylum

On Saturday, February 26, the police forced an entry into the storeroom attached to the Crawley factory and found the stirrup pump, carboys of acid, and a rubber apron bearing traces of blood. From a holster they took a .38 Webley revolver which, after being tested by a firearms expert, was shown to have been recently fired.

Haigh was then "invited" back to the police station to answer further questions. However, before many had been put to him, he, himself, asked one which was to set the pattern of subsequent events. "Tell me frankly," he asked his interrogators. "What are the chances of anybody being released from Broadmoor?"

Realizing he hoped to gain "sanctuary" in the notorious asylum for the criminally insane, the detectives refused to answer him. Haigh then drew heavily on the cigarette he was smoking and said dramatically: "If I tell you the truth you would not believe it. It sounds too fantastic."

Having thus set the scene he continued: "I will tell you all about it. Mrs. Durand-Deacon no longer exists. She has disappeared completely and no trace of her can ever be found again. I have destroyed her with acid. You will find the sludge that remains at Leopold Road, Crawley. Every trace has gone. How can you prove murder if there is no body? . . .

"I shot her in the back of the head. Then I went out to the car and fetched a drinking glass and made an incision, I think with a penknife, in the side of the throat and collected a glass of blood which I then drank."

Two days after putting the body into the acid drum Haigh returned to Crawley, he said, "to find the reaction almost complete" with nothing left of the body but a residue composed of the chemically reduced remains of flesh and bone.

"I emptied off the sludge with a bucket and tipped it on to the ground opposite the storeroom," Haigh explained in careful detail. Then he added: "I should have said that after putting her in the tank and pouring in the acid I went round to the Ancient Priors for tea."

Once more the police returned to Crawley and dug up and removed the patch of soil on to which Haigh said he had emptied the "sludge". When this was methodically sifted and examined at Scotland Yard's laboratory, it became clear that Haigh's assertion that no trace of Mrs. Durand-Deacon would ever be found was ill-based.

Among the 28 lbs. of melted body fat, the pathologists found 18 fragments of human bone, partly eroded by acid but still sufficiently preserved to exhibit traces of arthritis—and thus point to the victim having been an elderly person. In addition, a piece of hipbone was positively identified as female. But, most decisive of all, upper and lower dentures were discovered in an undamaged state, and were proved to have been made for Mrs. Durand-Deacon.

Even though Haigh had failed to "completely erase" the widow's body, his work looked like that of someone experienced in acid baths and killings. Indeed, the police soon learned that he had murdered and similarly disposed of five previous victims in recent years. The first was William Donald McSwann, a young amusement arcade operator, killed in 1944, whose mother and father Haigh shortly afterwards also dispatched. The others were a doctor and his wife, Archibald and Rosalie Henderson, done to death and destroyed in February 1948.

Scandalous case

In each case Haigh acquired the money and other property of his victims by highly skilful forgery. Long after their acid-burned remains had been buried, he wrote business and private letters in impeccable facsimiles of their handwriting, successfully staving off inquiries from relatives and friends.

In a letter postmarked Glasgow, Haigh wrote in a forged hand to Mrs. Henderson's housekeeper in London: "Dear Daisy: We are going to South Africa. Mr. John Haigh has the property now and you will hear from my brother, Arnold Burlin. I want to thank you for the splendid help you have always been and I am sure you must have been while we have been away. If you would like to write, our address until we settle down will be c/o the GPO, Durban, South Africa. Shall always be glad to hear from you. Yours sincerely, Rose Henderson."

In recalling the murders Haigh claimed that "in each case I had my glass of blood after I killed them." It soon became evident that his vampirish ritual would play an important part in his trial—on the charge of murdering Mrs. Durand-Deacon—as "proof" of his insanity. He was duly detained on remand at London's Brixton Prison, and it was then that the London *Daily Mirror* told its 15 million readers of Haigh's supposed activities.

On March 4, 1949, the tabloid appeared with the blazoning front page headline: "Vampire—A Man Held." Underneath, the story began: "The Vampire Killer will never strike again. He is safely behind bars, powerless to lure his victims to a hideous death . . ."

Silvester Bolam, the then editor of the *Mirror,* was brought—in the King's Bench Division of the High Court—before Lord Goddard, the Lord Chief Justice, and Judges Humphreys and Birkett and told: "In the long history of this class of case there has, in the opinion of this Court, never been a case approaching such gravity as this one of such a scandalous and wicked character."

Imposing what they described as "Severe punishment", the High Court judges sentenced Mr. Bolam to three months' imprisonment—in another part of that same jail in which Haigh was being held—and fined the newspaper £10,000, plus the costs of the case.

Once this had been settled, the law once again turned its attention to Haigh. On July 18, 1949, he was put on trial at Lewes, in Sussex. The prosecution was led by Sir Hartley Shawcross, the Attorney-General, and the defence by

EXHIBITS—pieces of bone and the decisive dentures—were carried to and from a pre-trial hearing in a syrup box.

Sir David Maxwell Fyfe—two eminent lawyers who had earned high international reputations for their work at the trial of Nazi war criminals in Nuremberg after World War II.

Despite lengthy legal wranglings over the definition of insanity and the alleged blood-drinking rites, Haigh was found guilty after only a 15-minute retirement by the jury, and sentenced to death.

There were no public expressions of pity for the departed John George Haigh, but there were many of curiosity. How was it, people wondered, that an intelligent boy from a good home should have grown up into such a hideous creature? At the age of 12 he had been an angelic-looking choirboy at Wakefield Cathedral, in Yorkshire, and his parents were devoutly religious Plymouth Brethren.

Brand of Satan

While awaiting execution Haigh wrote: "Although my parents were kind and loving, I had none of the joys, or the companionship, which small children usually have. From my earliest years my recollection is of my father saying: 'Do not' or 'Thou shalt not.' Any form of sport or light entertainment was frowned upon and regarded as not edifying. There was only condemnation and prohibition . . .

"It is true to say that I was nurtured on Bible stories but mostly concerned with sacrifice. If by some mischance I did, or said, anything which my father regarded as improper, he would say: 'Do

SMILING inanely rather than insanely, Haigh (below) made great efforts to convince the court that he was a lunatic. Hartley Shawcross (below inset) and Judge Humphreys (right) disagreed. Far right: a crowd gathers outside the jail as execution notices are posted.

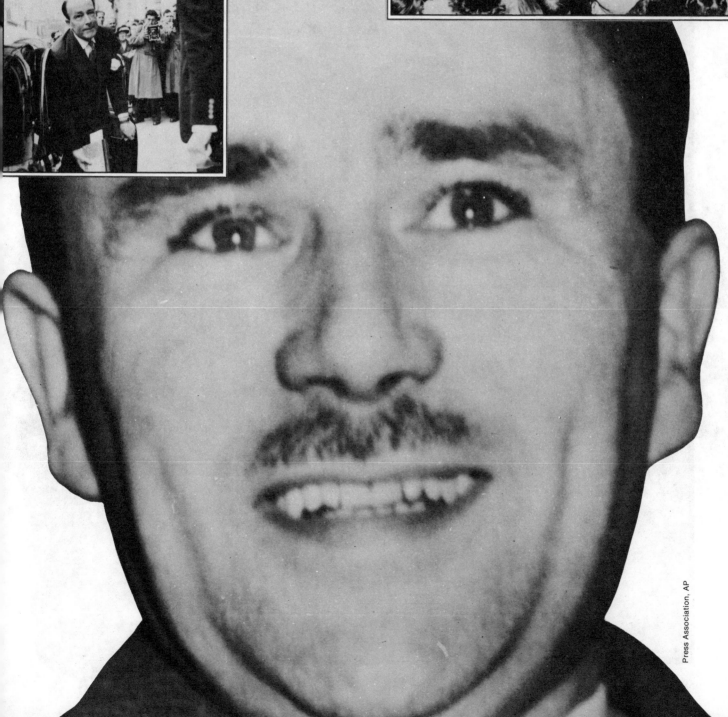

not grieve the Lord by behaving so.' And if I suggested that I wanted to go somewhere, or meet somebody, he would say: 'It will not please the Lord.' "

According to the same statement, Haigh's father told him that his mother was, literally, "an angel". So that no outside worldly evil might penetrate the sacred home, the couple had built a high wall around the garden of their tiny house in Outwood, Yorkshire. Mr. Haigh, who was a foreman electrician at a nearby colliery, had been struck by a piece of flying coal and, as a result, bore a blue scar on his forehead.

This, the father had explained to the son, was the brand of Satan. "I have sinned and Satan has punished me. If you ever sin, Satan will mark you with a blue pencil likewise." After that, in the night, before sleep came, young John George would pass his fingers, tremulously, across his own forehead to see if he, too, had yet been stamped by Satan's mark.

During his younger days, Haigh asserted, he suffered from dreams in which flowing blood figured prominently. After a car accident in March 1944, in which blood had streamed down his face and into his mouth, the dreams recurred.

"I saw before me," he said, "a forest of crucifixes which gradually turned into trees. At first there appeared to be dew, or rain, dripping from the branches, but as I approached I realized it was blood. Suddenly the whole forest began to writhe and the trees, stark and erect, to ooze blood . . . A man went to each tree catching the blood . . . When the cup was full he approached me. 'Drink,' he said, but I was unable to move."

The dream faded, later to become a waking nightmare for Haigh . . . and to bring eternal sleep to his victims.

THE IMAGINATION of a vampire . . . Haigh's weird, religious background may have turned him into a twisted killer.

THE LONELY HEARTS KILLERS

Raymond Fernandez and Martha Beck

He looked a charming man to the lonely widow anxiously waiting for his first visit. But Charles and "sister" Martha were after something else. . . .

Associated Press

Popperfoto

AT THE house in Byron Centre, a suburb of Grand Rapids, Michigan, all was excitement. Mrs. Delphine Downing, a 28-year-old widow, had led a lonely life since the sudden death of her husband a couple of years earlier. Her only consolation was her daughter Rainelle, now coming up to her third birthday, but Rainelle did not help to make the nights any shorter.

Now, however, it looked as if all that might change. She was awaiting a visit from the man she expected to fill the gap in her life. He was Charles Martin, a Hawaiian-born Spaniard who said that he had worked for British Intelligence during the war. That really did make him sound reliable. His letters – after they had been put in touch with each other through a Lonely Hearts Club – had been charming. Most important of all, he loved children, and Rainelle needed a father.

Charles proved to be everything she hoped for when he walked up the pathway to the house at 3435 Barn Center Road on the afternoon of January 19, 1949. He was slim, young, elegantly-dressed, and romantic-looking with his thin moustache and sensuous lower lip. "Rather like Charles Boyer," thought Mrs. Downing.

Rainelle, not so certain, hid behind her mother's skirts. "Hallo, Rainelle," said Charles, bending down with a winning smile. "Don't be a shy little girl." His words and gentle manner coaxed a smile from her in return. Mrs. Downing was enchanted. He really did love children.

Sex-crazed crook

Charles had not arrived alone. With him was his big, jovial sister, 28-year-old Nurse Martha. The widow was quick to reassure Martha that she was glad of her presence. "Charles on his own might have caused a bit of scandal with the local folks," she explained. "You know what it's like in these close-knit communities."

She would have been less happy had she had any inkling of the truth – that Charles was actually a sex-crazed crook named Raymond Fernandez, who made his living by seducing lonely women and swindling them out of their savings . . . that Martha, whom he had also met through a Lonely Hearts Club, was his passionate mistress, only too willing to satisfy his lust for perverted sex . . . and that Martha's insane jealousy over Fernandez's attentions to his victims had already turned both of them into murderers.

They moved into the widow's home where to Martha's rage – he was there to work, not enjoy himself – Fernandez quickly seduced their hostess. For the next five weeks he busied himself as Mrs. Downing's financial adviser, helping her to sell up property she owned before taking her to his home at Valley Stream, Long Island, and making her Mrs. Charles Martin.

And then the widow suddenly disappeared. Charles and Martha called on neighbours to reassure them: "Delphine has gone away for a while and we're looking after Rainelle for her." But the neighbours, who had always thought there was something "peculiar" about Charles and his sister, were not satisfied. They called the police.

The squad car which sped to 3435 Barn Center Road found the house empty. The policemen waited. Finally, Charles and Martha reappeared. "We've been to the pictures," they explained. No, they had no idea where Mrs. Downing had gone and when she might be back. In answer to further questions, Fernandez suggested: "Go ahead and search the house if you want to."

Damp spot

Deputy Sheriff Clarence Randle, one of the policemen, later said: "Somehow I had a hunch there had been a murder and that the body would be in the basement. We went down to the cellar. The first thing we saw was a damp spot of cement. It even had the outline of a grave. So we dug – and dug – and there we found them, not only Mrs. Downing but her little girl."

The widow had been forced to take an overdose of sleeping pills, then shot in the head. It was never to be established clearly who had actually pulled the trigger. Fernandez claimed at one point that he thought she was dying from the pill overdose, and had shot her as an act of euthanasia. On the other hand, it was suggested that Martha had fired the fatal shots: jealous because she believed Fernandez's "necessary" lovemaking had made Mrs. Downing pregnant.

No matter who was responsible, they were left with the problem of a disconsolate Rainelle, weeping continuously and asking over and over again: "Where's my Mummy?" In the end Fernandez couldn't stand it any longer. "You'll just have to do something about her," he said. Martha needed little prompting. She had never liked the child – and now she picked up the screaming little figure and calmly drowned her in a washtub.

Fernandez took the limp body down to the cellar, laid it on top of Mrs. Downing's in the deep pit he had dug and filled the hole in with cement. Then, their getaway planned for early the next day, he took his mistress off for a pleasant evening at the cinema.

But it quickly became clear that this was just the beginning of a horrifying story. Fernandez proved a boastful prisoner who made no attempt to hide how he had made his living. Lonely Hearts Clubs' lists of past and potential victims, found in his possession, were checked out by the police. By the night of March 2,

the Spaniard and his fat mistress had not only been charged with three murders, but were suspected of having committed another 17, and feared to have committed even more.

There was, for example, the case of Mrs. Jane Thompson, who had died at the end of a holiday with Fernandez at La Linea in Spain in October, 1947. The Spaniard, on his return, had given two versions of her death – firstly that she had been killed in a train crash, secondly that she had been the victim of a heart attack. La Linea police believed she had been poisoned, and had they been able to lay hands on him, were prepared to arrest Fernandez.

As it was, he was able to make his escape and, back in New York, produced a fake will laying claim to the apartment occupied by Mrs. Thompson's mother on 139th Street. First he moved in with her, but later he packed her off to live with a son so that he could have the flat to himself.

Then there was Myrtle Young. Fernandez, who already had a wife in Spain as well as his mistress Martha, went through a bigamous form of marriage with her on August 14, 1948, in Cook County, Illinois. Martha was, as usual, present, and – as usual – consumed with jealousy at the thought of Fernandez having to play the role of gallant lover.

When the "newlyweds" moved into a Chicago boarding-house after the ceremony, Martha moved in with them and – because of her "brother's" shyness – insisted on sharing the same bed as "the bride". When Myrtle protested, Martha, a frightening and dominating personality, fed her an overdose of barbiturates "to soothe her nerves".

She was unconscious for 24 hours. After she came to, but was still in a dazed state, the couple put her on a bus bound for her home town of Little Rock, Arkansas. She died shortly afterwards in hospital. At the time, however, the cause of death was presumed to be a liver complaint from which she suffered.

Marriage promise

Fernandez denied murdering either woman. In fact, he and Martha would admit to only one other killing apart from Mrs. Downing and her little girl. That was a 66-year-old widow, Mrs. Janet Fay, of Albany, New York. "I got 6000 dollars out of her just three weeks before moving in with Mrs. Downing," he boasted. Once he had his hands on the money, the widow was lured by the promise of marriage to her death at the new apartment Fernandez and his "sister" had rented at 15 Adeline Street, Valley Stream, Long Island. It was Martha who gave the police the details of the murder.

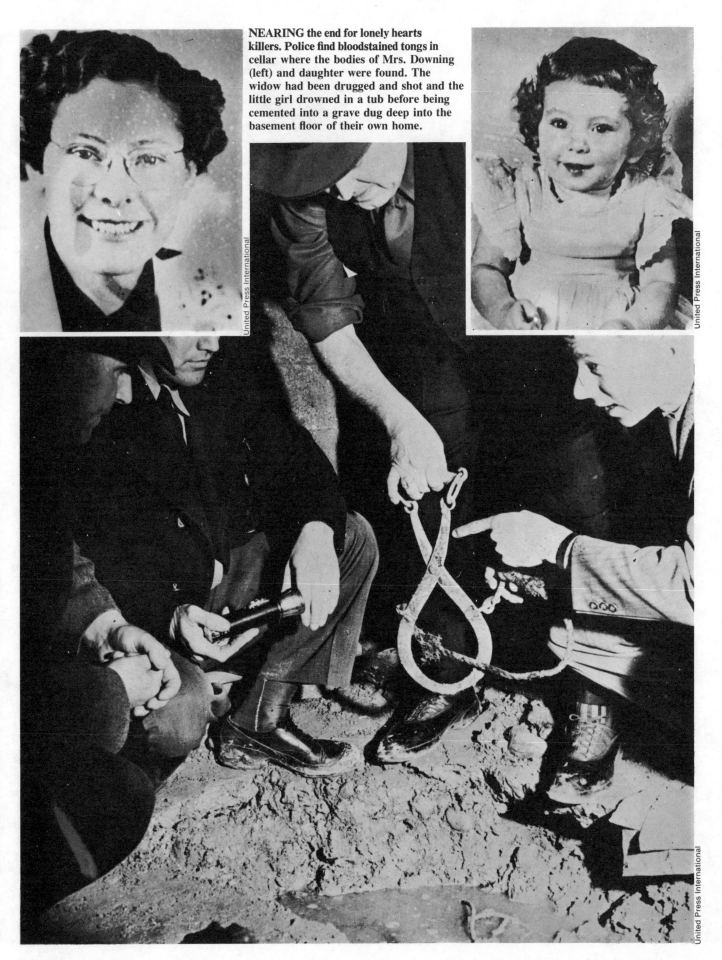

NEARING the end for lonely hearts killers. Police find bloodstained tongs in cellar where the bodies of Mrs. Downing (left) and daughter were found. The widow had been drugged and shot and the little girl drowned in a tub before being cemented into a grave dug deep into the basement floor of their own home.

United Press International

United Press International

United Press International

DEATH HOUSE . . . the apartment
building where Fernandez lived with Jane
Thompson and her mother. Jane died
mysteriously while on holiday with
Fernandez in Spain. On the murderer's
return Jane's mother "disappeared".

"I bashed her head in with a hammer in a fit of jealousy," she said. "I turned to Raymond and said: 'Look what I've done.' Then he finished the job off by strangling her with a scarf."

They had cleaned up the flat at once to stop blood dripping through to the apartment below, then made passionate love while the body of the murdered widow grew cold on the floor beside them. Next day, Fernandez bought a trunk, locked the widow's body in it and took it to his sister's home—where it was left in the cellar.

It was there for some time while Fernandez and Martha made arrangements to rent a house in the Queens district of New York as a disposal place for the body. Nobody had noticed the smell of the decaying corpse when the Spaniard came back to collect it. He and Martha buried the body in the basement of the rented house, cemented it over, and waited for four days for the cement to dry. Then they went back to the agent and said that the house was unsuitable.

"What was the address?" the police asked. Fernandez had no compunction about replying. He gave them the number on 149th Street, South Ozone Park, Queens. A few minutes later, Fernandez and Martha were calmly repeating details of the murder to the New York District Attorney over the telephone. Mrs. Fay's body was found, just as they had described, wrapped in brown paper and buried four feet down in the basement.

Fernandez and Martha would not have remained so calm and self-assured had they realized what lay behind the increasing police interest in the murder of Mrs. Fay. In Michigan there was no death penalty and, if convicted of the murder of Mrs. Downing and her little girl, the worst the couple could expect was a life sentence—which would probably mean freedom at the end of 16 years or so. It was this which had led the couple to talk so freely about their crimes.

Legal battle

In New York, however, the electric chair was still the penalty for first-degree murder. The authorities therefore set about getting Martha and her lover extradited on the grounds that, although they had been arrested in Michigan, the first murder they had admitted to—that of Mrs. Fay—had been committed in New York.

The couple's first intimation that they might have talked too much came when the Michigan Attorney General ordered a delay in their trial. They began an immediate legal battle to try to avoid extradition. The police had moved too quickly for them, however. Although the legal arguments were to last for more than a year, Martha and Fernandez

MYRTLE YOUNG: She was fed barbiturates and later, still in a daze, packed off in a bus to her home town in Arkansas. She died soon afterwards; but not before Fernandez had fleeced her of $4000. She had withdrawn the money in order to get married to the man who was to kill her.

THE HOUSE where Mrs. Janet Fay was brutally beaten to death. Subsequent occupant of house (right) places fishing reels where Mrs. Fay's body was found.

United Press International

United Press International

found themselves within a month in a Long Island prison, where Martha passed away the time by reading two crime novels a day.

They were finally brought to trial — charged for the time being only with the murder of Mrs. Fay — before Judge Ferdinand Pecora in New York at the beginning of July, 1949. The question at issue was not so much their guilt, as whether or not they were sane.

Twisted mind

The defence spared no efforts to try to prove that they were unbalanced and not responsible for their actions. Martha, it was said, had a twisted personality as a result of being repeatedly raped by one of her brothers when she was a child. Fernandez, once woman-shy, had been transformed into a sex-mad gigolo when he was accidentally struck on the head by a falling hatch while working aboard an oil tanker.

Martha — like Mrs. Fay and Mrs. Downing later — had come into his life via a Lonely Hearts Club in 1947. At the time she was a divorcee, Mrs. Martha Beck, who had just lost her job as matron of a crippled children's home in Pensacola, Florida. Not only was she lonely. She had two children to support — one

Martha and Fernandez on their way to death house at Sing Sing prison. "Let him who is without sin cast the first stone," she said without a trace of repentance.

illegitimate by a West Coast bus driver who had committed suicide rather than marry her.

Fernandez picked Martha's name out of the Lonely Hearts list for two reasons. She was, unlike most addicts of Lonely Hearts Clubs, a mere 26. She had also given her maiden name, Seabrook — and he regarded this as a good omen because he was a practitioner of Voodoo and, by a coincidence, (William) Seabrook was also the name of the author of *The Magic Island,* his Voodoo "bible". So he sent her his standard letter:

Dear Martha:

I hope you'll allow me the liberty of addressing you by your Christian name. To tell the truth, I don't quite know how to begin this letter to you because, I must confess, this is the first letter of this sort I have ever written.

Would you like to know a little about me? I'm 31 and I've been told I'm not a bad-looking fellow. I am in the importing business from Spain, my mother country. I live alone here in this apartment, much too large for a bachelor,

but I hope some day to share it with a wife.

Why did I choose you for my debut friendship letter? Because you are a nurse and therefore I know you have a full heart with a great capacity for comfort and love.

Your friend,
Raymond Fernandez.

A month later she came, by invitation, to New York. It was a disappointed Fernandez who received her at the 139th Street apartment, which had once belonged to Jane Thompson's mother. Not only did Martha seem a poor bet financially: her appearance was repellent — fourteen-and-a-half stone, treble chin, mop of dark, unruly hair, heavy make-up. The long fashions of the era did nothing for her, although she usually wore black in an effort to make herself seem slimmer than she was.

Handsome lover

Fernandez tried to break with her not long after that first meeting. But Martha refused to be shaken off. To outsiders he might seem — with his long, sallow Spanish face, thin moustache, and receding hairline concealed by a toupee — like a seedy, dancehall gigolo. She saw him with different eyes. He was the handsome lover she had dreamed about all her life —the embodiment of all the romantic heroes she had read about in the true-story magazines, she devoured like a drug.

She was mad about him right from the beginning. At their very first meeting she allowed him the pleasure of her obese body—and when he later attempted to ditch her, she tried to gas herself. Fernandez's response was not merely to take her back. He also revealed to her how he made his living.

Her jealousy

She was not horrified. "That's all right," she told him, snuggling up to him in bed. "I don't mind, darling. We can work together. I can pretend I am your sister. We can be together always. And I can help to persuade the women to put their trust in you."

Which was how they worked, fleecing an average of one new victim a month. Even to Fernandez, the number seemed incredible. Yet the lonely women caught in his net—when, otherwise, they seemed condemned to a solitary life—were anxious to please. If they had any misgivings, the Spaniard and his "sister" proved a persuasive team.

The one factor that he could never control, however, was Martha's all-consuming jealousy. She wanted the money that meant a nice modern home with a refrigerator and all the other contemporary comforts. But the thought of her beloved Fernandez caressing the bodies of other women, and making love to them as part of the swindle, drove her mad. Eventually, it drove both of them to murder.

One of the remarkable aspects of the case is that Fernandez had any energy left to satisfy the desire of his victims. Martha had a voracious sexual appetite. Anything and everything went. As part of the defence's attempt to make them seem unbalanced, no detail of their bizarre sexual experiences together was withheld from the court. The details of their carnality and bestiality were so lurid that not even the most outspoken newspapers felt they could publish them.

Kissed him

An indication of Martha's passion for her lover was given when she appeared —wearing a silk dress, green shoes, bright red lipstick and thick rouge on her sagging cheeks—to give evidence for the first time. She rushed across the courtroom, cupped Fernandez's chin in her hands, and kissed him passionately, first on the mouth, then on his face and head. He was covered in lipstick before court officials could pull her away. "I love him, and I always will," she yelled as she was dragged to the witness-stand.

HEADLINE MURDERER . . . Fernandez reads the story of his own case as a way of passing time in jail. His only regret was separation from "sexy" Martha.

It was three weeks before the jury retired to consider their verdict, by which time the court testimony amounted to some 45,000 pages. It took the jury all night to reach a conclusion. In the middle of their deliberations they had to return to hear a confession by Fernandez. At times he had complained that Martha was the sole culprit and deserved to die. Now he pleaded for her release because he wanted to confess that he, and he alone, was the killer.

Ultimately, the jury found them both guilty of first-degree murder. They appealed, Raymond changing his plea to one of insanity, but reverting to his original response to the charge—that he had been a mere accessory after the fact—when psychiatric reports indicated that he was of perfectly sound mind.

During the long months they spent in Death Row at Sing Sing awaiting the hearing of their appeals, Martha and Fernandez corresponded regularly. One of her most treasured possessions was a letter from her Latin Romeo saying: "I would like to shout my love for you to the world."

Finally, their appeals were rejected and the date of their execution was fixed for the night of March 8, 1951. Both, at the end, seemed calm and unrepentant. Fernandez entered the execution chamber in the company of a Roman Catholic priest at 11.12 p.m. "I am going to die," he said calmly. "That is all right. As you know, that's something I've been prepared for since 1949. So tonight I'll die like a man."

Martha followed him 12 minutes later. It had been decided that she should be the last to go to the chair because she was the more unlikely to break down in the face of impending death. Her last statement to the world was an attack on everyone who had judged her harshly.

It said:

"What does it matter who is to blame? My story is a love story, but only those tortured with love can understand what I mean. I was pictured as a fat, unfeeling woman. True, I am fat, but, if that is a crime, how many of my sex are guilty?

"I am not unfeeling, stupid or moronic. The prison and the death house have only strengthened my feeling for Raymond, and in the history of the world how many crimes have been attributed to love? My last words and my last thoughts will be: Let him who is without sin cast the first stone."

DEATH IN THE FAMILY

ARREST BY RADIO

Dr. Crippen

A PATHETIC man . . . hen-pecked and humiliated by a wife who preferred her lovers to her husband. But Crippen turned into an unrepenting poisoner. He fled the country with his mistress – disguised as his son. But when they landed in Canada, the police were waiting . . .

EVERYONE aboard the S.S. *Montrose* considered them to be a most considerate and devoted couple—the father and son who were travelling to start a new life in Canada. Mr. and Master Robinson—to use the names they gave to the purser—were never seen apart, and although they were polite and agreeable they spoke to no one unless they had to.

During the day they sat together on deck, chatting quietly about the sea, the weather, and the marvels of the recently installed Marconi wireless aerial which crackled above their heads sending messages both ways across the Atlantic.

At meal-times their concern for each other was even more marked. Mr. Robinson made an inordinate fuss of the boy—a shy, delicately-built youth who appeared to be in his mid-teens.

Mr. Robinson was quick to crack nuts for his son, to help him cut up his meat, and to give him half of his own helping of salad. Master Robinson thanked his father in a low gentle voice, and ate his food in a fastidious, almost ladylike way.

But as the voyage continued, one person on the ship found the Robinsons a little too loving to be true. Captain Kendall's suspicions were first aroused when he noticed that Master Robinson's trousers were too large for his slender body, and were held in place by means of a large safety-pin.

Long wavy hair

Added to that, there was the slouch hat which sat somewhat incongruously on top of the boy's long brown hair—the locks so soft they could be a girl's.

But what really set the captain thinking was the regularity with which Mr. Robinson kept on fondling his son, squeezing his hand and kissing him tenderly on the cheek.

Captain Kendall was an avid newspaper reader and knew that the *Daily Mail* was offering a reward of £100 for information concerning the whereabouts of the suspected wife-killer, Dr. Hawley Harvey Crippen. Crippen was said to be on the run with his mistress, Ethel Le Neve, and Scotland Yard detectives were on their trail.

According to the press, American-born Dr. Crippen—who stood at only 5 feet 4 inches—could be identified by his sandy moustache, balding hair, gold-rimmed glasses and false teeth.

Except for the teeth—which Captain

THE VICTIM... Belle Crippen (left) was left mutilated and buried in a cellar while her husband and his mistress Ethel Le Neve (inset, left) fled to Canada on the S.S. Montrose (right). But Captain Kendall (inset right) became suspicious. And, for the first time, radio caught a killer....

Kendall had not been able to examine—this was a perfect description of the man calling himself John Philip Robinson. On the second night out from Antwerp, the captain made a point of inviting the Robinsons to dine at his table.

The ship's master was at his best, cracking jokes, telling humorous naval stories, making Mr. Robinson open his mouth and throw his head back in laughter. Under cover of the merriment, the captain looked closely at his guest's undeniably false teeth.

When the joviality had died down, and the meal was over, Captain Kendall excused himself, hurried to the wireless room, and sent an urgent radio message to the authorities in London:

Criminal history

"Have reason to believe Dr. Crippen and Miss Le Neve are travelling as passengers on my ship. They are posing as father and son and should reach Quebec on July 31. Await instructions. Kendall."

The year was 1910, and it was the first time in criminal history that such a message had been sent by wireless. It was sufficient to make Chief Inspector Walter Dew of Scotland Yard book a passage on the *Laurentic,* a faster vessel than the *Montrose* and one which would reach Canada before her.

For the rest of the voyage, the captain kept the suspect couple under close surveillance. If Crippen knew he was being watched he gave no outward sign of it, and nor did he look the kind of man who was soon to appear at the Old Bailey accused of murdering and mutilating his buxom American wife, Cora.

The marital problems of Hawley Harvey Crippen began some while after he and his wife left New York, where he

practised as a doctor, and came to live at 39 Hilldrop Crescent, Camden Town, in North London.

At the time Crippen was employed as the manager of an American patent medicine company with an office in London's Shaftesbury Avenue. By 1907—seven years after their arrival—the 45-year-old physician found that his boisterous, full-bosomed wife was beginning to irritate him, in two deadly ways.

First of all there were constant and steadily increasing sexual demands, which took more out of him than he was willing to give. Then, and even worse, there was her grandiose ambition to become an opera star.

As a classical singer Cora—or Belle Elmore as she called herself professionally—made a fairly indifferent chorus-girl. Her voice matched that of her personality, and was loud, vulgar, unsubtle and lacking in feminine charm.

This obvious dearth of talent, however, did not prevent her joining and becoming treasurer of the Music Hall Ladies' Guild, and filling her three-storied terrace-house with a collection of so-called artistes—mainly low comedians and third-rate vocalists like herself.

Flamboyant characters

In comparison to these flamboyant but shallow characters, Dr. Crippen seemed even more mild-mannered, self-effacing and meek. His place in Cora's bed was taken by an American entertainer Bruce Miller, and he found himself reduced to the status of unpaid domestic servant.

To pay for her costumes, stage attire, and blonde wigs, Cora took in a succession of theatrical lodgers. Too lazy to look after these boarders herself—and too mean to employ a maid—she forced

Syndication International

expected to act as a stand-in whenever she was without an admirer, and he took to staying her passion with hyoscine—a poisonous drug used as a nerve-depressant and hypnotic.

On January 17, he bought five grains of the narcotic from a chemist and two weeks later invited two of Cora's music hall friends, Mr. and Mrs. Paul Martinetti to dinner. The meal broke up at 1.30 on the morning of February 1st. The Martinettis bade a genial goodnight to Cora who had been in typical form all evening—flattering her guests and speaking angrily to her husband.

Although they didn't know it, the Martinettis were not to exchange theatrical gossip with Cora again. A month afterwards Crippen pawned some of his wife's jewellery for £80, and wrote to the Ladies' Guild explaining that she could no longer attend their meetings as she had gone to stay with a sick relative in America.

At the time nothing was thought of this, although plucked eyebrows were raised when Ethel Le Neve moved into 39 Hilldrop Crescent and was seen in the district wearing clothes and furs belonging to the absent Cora.

In fact, Mrs. Crippen was not far away. Her fleshly remains were buried in the cellar, wrapped in a man's pyjama jacket containing quicklime, while her bones had been filleted from her body and burnt in the grate which her husband had spent so many hours cleaning on his hands and knees.

The death notice

On March 26, Crippen inserted a notice of his wife's death in the *Era* magazine. "She passed on of pneumonia," he told sympathisers, "up in the high mountains of California."

This story was accepted, and Crippen might well have been left to marry his Ethel and live lovingly ever afterwards. What happened next, however, is beyond rational explanation—unless his actions are viewed as an unconscious Freudian desire to draw attention to his crime and be caught.

He took Ethel to a ball given by the Music Hall Ladies' Guild at which she prominently displayed a diamond clip which had last been seen decorating Cora's ample chest. Reports of this "tastelessness" were passed on to Scotland Yard, and in July Chief Inspector Dew visited Crippen at his home.

The quietly-spoken doctor then confessed that Cora was not lying in a grave on the west coast of America. She had,

THE HUNTERS . . . Detective Sergeant Mitchell and wardresses Miss Stone (left) and Miss Foster set off for Canada to arrest Crippen and Le Neve.

her husband to rise each morning at dawn.

Outwardly uncomplaining, Crippen went down to the kitchen where he blacked the grate, cleaned-out and set the fire, made the tea and polished the "paying guests'" boots.

These tasks done, he left the house, went to his office, and consoled himself with the modest, undemanding love offered to him by Ethel Le Neve, whom he had recently engaged as a book-keeper and secretary.

Ethel, aged twenty-four and unmarried,

was everything Cora was not—demure, understanding, sympathetic and genteel. She cared for Crippen in a way that made him feel a man again and not a flunkey. Most important of all, she was the one person with whom he could discuss his shameful and humiliating home life.

Three years passed in this way—with Crippen and Ethel meeting and consummating their love in cheap hotel rooms in London. Apace with this, Cora's conceit reached almost manic proportions, and resulted in her being booed off the stage at her one professional appearance at the Bedford Music Hall in Camden Town.

By 1910 it was clear that things could not continue as they were. To satisfy Cora's sexual appetite, Crippen was still

THE GUESTS . . . Paul Martinetti and his wife were the last people – apart from Crippen – to see Belle alive. They were guests of the Crippens at Hilldrop Crescent (right).

IN DISGUISE . . . Ethel Le Neve (left) dressed as Crippen's son. But she was really his mistress. An eagle-eyed captain spotted her wavy hair and soon police were sailing out to take Crippen to face trial (above).

he claimed, run away with her old flame, Bruce Miller. The couple were living somewhere in America, and only pride had stopped him from publicly admitting this.

This seemed a reasonable explanation, but even so the inspector insisted on searching the house from cellar to attic. Apart from her gaudy clothes no physical trace of Cora was found and the detective went away satisfied.

Crippen was not under any definite suspicion, and could have remained where he was without further interference from the police. He could not, however, believe that the inspector really accepted his story.

He felt he would be arrested at any moment and charged with the crime he had so painstakingly committed. To avoid this possibility, he obtained a boy's outfit for Ethel, and fled with her to Rotterdam. On July 11, while they were still in Holland, Inspector Dew returned to Hill-

drop Crescent to check a date in the account of Cora's alleged desertion.

To his surprise, he found that the house was empty and learnt that Crippen and his "housekeeper" were not expected back. Dew immediately sensed that the building had at least one occupant — Cora, or whatever was discovered to be left of her.

Pieces of flesh

This time Dew's investigation included the digging up of the cellar and the uncovering of a man's pyjama jacket, parts of a human buttock, pieces of skin and bits of muscle, and chest and stomach organs. Although the remains were sexless, old scar tissue showed that the subject had undergone an abdominal operation.

This tallied with what little was known of Cora, and on July 16th, a warrant was issued for the arrest of Crippen and Miss Le Neve. Four days after this — without knowing that the search for them was on — they boarded the *Montrose* at Antwerp and began their extraordinary but unsuccessful deception as father and son.

After Captain Kendall had sent his first radio message, he kept abreast of the

ON TRIAL . . . Crippen and his mistress in the dock (top) facing murder charges. Some of Mrs. Crippen's friends (above) were called as witnesses and the deadly doctor was sentenced to death. But Ethel Le Neve went free . . .

developments as Inspector Dew and his sergeant sailed from Liverpool. Their ship forged ahead of the *Montrose* at the entrance to the St. Lawrence River.

The *Montrose* arrived in Canadian waters early in the morning of July 31. At 8.30 a.m. the pilot boat came alongside, and Dew and Sergeant Mitchell boarded the liner. They were accompanied by a chief inspector of the Canadian police, and posed as river navigators.

They were taken straight to Captain Kendall's cabin, and there brought face to face with the self-styled John Philip Robinson. Dew wasted no time in bothering with questions of identity of disguise.

Wife mutilated

"Good morning, Dr. Crippen," he said briskly. "I am Chief Inspector Dew of Scotland Yard. I believe you know me."

Crippen blanched, but found the voice to say: "Good morning, Mr. Dew."

The detective gazed down at the small, clerkish-looking fugitive and told him: "I am arresting you for the murder and mutilation of your wife Cora Crippen in London on or about February 2 last."

Crippen made no reply, and Dew went out to find and charge Ethel. The run-

Mary Evans

away lovers were then taken on to Quebec and a month later brought back to England, London, and the Old Bailey.

The doctor was the first of the two to be put before a jury, and his five-day trial opened on October 18, 1910. From the start it was clear that he had no chance of being acquitted. He seemed indifferent to his own fate, and his main concern was for Ethel, whom he swore knew nothing of Cora's murder.

After duly being pronounced guilty,

WIFE-KILLER Crippen, his life in ruins, was only too happy to leave a world where he had known only the briefest moments of happiness.

he waited feverishly to hear how Ethel had fared on a charge of being an accessory. As it turned out, he had nothing to fear.

Her trial four days later was almost a formality for her defence counsel, the brilliant and foxy F. E. Smith. He chal-

lenged the prosecution to prove that she was anything other than innocent. The case against her failed, and she was found not guilty and discharged.

For Crippen there was little to live for—even if his neck had been spared. Without Ethel—who disappeared without trace from the public eye—he wished only to die, and to do so quickly.

He was hanged on November 23, and his last request was that a photograph of her be buried with him.

A VERDICT REVERSED

Dr. Sam Sheppard

HE FOUGHT hard to prove his innocence. And eventually Dr. Sam Sheppard (right) was freed from jail. So who did batter his pretty wife to death and leave her slumped in her blood-spattered bedroom (inset)?

WHEN Dr. Samuel Sheppard stepped into the dingy grey building that housed Cuyhoga County criminal court on October 24, 1966, his surroundings must have been only too familiar. He had been there before, 12 years ago, on the same charge: the brutal murder of his own wife, Marilyn, who had been battered to death in the early hours of July 4, 1954.

The first trial had been the longest murder trial in American history. For over 2 months, from October 18, 1954, until December 21, 1954, the jury had been battered with torrents of words. Accusations, pleadings, denials and passionate legal arguments had rattled across the courtroom like machine-gun fire.

Silver-haired Judge Edward Blythin presided over the proceedings like a man suffering from shell shock. Before his eyes he had watched the court transform from a solemn house of justice into what seemed like a circus. Camera bulbs flashed continuously, television crew men hurried back and forth loudly whispering directions to each other and the press gallery was in constant noisy movement as journalists hastened to telephone their editors with news of the latest developments.

Amid the hubbub, the father of the accused, Dr. Richard Allen Sheppard and Sam's two brothers, Stephen and Richard, sat solemnly at the back of the court. As they awaited the jury's verdict on the final day they looked as tense and drawn as Sam himself.

Damaging innuendo

There was a sudden hush as Judge Blythin entered and resumed his seat. William J. Corrigan, Sheppard's tough, veteran attorney followed, looking grim. Then came John J. Mahon, leader of the prosecution, his assistants Saul S. Danaceau and Thomas Parrino—whose verbal skill and gift for damaging innuendo had left Samuel Sheppard bewildered and exhausted.

As they filed in, not one of the jury so much as glanced at Sheppard. Defending counsel Corrigan placed his hand on Sheppard's shoulder and prepared him for what was to come. "I think we've lost," he whispered.

Corrigan was right. Sheppard was found guilty of second-degree murder and sentenced to life imprisonment.

But the nightmare that started on July 4 had only just begun. For the conviction unleashed a chain reaction of tragedies both on the Sheppard family and on others involved in the case. A month after the trial Sheppard's mother committed suicide overcome by grief at the fate of her son whom she believed innocent; shortly afterwards Sam's father died, his health broken by the worry and disgrace. The murdered woman's family suffered

WEDDING DAY . . . Dr. Sam and his wife, Marilyn (above). They moved into the luxurious Ohio house (right) where the bride was to be beaten to death . . .

equally, culminating in a further suicide: that of Marilyn's father. Even a member of the jury, depressed and exhausted by the strain of the ordeal and the sensation surrounding it, had taken his life.

For the case had divided the state of Ohio as it was to divide the nation. Was Sheppard a ruthless wife-killer as the verdict indicated, or the victim of a cruel miscarriage of justice?

The tale unfolded to the jury was a complex one; and reasoned judgement was made infinitely more difficult by the press which had conducted, from the start, a powerful vendetta against Sheppard, his family and the comfortable background from which they came.

Screaming headlines had fomented suspicion and dislike long before Dr. Sam set foot in court. The *Cleveland Press* was one of the worst offenders. WHY ISN'T SAM SHEPPARD IN JAIL? its banner headlines demanded.

In effect, the *Cleveland Press* had pointed to Dr. Sheppard as the murderer, and implied that his family and friends were using their influence to shield him.

When, as a result of the hysterical press campaign against him, Sam Sheppard was finally arrested, his family continued to suffer threats, insults, and anonymous telephone calls at all hours of the day and night from people fired to anger by what they had read in their local newspapers.

The trial itself proved a sort of public entertainment; each instalment was an event eagerly awaited and discussed; newspapers sold by millions and television items were given peak viewing.

At 30, Sam was a brilliant neurosurgeon and the youngest son of Dr. Richard A. Sheppard, a general surgeon and osteopath who had founded Cleveland's Bay View Hospital. Sam worked there with his father and two brothers, Richard and Stephen. He had married pretty Marilyn Reese in 1945 and later bought a pleasant, four-bedroom house for them near the hospital. The house was perched nearly a hundred feet above the winding shore of Lake Erie and included a private beach. It was, like the Sheppards themselves, typically suburban, fashionable and expensively middle-class.

The court heard how, on the evening of July 3, 1954, Samuel Sheppard and his wife had entertained Mr. and Mrs. Ahern to dinner at their house. Afterwards Chip, the Sheppard's young son, was put to bed and the two couples sat down to chat, drink, and watch television.

By 12.30 p.m. everyone was tired and the Aherns were shown out by Marilyn alone because Sam, who had had a tough day at the hospital, had already fallen asleep on the couch. What happened afterwards depended solely upon the evidence of one witness, Samuel Sheppard; and the story he told, though it never varied over the years, was undeniably vague.

Marilyn left Sam lying on the couch downstairs and went up to bed. Some time later, according to his testimony, he was awakened by the sound of her screams, rushed upstairs and was struck down from behind.

"The next thing I knew was coming to, a very vague sensation, in a sitting position right next to Marilyn's bed, facing the hallway, facing south." He looked at his wife, realized she was "in very bad condition" and felt that she was "gone". Fearful for his son he went into Chip's room and "in some way evaluated that he was all right".

Hearing a noise downstairs he dashed down in time to see a shadowy figure fly through the back door and make for the beach. Sam gave chase, and managed to grasp the figure from behind but was again knocked unconscious.

This time when he regained his senses he was lying face down on the edge of the lake with most of his body in the water. He staggered to his feet, frozen and dripping wet, lurched once more towards the house, and went upstairs.

There he saw, in the dawn light, that Marilyn had been "terribly beaten". He thought he determined that she was dead. Then, at 5.45 a.m. he phoned his friend and neighbour J. Spencer Houk, mayor of the town:

"For God's sake, Spen, come quick!" he gasped. "I think they've got Marilyn!"

Missing morphine

But, as the prosecution pointed out, there were some puzzling gaps in the story. The T-shirt he was wearing had disappeared. Why and where? Why had his medical case been found upside down, the contents spilled and a box of morphine ampoules missing? If he had been lying with his head on the shore of the lake, why was there no sand in his hair?

When Mayor Houk arrived, accompanied by his wife, he found Sheppard stripped to the waist, sodden wet, slumped in a chair. Mrs. Houk rushed upstairs. She found the victim lifeless in her blood-soaked bed, pyjama top drawn over her breasts, outspread legs dangling under the crossbar of the fourposter.

The entire room was spattered with blood. Marilyn's skull showed that she had been beaten savagely on the head with a blunt instrument—35 times, the authorities said later.

The police arrived, followed by Sheppard's brother, Dr. Richard Sheppard, and finally the coroner, Dr. Samuel Gerber. From the start Gerber was sceptical. The displaced drawers and ransacked con-

The Plain Dealer

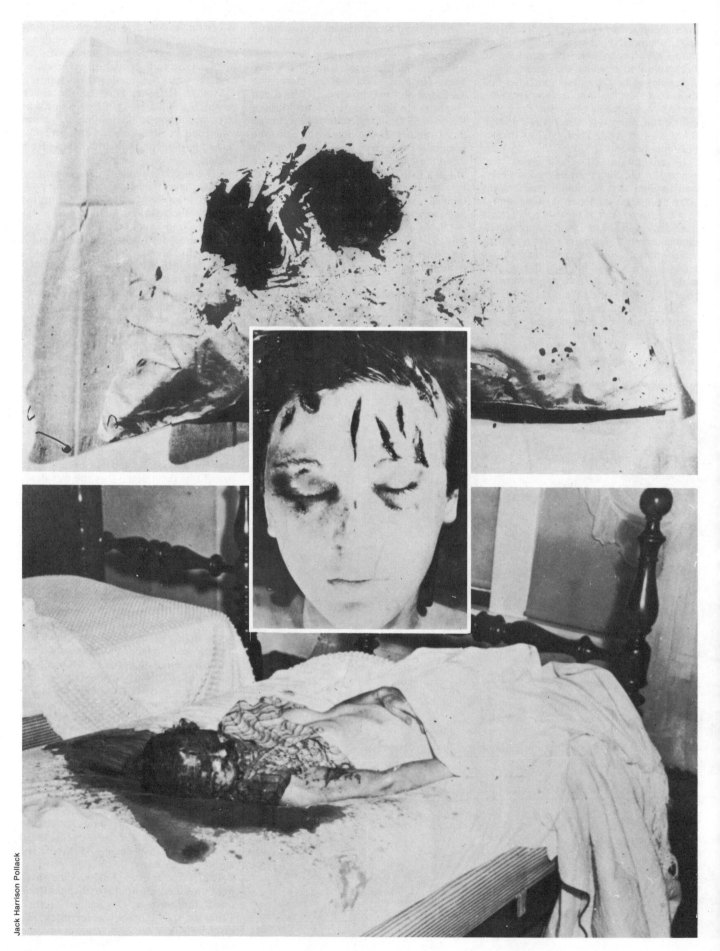

Jack Harrison Pollack

tents seemed like a clumsy attempt to simulate a burglary.

He put Marilyn's death at between 3 a.m. and 4 a.m.—which would have given Samuel Sheppard nearly three hours at least in which to remove evidence and arrange the house to suit his story.

Richard broke the news to his brother that Marilyn was indeed dead. Mayor Houk, however, gave the jury a much more damaging account of their dialogue. According to him Richard had said, "Did you do this, Sam?"—implying that even Sam's own brother thought him capable of such an act.

Bloodstained watch

The jury heard of other oddities. Searchers found, among the shrubs near the house, the canvas bag Sam used on his boat. Inside the bag were his wristwatch, slightly bloodstained, his fraternity ring, and the keys and chain that were normally affixed to his trousers.

How had the bag arrived there with its contents? Had it been left there by the attacker? If so, why? Or had Sam left it there himself in some vague attempt to misguide the police?

These questions were never answered. Others were never asked. Where, for example, had the fragment of torn red leather come from which was found under Marilyn's bed? Fibres found under her fingernails were produced in court. But neither prosecution nor defence sought to explain their origin.

A fragment of tooth was ignored as evidence, although it appeared that it may have broken off as Marilyn bit her attacker who withdrew his hand with force; and Dr. Sam had no scratches or bites on his hands or arms.

In the end three things were responsible for the jury's verdict of guilty. The first of these was the evidence given in court by the coroner, Dr. Samuel R. Gerber. He testified that the bloody "imprint" on the pillow case beneath Marilyn's head was caused by a "surgical instrument". The murder weapon had never been found in spite of intensive searches by the police.

In its absence what could be better than a testimony from the respected coroner that it was a surgical instrument, the kind of instrument, in fact, which only a surgeon such as Dr. Sheppard was likely to possess?

Gerber never explained and was never asked what kind of surgical instrument he

BEATEN TO DEATH . . . How police found the body of Marilyn Sheppard. The bloodstained pillow (top) was produced as evidence when her husband was put on trial. But the murder weapon and "a surgical instrument" that left a bloody imprint on the pillow were never found by police.

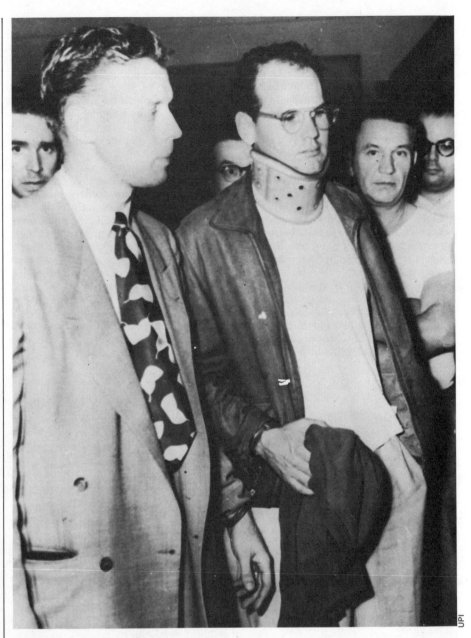

UNDER ARREST . . . Dr. Sam, handcuffed to a detective, is led to his trial. It was the first of many courtroom appearances before he was cleared.

had in mind. Nor was one ever produced; but the jury were greatly impressed.

The second factor was Sheppard's penchant for extramarital affairs—which he had, at first, denied. This was taken up with great enthusiasm by the media and provided the prosecution with a perfect motive. Sheppard had been having an affair with a young colleague, Susan Hayes. Perhaps he wanted his wife out of the way. And if Sheppard could lie about marital infidelity, the prosecution suggested, would he not also lie about killing his wife?

Finally, and perhaps most important of all, there was the influence of the press, not only on the public in general, but also on the jury—whose members had followed the case with interest as reported in local newspapers before the trial and even during it. And the local press had been particularly vindictive towards Sheppard.

But if the press campaign against him had helped to secure a conviction in 1954, it was the main reason why Sheppard secured a new trial in 1966. For, on June 6 of that year the U.S. Supreme Court overthrew his murder conviction on the grounds that "prejudicial publicity" had deprived him of a fair trial. It was the first decision of its kind in American legal history.

For most of the intervening 12 years, Sheppard had been in jail. But he had remained firmly in the news. Firstly, there were the repeated efforts at every level—local, state, and federal courts—to secure a new trial. Again and again William Corrigan, Sam's fighting lawyer, saw his efforts fail; but Sam was still in jail when Corrigan died in 1961.

Then, in 1963 there was another bizarre development. A wealthy young German divorcée from Düsseldorf, who had been corresponding with Sam Sheppard after reading about his case, decided to come to the United States to see him.

Ariane turned out to be stunningly beautiful, and at their first meeting in Ohio's Marion penitentiary the couple gave each other love tokens in the presence of the prison guards, as a symbol of their engagement.

Once more the press latched on. Wherever she went, cameras flashed and reporters barked their questions. Was this some stunt engineered by Sheppard's new lawyer, Lee Bailey?

Bailey was shrewd, young, dynamic, ambitious for success, hardworking and, above all, a masterly manipulator of publicity. If publicity had put Sheppard in, perhaps it would also help to get him out. In any event, once the flamboyant Boston

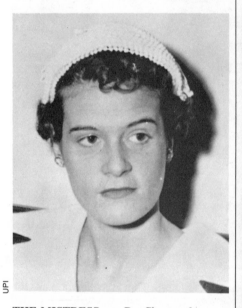

THE MISTRESS . . . Dr. Sheppard, pictured right with his father during the first trial, made love with pretty Susan Hayes (above), a technician at the osteopath's hospital. At first, he denied having any extramarital affairs. But before he stood trial, his secrets were out . . .

lawyer had taken over the case Sam Sheppard was rarely out of the news for any length of time.

Bailey vowed to secure a retrial. And he did. But after the Supreme Court decision the press were very wary of attacking Dr. Sam, and the coverage was guarded and often sympathetic.

So it was that on October 24, 1966, Dr. Samuel Sheppard—now remarried to the glamorous Ariane—stood trial for the

second time, in the same place, for the same murder.

Judge Francis Talty entered the courtroom first. Handsome and grey-haired, he was known to be tough but scrupulously fair. It was he who ordered all photographers and movie cameramen to stay outside the court building, and forbade newsmen to seek information from anyone directly involved in the case.

An imposing figure

Next came the prosecutors, John T. Corrigan—no relation to Sheppard's first defence lawyer, William J. Corrigan—and his assistant Leo Spellacy. They were both highly skilled courtroom performers and looked confident right from the start.

But then so did the two who followed: Sheppard's prime defence laywer, the youthful F. Lee Bailey, and his boyish, crew-cut assistant Russ Sherman. Bailey was an imposing figure; his suits were impeccable, almost too impeccable some said, and his tone of voice resonant and sure. Perhaps a little too sure.

Finally Dr. Samuel Sheppard appeared —not to the flashing cameras and buzzing whispers of anger and innuendo, as before, but to a court that seemed eerily silent. Sam looked fit, but his tightly drawn lips were a clear sign of the strain he was undergoing.

This was his last chance to prove his innocence. If the jury found him guilty this time he would be guilty forever; even when finally released from jail he knew that society would never take him back. He would remain an outcast, a convicted murderer, for the rest of his life.

Sergeant Robert Schottke, one of Cleveland's best homicide detectives, was the first important prosecution witness to take the stand. He had been the first to accuse Dr. Sam back in 1954, and this "coup" had helped to make his name as a brilliant officer.

In the cross-examination Bailey fired at him with both barrels. He referred to the canvas bag containing Sam's blood-smeared watch, ring and key.

"Did you realize that Marilyn's killer

had probably left prints on those items of jewellery?"

Schottke admitted that this was probably true.

"And did you . . . ascertain just what prints were there before accusing *anyone* of this murder?"

There was a pause; and then a faint but audible, "No".

A defence victory

Bailey then asked the witness about the injuries which Sheppard received at the hands of the supposed attacker. Schottke admitted that he had not inquired whether Sam could have inflicted the injuries himself, or whether they *must* have been inflicted by someone else.

The astute lawyer pounced. "So you accused the doctor without finding out whether it could have been him or not?" he snapped. Schottke nodded agreement. It was an opening victory for the defence.

Next on the stand was Dr. Samuel Gerber, the coroner. He, too, had become well-known since the 1954 trial, and had

ON TRIAL . . . Medical technologist Mary Cowen and prosecutor Thomas Parrino (above) discuss spots of blood found on Dr. Sheppard's watch. The blood riddle baffled lawyers at the first trial (right), but 12 years later, the doctor's counsel found an answer that convinced a jury.

lectured all over the country on the Sheppard case always "proving" that Dr. Sam was guilty. Bailey went straight to the crux of Gerber's argument: the bloodstained pillow which showed, according to the coroner, the imprint of a "surgical instrument".

Gerber admitted at once that he had never seen an instrument of the sort he had in mind, though he had certainly looked.

"Tell the jury, Doctor, where you have searched for the instrument during the last 12 years."

"All over the United States."

Delighted, Bailey feigned an expression of surprise, "Please tell us what you found," he demanded of the coroner.

Gerber shook his head sadly. "I didn't find one."

There was a murmur of astonishment round the court. Even Judge Talty reacted. Corrigan and Spellacy looked as if they were on the point of choking their star witness with the blood-smeared pillow.

"Did you, Coroner Gerber, once say, about a month before Marilyn Sheppard was murdered, that you intended someday to 'get' the Sheppards?"

"Any man who says that is a liar!" Gerber shouted back. But to the jury he was now a blusterer more interested in convenience than the truth.

The trial was going well for Sheppard, and everyone both inside and outside the courtroom knew it. The odds in Las

Vegas were approaching 20-1 for Dr. Sam's acquittal. But the prosecution had another ace. They called Mary Cowan, Gerber's assistant.

It was she who had examined the contents of the canvas bag, and she came to court with colour transparencies of the objects found inside. She flashed onto the screen the picture of Dr. Sam's watch as it was then, speckled with blood. These speckles, she testified, were caused by "flying blood".

It was a tense moment. The speckles must have appeared on the watch while Sheppard was beating his wife to death, argued Corrigan—there was "no other way" it could have happened.

The flying blood

It was Bailey's turn to look worried. He questioned Mary Cowan on every aspect of her testimony, but failed to make her change it. The longer the trial proceeded the more it became obvious that the entire case hung on the "flying blood" theory. When he was not in court, Bailey spent his whole time, questioning Sam, probing, searching for an answer to the riddle.

How had the blood spots appeared on the watch? Bailey, Sherman, and Sheppard spent hours examining every possibility, casting their minds back to the damning transparency. Typically, it was Bailey who found an answer.

He remembered seeing minute particles of blood on the *inside* of the watch band. So, he concluded, the blood must have got onto the watch after it had been removed from Sam's wrist.

It was a clever argument and the jury accepted it. From then on the defence

UPI

carried all before it. Bailey, his confidence restored, summed up on Tuesday November 15 by dismissing the prosecution's case as "ten pounds of hogwash in a five-pound bag".

No happiness

On the following day the jury declared Dr. Samuel Sheppard "not guilty".

But life outside prison brought him none of the happiness for which he had fought so long. He made numerous efforts to be reinstated in the medical register; but prejudice against him remained and it was more than a year before he was able to resume his practice. When he did begin medical work again he found that many of his patients distrusted him and were only too eager to sue him for negligence. Finally he was forced out of the profession because no insurance company would continue to cover him.

WIFE No. 2 . . . Dr. Sheppard and Ariane (above and top) celebrate after he is eventually cleared. But their happiness did not last . . .

Meanwhile Ariane sued him for divorce, claiming that he threatened her and carried a heavy axe and a knife.

Frantic bride

Later, Sheppard met up with an athlete called Strickland and turned to professional wrestling to earn a living. He also got married for the third time—to Strickland's pretty 19-year-old daughter. But his efforts to regain a place in society were all in vain. Six months after his marriage his health began to decline and, ignoring his frantic bride's pleas to see a doctor, he died a sad and inwardly lonely man on April 6, 1970.

The coroner's verdict was death by natural causes. But perhaps he wanted to die, as those near him suggested, worn out by society's rejection of him and the hopelessness of his struggle to re-establish himself.

92

MAD MURDERERS?

A MURDER IN SOCIETY

Leopold and Loeb

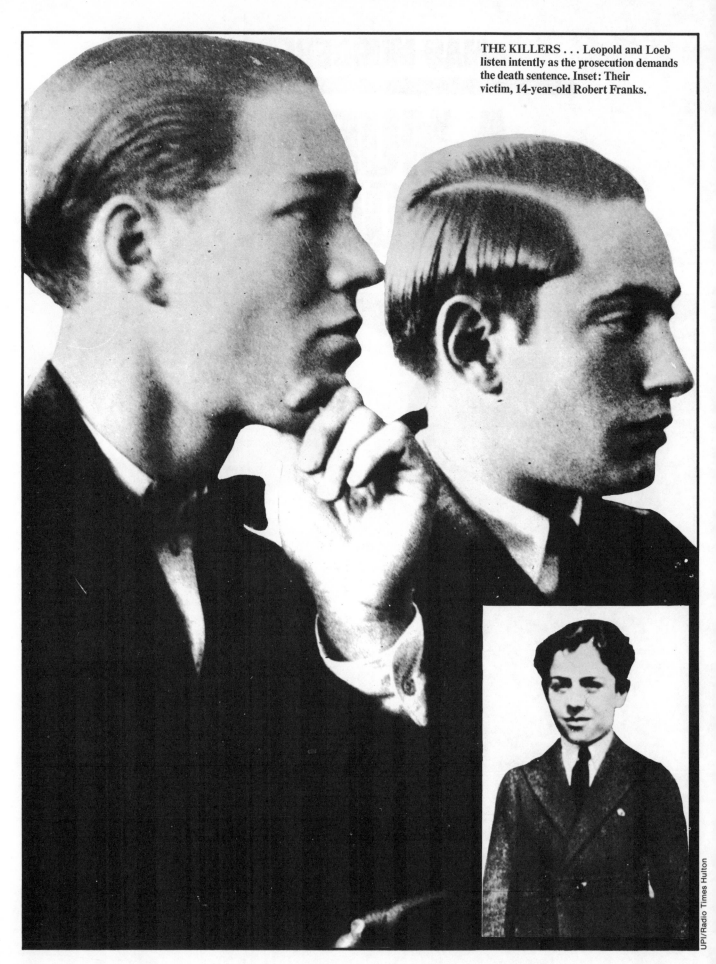

THE KILLERS . . . Leopold and Loeb listen intently as the prosecution demands the death sentence. Inset: Their victim, 14-year-old Robert Franks.

UPI/Radio Times Hulton

94

WHEN on May 31, 1924, the news that 18-year-old Richard "Dickie" Loeb—the son of a vice-president of the mail order firm of Sear Roebuck & Co.—had confessed to the most dastardly and bizarre crime of the decade—the kidnapping and murder of 14-year-old Robert Franks, son of a millionaire businessman—many a young debutante shed bitter tears. Dick, irresistible, charming Dick, could not have committed the horrible deed. And if he had surely it must have been—couldn't the prosecutor understand this—under the nefarious influence of his closest friend and ally, the somewhat sinister Nathan "Babe" Leopold Jr.

Superman philosophy

Dick might have been a bit crazy, wild—but he was young and rich and you had to expect that. Leopold, aged 19, was another make of man altogether. He was somewhat peculiar. His head was always in books. The "Crazy Genius" his classmates called him on account of his prodigious intellectual prowess. Everybody was sure that Leopold—who believed in the German philosophy of the "superman"—must have masterminded the whole operation. But there was no gainsaying the confession. Richard Loeb and Nathan Leopold Jr., of Chicago's finest set, had without compunction taken the life of young Robert Franks.

The trial promised to be the most spectacular in Chicago's history. The protagonists were rich, young, handsome and very intelligent. The counsel for the defence, Clarence Darrow, had established a reputation as America's most provocative attorney, the scourge of prosecutors all over the land. "Attorney for the damned" they called him, but "what", the massed audience wondered, "could he do for Leopold and Loeb?" After all Mr. Crowe had a watertight case; the lads had spoken freely and without reserve—not the smallest detail of the crime remained hidden. There could be no doubt about the charge—murder in the first degree.

Heavily guarded

It was no surprise—when on July 21, 1924, the trial opened—that the spacious Criminal Court of Cook County was crowded with members of the press and fascinated onlookers. The defendants, heavily guarded by bailiffs and deputy sheriffs, sat with counsel at a table before the Bench. Except for a few whispered conversations with their attorneys, and when testifying, they maintained a stony-faced silence throughout the trial. Their relatives sat grief-stricken to the left of the bench. They had not yet recovered from the shock.

The first surprise of the trial came early. The charges were read out and the de-

Brown Brothers

fendants asked how they pleaded. "Guilty" was the reply. A murmur of astonishment ran through the crowd. Everyone had expected a plea of not guilty on an insanity defence.

Most taken aback was the State's Attorney Robert E. Crowe. The custom in American courts is that a plea of guilty on a capital charge is only entered as the result of an agreement with the prosecution that—in consideration of the saving of trouble and expense—the State will not demand the death penalty, but will be satisfied with a sentence of imprisonment. In this case no such agreement had been concluded—indeed the prosecution neither needed it nor was willing to make such a concession to the defence in view of the public opinion which had been greatly incensed by the brutality of the crime.

It was not without justice, however, that 67-year-old Darrow had achieved his great fame. He was a shrewd and capable judge of people and situations. He knew that if his clients pleaded not guilty they would have to face a jury. He knew that in the present climate of horror and revulsion—not to mention the more subtle influence of racial prejudice—the jury would be hostile. Equally inevitably the trial would end with a mandatory death sentence for his clients. On a plea of

ANGRY CROWDS surround the undertaker's where Robert Franks's mutilated body was taken. In their minds, there could be only one sentence: death.

guilty Darrow could hope to convince the judge, Chief Justice John B. Caverly, that there were mitigating circumstances, and thus save his clients from the gallows.

The State's Attorney was surprised, but not upset, by Darrow's move. He felt certain about his case. Here were prey that would not be snatched from the hanging rope. Over a period of eight days the State presented its case (under the law of Illinois the State must prove the crime even on a plea of guilty).

The most important prosecution witnesses were the defendants themselves. They had already confessed, eagerly and at length, to the State's Attorney. But the details of the crime had to be meticulously reiterated in the courtroom. "Now, Nathan," said Crowe in a fatherly manner, "I just want you to go on in your own way and tell us the story from the beginning, tell us the whole thing."

Leopold's high, reedy voice dominated the courtroom—where the silence was broken only by the occasional cough or gasp of horror. "We planned a general thing of this sort as long ago as last

November," began Leopold, hesitantly. The hesitancy, however, soon gave way to a kind of childish excitement as he launched into his story.

He told of the various plans discussed — should they kidnap the father of one of themselves? — and rejected. Finally, they agreed to leave the victim to chance, and began to lay their plans which could be adapted to any circumstances.

To this end Leopold stayed in the Morrison Hotel in Chicago checking in under the name of Morton D. Ballard, in which name he received mail, opened a banking account, and hired a car.

Bottle of chloroform

He and his confederate also bought a chisel with which to knock their victim unconscious, a rope with which to strangle him, some cloth for covering the body, a bottle of chloroform in case of emergency, and a bottle of hydrochloric acid with which to mutilate the victim's features.

At the same time Leopold used a stolen Underwood typewriter on which to write a letter informing the victim's father that his son had been kidnapped and demanding a ransom of $10,000 in old bills. ("Any attempt to include new or marked bills will render the whole venture futile.")

The money was to be placed in a large cigar box and to be delivered according to the kidnappers' subsequent telephoned instructions. If these were carefully followed and the police were not alerted, "We can assure you that your son will be safely returned to you within six hours after our receipt of the money".

On the afternoon of May 21, 1924, Leopold left his home in the hired car with Loeb in the passenger seat in search of a victim. Near the corner of 49th Street and Ellis Avenue they espied young Franks. They stopped and Loeb spoke to Franks. "Come in a minute," he said, "I want to ask you about a certain tennis racquet." Franks did as he was asked and got into the car. He was also asked if he minded driving around the block, and he said no.

"I stepped on the gas then," said Leopold, his voice becoming hoarse from the strain, "and Dick hit Bob on the head with the chisel and stuffed the cloth into his mouth. I think he must have died pretty soon afterwards."

By now Leopold was so wrapped up in the story of the murder that he did not notice Loeb grimace as he mentioned that it was Loeb, and not he, who had actually killed the young Franks. This was the only open point of dissension between the otherwise fast friends. (The friendship was quickly mended once they were jailed. Leopold approached Loeb in the prison yard extending his hand and said, "Dick, we've quarrelled before, and made up, let's forget and start again.")

Once Franks was dead, Leopold went on, the car was driven to a piece of waste land known as Hegewich to the south of the city, where Leopold used to go bird-watching. There the unfortunate Franks's body was stripped, disfigured with acid and thrust into a drain where the murderers thought that it would be submerged and washed away. They then buried their victim's shoes and leather belt, threw away the chisel, destroyed the cloth and burned the rest of the boy's clothes in the cellar of the Loeb house. After that they mailed the ransom letter which was signed "George Johnson" to Mr. Jacob Franks, Robert's father.

Bloodstained car

Next morning the two killers met at the University, and together went to the Leopold house where the hired car had been left in the driveway. Finding some bloodstains inside the car, they set to work to remove them with a mixture of soap and water and petrol. Leopold's chauffeur, who was standing by, offered to help. But the lads hurriedly assured him that it was just some red wine they spilled the previous night, and that they would soon be finished cleaning it.

"After we had cleaned the car," Leopold continued, "we went to a phone booth and telephoned Mr. Franks. I did the talking because he might have recognized Dick's voice. Bobby was some kind of distant cousin of his. Well, I told Mr. Franks 'This is Johnson calling' and asked him to take the money to a certain drug store where he would find a letter waiting for him.

"Dick and I had talked a lot of how to do the pick-up, and we finally decided to ask the father to board a south-bound train and throw the box out of the window as it passed the Champion Manufacturing Company at 74th Street and the I.C. Railroad tracks. Anyways, that's what the letter told him to do but he never did it because by then the police had found the body and informed him of the fact.

"The story made a big stink in the papers but I didn't think that I could be connected with it in any way. At least not until the police came to the house with my spectacles. You know, I had completely forgotten about them. I must have dropped them out at Hegewich. In any case I did not think they were mine at first and invited the police to search my home.

Radio Times Hulton

AT THE WHEEL . . . Leopold in the car he and Loeb hired before they killed little Robert Franks. After they had bundled the disfigured body into a drain, they sent his father a ransom note (right) . . . under a false name. Divers were called in (opposite, top) to search for the typewriter used for the letter to Mr. Franks.

Dear Sir:

Proceed immediately to the back platform of the train. Watch the east side of the track. Have your package ready. Look for the first LARGE, RED, BRICK factory situated immediately adjoining the tracks on the east. On top of this factory is a large, black watertower with the word CHAMPION written on it. Wait until you have COMPLETELY passed the south end of the factory - count five very rapidly and then IMMEDIATELY throw the package as far east as you can.

Remember that this is your only chance to recover your son.

Yours truly,

GEORGE JOHNSON

MR JACOB FRANKS

Should anyone else find this note, please leave it alone. The letter is very important.

"When the search failed to reveal my spectacles I knew that the police had mine. I still didn't admit to anything until Mr. Crowe told me that Dick had confessed to the kidnapping. I guess there was no use hiding anything then."

In all 80 witnesses were produced and gave their damning evidence. Counsel for the defence sat, for the most part, impassively through the barrage of facts and testimonies. Their play would come later.

On July 30 the State rested its case Now was to come the first major battle of the trial. Should evidence of mitigating circumstances be introduced into a trial where the defendants had pleaded guilty? It was a thorny legal question which had, so far, never been satisfactorily answered. Was there such a thing as degrees of mental responsibility short of insanity in the *legal* sense?

"No," claimed the State's Attorney, "there is nothing in law known as degrees of responsibility. You are either entirely responsible for all the consequences of your act, or you are not responsible at all."

The defence held otherwise. They could not argue insanity because of the guilty plea (under state law an insane person cannot be held responsible for his crimes), but they did argue that proof of mental abnormality must be considered by the court in mitigation.

For three days the controversy raged. If the decision went to the State the defence could pack up its bags and Leopold and Loeb would soon find themselves marching to the gallows. The prospects were dim. Crowe knew he had public opinion behind him, and that the pressure was on the judge to sustain the prosecutor's objection. Chicago wanted blood retribution.

The decision came on the third day. In a statement read out to a hushed and tense courtroom Judge Caverly declared that "the court is of the opinion that it is his duty to hear any evidence that the defence may present, and it is not for the court to determine in advance what it may be."

Mental abnormality

Darrow had won the first round. But the real struggle was just about to begin. It was one thing to present evidence of mental abnormality, another to prove the truth of it. In anticipation of an insanity plea the prosecution had already lined up a battery of expert witnesses — including four well-known psychiatrists and neurologists — to counter whatever claims the defence would present.

For days thereafter the courtroom became the jousting ground for the two opposing groups of psychiatrists ("alienists" as they were then known). The air was thick with psychological terms — split personality, abnormal fantasies, paranoia, subconscious; terms which were new and had not entered the general vocabulary.

It reached the point that Crowe was to complain in his summation that: "I have heard so many big words and foreign words in this case that I sometimes thought that perhaps we were letting error creep into the record, so many strange, foreign words were being used here, and the constitution provides that these trials must be conducted in the English language."

Cunning and trickery

The leading "alienist" for the defence was Dr. William A. White, the Superintendent of St. Elizabeth's Hospital for Mental Diseases in Washington, D.C. (Crowe was to make much of the fact that the defence alienists were brought from the east, playing on the Mid-Westerner's association of the east with cunning and trickery, not quite honest-to-goodness American.)

The gist of Dr. White's and his associates' statements was that Leopold and Loeb, due to innate constitutional factors in combination with an unhealthy and restricted childhood, developed abnormal fantasy lives which increasingly substituted for normal emotional growth.

Loeb would often fantasize at being a famous criminal locked in jail and brutally beaten by his captors. "I was abused, but it was a pleasant thought," said Loeb.

Leopold, the super-intellect, decided at an early age to suppress all emotion. The defence alienists stated that he represented a "picture of a special abnormal type, the paranoid psychopathic personality". As soon as the defence witnesses had vacated the stand they were occupied by the prosecution's experts. The first witness for the prosecution to be called was Dr. Hugh T. Patrick, a Chicago neurologist.

After recounting the details of his interviews with Leopold and Loeb he was asked, "Have you an opinion from the observation and examination as detailed, as to whether the defendant, Richard Loeb, was suffering from any mental disease at that time?"

"Yes," he answered.

"What is that opinion?"

"My opinion is that he showed no evidence of mental disease," declared Dr. Patrick. He went on to state that "unless we assume that every man who commits a deliberate, cold-blooded, planned murder must, by that fact, be mentally diseased there was no evidence of any mental disease."

One by one the State's experts, prodded by Crowe, recited the litany of guilt. "Have you an opinion?" . . . "Yes . . . No evidence of mental disease."

Deadlock. Two equally distinguished groups of psychiatrists had given diametrically opposed views on the question of the mental health of Nathan Leopold and Richard Loeb. Their fates hung in the balance. To which side would the judge incline his ear? That, it seemed, would depend on the summation speeches.

The second and most decisive battle of the courtroom drama was about to begin. Speaking for the defence was the formidable Clarence Darrow whose silver tongue had more than once saved the day in apparently hopeless cases. But never before had guilt been so obvious and public pressure so demanding. To win a reprieve for his clients he would have to pull out all stops.

On his side he had the contested opinion of three expert witnesses. Against him stood State's Attorney, Robert Crowe, an able prosecutor with a reputation for sending criminals to their death; the natural revulsion evoked by the senseless crime, and a prejudice against the rich which coalesced into a public demand for a speedy resolution to the trial: resolution by hanging!

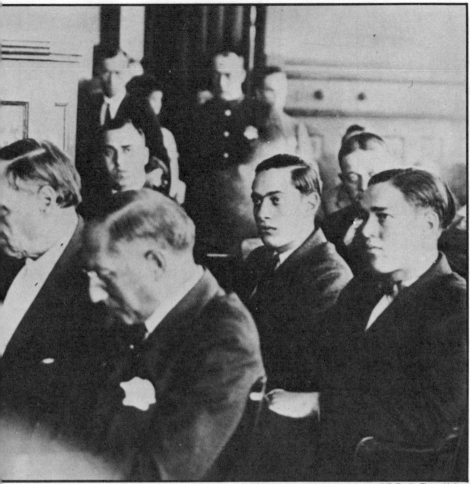

THE LAWYERS (above) argue out the
vital question . . . were the killers
mentally ill? NO . . . said State
Attorney Robert Crowe (inset, above).

YES . . . said the boys' lawyer
Clarence Darrow, seen below hearing
that his clients will not be executed.
His brilliant mercy plea had succeeded.

Even some half-century after the trial,
Clarence Darrow's masterly summation
contains a magnetic, near hypnotic force.
How much more powerful it was in that
hot and dusty courtroom in the early days
of August 1924, as the crowd sat spell-
bound, listening to the master defend the
lives of "these hated, despised outcasts".

All the tricks of oratory were brought
to play, from biting irony (of the assistant
prosecuting attorney Joseph Savage,
Darrow said, "did you pick him for his
name or his ability . . ."); to cold logic,
and finally, compassionate enjoinder. His
knowledge of the law was vast and he let
loose a pyrotechnical display of prece-
dents for mercy in cases such as the
present one.

Argument demolished

With quick, sharp jabs he demolished
the State's argument that the boys had
killed for money. They had killed simply
for the experience. It was obvious that
the boys were mentally ill, "that somewhere in the infinite processes that go to
the making up of the boy or man something slipped".

But the main thrust of Darrow's argument was against capital punishment. "I
hate killing and I hate it no matter how
it is done," he declared. He asked the
judge to consider why it was that capital
punishment still existed in civilized
countries and in reply to his own question
he answered:

"You can only hang them because back
of the law and back of justice and back of
common instincts of man, and back of the
human feeling for the young, is the hoarse
voice of the mob which says 'Kill'."

For three days Darrow argued his case,
leading the judge through all the emotions
known to man—joy, hate, anger, and
finally compassion. And with a final,
passionate enjoinder to the judge to consider the future he rested his case.

"I know the future is on my side. Your
Honor stands between the past and the
future. You may hang these boys; you
may hang them by the neck until they
are dead. But in doing it you will turn
your face toward the past. In doing it you
are making it harder for every other boy
who in ignorance and darkness must
grope his way through the mazes which
only childhood knows. In doing it you
will make it harder for unborn children.

Vision, hope, and fate

"You may save them and make it
easier for every child that some time may
stand where these boys stand. You will
make it easier for every human being
with an aspiration and a vision and a
hope and a fate. I am pleading for the
future; I am pleading for a time when
hatred and cruelty will not control the
hearts of men. When we can learn by

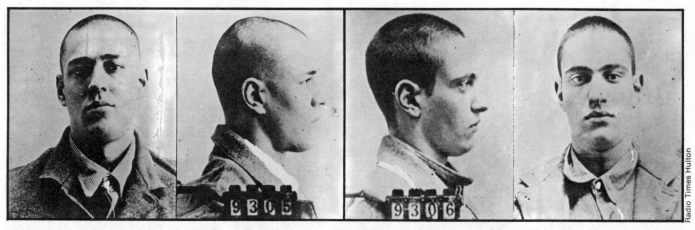

reason and judgment and understanding and faith that all life is worth saving, and that mercy is the highest attribute of man."

It might be expected that the State's Attorney, when he wound up for the prosecution, would have countered the defence lawyer's eloquence with a sober repetition of the facts, and calmly pointed out the weaknesses in his opponent's plea in mitigation. Instead Mr. Crowe attempted to rival Darrow's rhetorical extravagances in language which, however well it might have gone down with a jury, was quite unsuitable when addressing a judge.

Indeed, he got so far carried away in his concluding remarks that he implied that if any sentence short of death was passed on the prisoners, it would be regarded by the general public as proof that the court had been bribed. Not unnaturally Judge Caverly took the strongest possible exception to this observation "as being a cowardly and dastardly assault upon the integrity of this court", and ordered it to be stricken from the record.

Mr. Crowe's folly, added to Clarence Darrow's brilliant summation, had their effect upon the judicial bench. When it came to the final moments in this extraordinary courtroom drama, Judge Caverly announced that chiefly because of the prisoners' youth he did not intend to sentence them to death. Instead they would both be imprisoned for life in the Joliet penitentiary on the murder charge, with a recommendation to the authorities not to admit them to parole.

On the kidnapping charge they were both sentenced to 99 years, this sentence to operate even if—contrary to the judge's recommendation—they were eventually paroled on the murder conviction. The kidnapping sentence caused some surprise, since it meant that neither Leopold nor Loeb could ever be released except as the result of a special amnesty.

The trial requires a footnote. While Clarence Darrow added another triumph of advocacy to his already impressive list, Judge Caverly became the most abused judge in Chicago and had to be accorded police protection for long afterwards. Richard Loeb, who developed homosexual tendencies in Joliet, was killed as the result of a homosexual brawl with another inmate in the prison baths on January 28, 1936.

On the other hand, Nathan Leopold served $33\frac{1}{2}$ years of his sentence, during which time he organized the library of the penitentiary, learned thirty-seven languages and became an authority on many subjects, finally offering himself as a guinea pig for medical research into a new anti-malaria drug. His excellent prison record earned him his freedom.

Leopold was released from Joliet in 1958 and went to Puerto Rico where he became a laboratory technician in a missionary hospital at a salary of ten dollars a month. He later entered the University of Puerto Rico and took a master's degree. He then worked for the San Juan Health Department, and in 1961 he married a doctor's widow. After a dozen years of useful service to the local community he died on August 19, 1971.

Thus, as Judge Caverly had endeavoured to make sure in passing sentence, were the ends of justice satisfied and the interests of society safeguarded.

FREEDOM FIGHTER William Byron talks to Leopold in jail (left) about his plea for parole. Top of page: Official prison pictures of Loeb (left) and Leopold.

THE VAMPIRE OF DUSSELDORF

Peter Kurten

Deutsche Presse

His mild manners and soft-spoken courteousness placed him above suspicion, and to most people he appeared to be totally harmless. Yet his bourgeois exterior concealed one of the most brutal sadists of modern times . . .

AS NIGHT fell across the city that had lived through a year of terror, the streets rapidly emptied. People hurried through the narrow lanes to their homes. Children were plucked from playgrounds and sent to bed. Doors were bolted and curtains drawn. The people were in dread of a creature—a vampire—which had no face, no name, no shape. Already, it had committed 46 violent crimes, displaying every kind of perversion. Five bodies had been taken to the mortuary. But still it remained little more than a spectre.

As the lights went out on the night of August 23, 1929, the people of Düsseldorf, in the German Rhineland, felt almost inured to horror. Nothing more, they thought, could shock them now. As they slept fitfully, they little foresaw that the next few hours would demonstrate the full bestiality of the man they had labelled The Düsseldorf Vampire.

There was one bright and cheerful patch of light that evening. In the suburb of Flehe, hundreds of people were enjoying the annual fair. Old-fashioned merry-go-rounds revolved to the heavy rhythm of German march tunes, stalls dispensed beer and *würst*, there was a comforting feeling of safety and warmth in the closely-packed crowd.

A shadow

At around 10.30, two foster sisters, 5-year-old Gertrude Hamacher and 14-year-old Louise Lenzen, left the fair and started walking through the adjoining allotments to their home. As they did so a shadow broke away from among the beansticks and followed them along a footpath. Louise stopped and turned as a gentle voice said:

"Oh dear, I've forgotten to buy some cigarettes. Look, would you be very kind and go to one of the booths and get some for me? I'll look after the little girl."

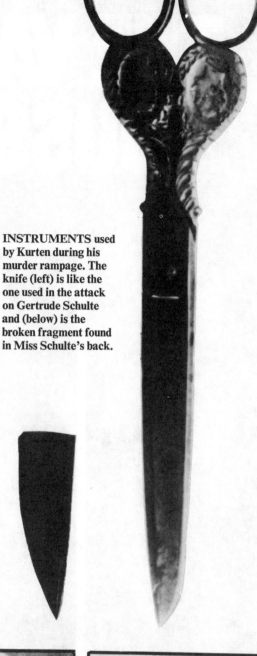

INSTRUMENTS used by Kurten during his murder rampage. The knife (left) is like the one used in the attack on Gertrude Schulte and (below) is the broken fragment found in Miss Schulte's back.

Louise took the man's money and ran back towards the fairground. Quietly, the man picked up Gertrude in his arms and carried her behind the beanpoles. There was no sound as he strangled her and then slowly cut her throat with a Bavarian clasp knife. Louise returned a few moments later and handed over the cigarettes. The man seized her in a stranglehold and started dragging her off the footpath. Louise managed to break away and screamed "Mama! Mama!" The man grabbed her again, strangled her and cut her throat. Then he vanished.

Twelve hours later, Gertrude Schulte, a 26-year-old servant girl, was stopped by a man who offered to take her to the fair at the neighbouring town of Neuss. Foolishly, she agreed. The man introduced himself as Fritz Baumgart and suggested they take a stroll through the woods. Suddenly, he stopped and roughly attempted sexual intercourse. Terrified, Gertrude Schulte pushed him away and screamed, "I'd rather die!"

The man cried "Well, die then!" and began stabbing her frenziedly with a knife. She felt searing pains in her neck and shoulder and a terrific thrust in her back. "Now you can die!" said the man and hurled her away with such force that the knife broke and the blade was left sticking in her back. But Gertrude Schulte didn't die. A passer-by heard her screams and called the police and an ambulance. By then, the attacker had disappeared.

In barely more than half a day, the Düsseldorf maniac had killed two children and attempted to rape and kill another woman. The citizens were stunned as they read their morning papers. Day by day, the attacks continued. Their increasing frequency and ferocity convinced medical experts that the Vampire had lost all control of his sadistic impulses.

In one half-hour, he attacked and wounded a girl of 18, a man of 30, and a woman of 37. The Bavarian dagger gave way to a sharper, thinner blade and then to some kind of blunt instrument. It was the bludgeon that hammered to death two more servant girls, Ida Reuter and Elisabeth Dorrier; the thin blade that killed five-year-old Gertrude Albermann, her body shredded with 36 wounds.

SAVAGED by the Vampire . . . (below from left to right) Ida Reuter, Frau Meurer, Gertrude Albermann, Christine Klein, Maria Hahn and Gertrude Schulte. The latter survived but Kurten (left) fled before her rescuers could spot him.

All Deutsche Presse

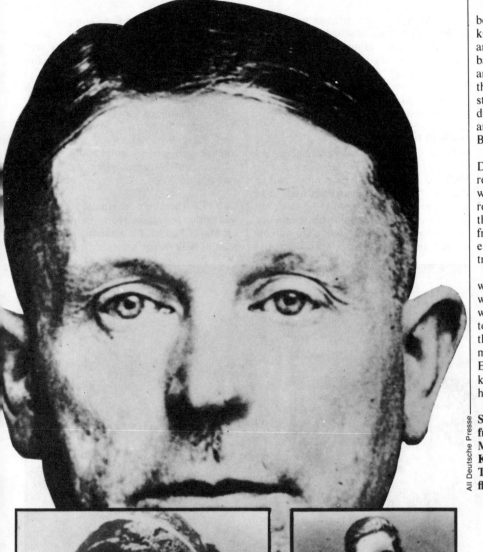

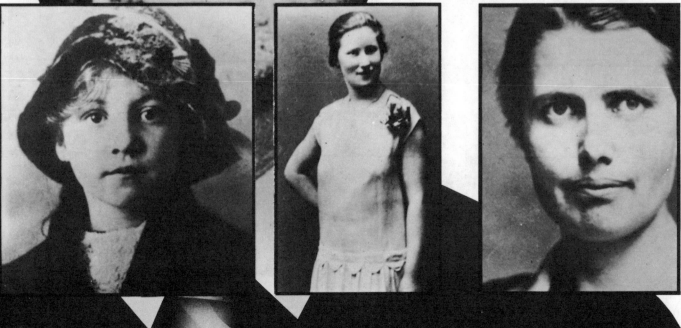

Mettmannerstrasse

Twenty miles away, in the cathedral city of Cologne, a 21-year-old "domestic" named Maria Budlick read the anguished headlines and said to a friend: "Isn't it shocking? Thank goodness we're not in Düsseldorf."

A few weeks later, Maria Budlick lost her job. On May 14, she set out to look for work and boarded a train for Düsseldorf . . . and an unwitting rendezvous with the Vampire.

On the platform at Düsseldorf station, she was accosted by a man who offered to show her the way to a girls' hostel. They followed the brightly-lit streets for a while, but when he started leading her towards the dark trees of the Volksgarten Park she suddenly remembered the stories of the Monster, and refused to go any farther. The man insisted and it was while they were arguing that a second man appeared, as if from nowhere, and inquired softly: "Is everything all right?" The man from the railway station slunk away and Maria Budlick was left alone with her rescuer.

Walk in the woods

Tired and hungry, she agreed to accompany him to his one-room flat in Mettmannerstrasse, where she had a glass of milk and a ham sandwich. The man offered to take her to the hostel, but after a tram ride to the northeastern edge of the city, she realized they were walking deeper and deeper into the Grafenburg Woods. Her companion stopped suddenly and said:

"Do you know now where you are? I can tell you! You are alone with me in the middle of the woods. Now you scream as much as you like and nobody will hear you!"

The man lunged forward, seized her by the throat and tried to have sexual intercourse up against a tree. Maria Budlick struggled violently and was about to lose consciousness when she felt the man's grip relax. "Do you remember

GENTLE vampire's apartment . . . It was to this humdrum room that Kurten led Maria Budlick for a sandwich and a glass of milk before attacking her.

Deutsche Presse

where I live?" he asked. "In case you're ever in need and want my help?" "No," gasped Maria, and in one word saved her own life and signed the death warrant of the Düsseldorf Vampire. The man let her go and showed her out of the woods.

Misdirected letter

But Maria Budlick *had* remembered the address. She vividly recalled the nameplate "Mettmannerstrasse" under the flickering gaslight. And in a letter to a friend the next day, she told of her terrifying experience in the Grafenburg Woods with the quiet, soft-spoken man. The letter never reached her friend. It was misdirected and opened by a Frau Brugman, who took one look at the contents and called the police.

Twenty-four hours later, accompanied by plainclothes detectives, Maria Budlick was walking up and down Mettmannerstrasse trying to pinpoint the quiet man's house. She stopped at No. 71. It looked familiar and she asked the landlady if "a fair-haired, rather sedate man" lived there. The woman took her up to the fourth floor and unlocked a room.

It was the same one in which she had drunk her milk and eaten her sandwich two nights earlier.

She turned round to face even more conclusive proof. The quiet man was coming up the stairs towards her. He looked startled, but carried on to his room and shut the door behind him. A few moments later, he left the house with his hat pulled down over his eyes, passed the two plainclothes men standing in the street and disappeared round a corner.

Maria Budlick ran out and told the officers: "That's the man who assaulted me in the woods. His name is Peter Kurten." So far, nothing linked Kurten with the Vampire. His only crime was suspected rape. But he knew there was no longer any hope of concealing his identity. Early the following morning — after meeting his wife as usual at the restaurant where she worked late — he confessed: "I am the Monster of Düsseldorf."

On May 24, 1930, Frau Kurten told the story to the police, adding that she had arranged to meet her husband outside St. Rochus Church at three o'clock

that afternoon. By that time the whole area was surrounded by armed police. The moment Peter Kurten appeared, four officers rushed forward with loaded revolvers. The man smiled and offered no resistance. "There is no need to be afraid," he said.

Grisly exhibits

After exhaustive questioning, during which he admitted 68 crimes — not including convictions for theft and assault, for which he had already spent a total of 20 years in prison — the trial of the Düsseldorf Vampire opened on April 13, 1931. He was charged with a total of nine murders and seven attempted murders.

Thousands of people crowded round the converted drillhall of the Düsseldorf police headquarters waiting to catch their first glimpse of the depraved creature who had terrorized the city. A special shoulder-

SIXTEEN names appeared on the police list of "vampire" victims of whom nine were murdered. At the trial, Kurten related the details with obvious relish.

Lfd. Nr.	Name des Opfers	Anklagebehörde Straftat	Beantragte Strafe	Anträge des Verteidigers	Urteil des Schwurgerichts	Gesamturteil
1	Kind Christine Klein	Mord Die unzüchtigen Handlungen sind verjährt	Todesstrafe	Totschlag daher bereits verjährt	Todesstrafe	
2	Frau Berta Kühn	Mordversuch in Tateinheit mit versuchter Vornahme unzüchtiger Handlungen	10 Jahre Zuchthaus	gefährliche Körperverletzung	10 Jahre Zuchthaus	
3	Kind Rosa Ohliger	Mord in Tateinheit mit gewaltsamer Vornahme unzüchtiger Handlungen	Todesstrafe	Totschlag	Todesstrafe	
4	Maschinist Rudolf Scheer	Mord	Todesstrafe	Totschlag keine Ueberlegung	Todesstrafe	
5	Hausangestellte Maria Hahn	Mord in Tateinheit mit gewaltsamer Vornahme unzüchtiger Handlungen	Todesstrafe	Totschlag keine Ueberlegung	Todesstrafe	
6	Fräulein Anna Goldhausen	Mordversuch	10 Jahre Zuchthaus	gefährliche Körperverletzung	10 Jahre Zuchthaus	Urteil: 9 x zum Tode, 15 Jahre Zuchthaus, Stellung unter Polizeiaufsicht und Aberkennung der bürgerlichen Ehrenrechte auf Lebzeit.
7	Frau Mantel	Mordversuch	5 Jahre Zuchthaus	gefährliche Körperverletzung	5 Jahre Zuchthaus	
8	Arbeiter Kornblum	Mordversuch	5 Jahre Zuchthaus	gefährliche Körperverletzung	5 Jahre Zuchthaus	
9	Kind Hamacher	Mord in Tateinheit mit gewaltsamer Vornahme unzüchtiger Handlungen	Todesstrafe	keine Ueberlegung Totschlag	Todesstrafe	
10	Kind Luise Lenzen	Mord in Tateinheit mit gewaltsamer Vornahme unzüchtiger Handlungen	Todesstrafe	keine Ueberlegung Totschlag	Todesstrafe	
11	Gertrud Schulte	Mordversuch in Tateinheit mit versuchter Notzucht	15 Jahre Zuchthaus			
12	Hausangestellte Ida Reuter	Mord in Tateinheit mit vollendeter Notzucht	Todesstrafe			
13	Hausangestellte Elisabeth Dörrier	Mord in Tateinheit mit gewaltsamer Vornahme unzüchtiger Handlungen	Todesstrafe			
14	Frau Meurer	Mordversuch in Tateinheit mit versuchter Vornahme unzüchtiger Handlungen	10 Jahre Zuchthaus			
15	Frau Wanders	Mordversuch in Tateinheit mit vollendeter Vornahme unzüchtiger Handlungen	5 Jahre Zuchthaus			
16	Kind Gertruden Albermann	Mord in Tateinheit mit gewaltsamer Vornahme unzüchtiger Handlungen	Todesstrafe			
			Gesamte beantragte Strafe siehe Urteil.		Gesamtstrafe: 9 x zum Tode 60 Jahre Zuchthaus	

Straftaten und Urteil im Mordprozeß gegen Peter Kürten 13.4.–22.4.1931.

Deutsche Presse, Hauptstaatsarchiv Düsseldorf

high "cage" had been built inside the courtroom to prevent his escape and behind it were arranged the grisly exhibits of the "Kurten Museum" – the prepared skulls of his victims, showing the various injuries, knives, scissors and a hammer, articles of clothing, and a spade he had used to bury a woman.

The first shock was the physical appearance of the Monster. Despite his appalling crimes, 48-year-old Peter Kurten was far from the maniac of the conventional horror film. He was no Count Dracula with snarling teeth and wild eyes, no lumbering, stitched-together Frankenstein's Monster. There was no sign of the brutal sadist or the weak-lipped degenerate. With his sleek, meticulously parted hair, cloud of Eau de Cologne, immaculate suit, and well-polished shoes, he looked like a prim shopkeeper or minor civil servant.

It was when he started talking that a chill settled over the court. In a quiet, matter-of-fact voice, as if listing the stock of a haberdasher's shop, he described his life of perversion and bloodlust in such clinical detail that even the most hardened courtroom officials paled.

Drunken brute

His crimes were more monstrous than anyone had imagined. The man wasn't a mere psychopath, but a walking textbook of perverted crime: sex maniac, sadist, rapist, vampire, strangler, stabber, hammer-killer, arsonist, a man who committed bestiality with animals, and derived sexual satisfaction from witnessing street accidents and planning disasters involving the deaths of hundreds of people.

And yet he was quite sane. The most brilliant doctors in Germany testified that Kurten had been perfectly responsible for his actions at all times. Further proof of his awareness was provided by the premeditated manner of his crimes, his ability to leave off in the middle of an attack if disturbed, and his astonishing memory for every detail.

How did this inoffensive-looking man become a Vampire? In his flat, unemotional voice, Kurten described a life in which a luckless combination of factors –heredity, environment, the faults of the German penal system – had conspired to bring out and foster the latent sadistic streak with which he had been born.

Kurten described how his childhood was spent in a poverty-stricken, one-room apartment; one of a family of 13 whose father was a drunken brute. There was a long history of alcoholism and mental trouble on the father's side of the family, and his father frequently arrived home drunk, assaulted the children and forced intercourse on his mother. "If they hadn't been married, it would have

been rape," he said. His father was later jailed for three years for committing incest with Kurten's sister, aged 13.

Bestiality

Kurten's sadistic impulses were awakened by the violent scenes in his own home. At the age of nine, a worse influence took over. Kurten became apprenticed to a dogcatcher who lived in the same house, a degenerate who showed him how to torture animals and encouraged him to masturbate them. Around the same time, he drowned a boy while playing on a raft in the Rhine. When the boy's friend dived in to rescue him, Kurten pushed him under the raft and held him down until he suffocated, too.

His sexual urges developed rapidly, and within five years he was committing bestiality with sheep and goats in nearby stables. It was soon after that he "be-

came aware of the pleasure of the sight of blood" and he began to torture animals, achieving orgasm stabbing pigs and sheep.

The terrible pattern of his life was forming. It only needed one more depraved influence to transfer his sadistic urges from animals to human beings. He found it in a prostitute, twice his age, a masochist who enjoyed being ill-treated and abused. His sadistic education was complete and they lived together for some time.

Far from straightening him out, a two-year prison sentence for theft left him bitter and angry at inhuman penal conditions – particularly for adolescents – and introduced him to yet another sadistic refinement, a fantasy world where he

ENCAGED in court, Peter Kurten looked anything but a savage killer. He was smartly dressed, polite and tranquil.

could achieve orgasm by imagining brutal sexual acts. He became so obsessed with these fantasies that he deliberately broke minor prison rules so that he could be sentenced to solitary confinement. It was the ideal atmosphere for sadistic daydreaming.

Shortly after being released from prison, he made his first murderous attack on a girl during sexual intercourse, leaving her for dead in the Grafenburg Woods. No body was ever found and the girl probably crawled away, keeping her terrible secret to herself. More prison sentences followed, for assault and theft. After each jail term, Kurten's feelings of injustice were strengthened. His sexual and sadistic fantasies now involved revenge on society.

THE EVIDENCE . . . Kurten, it turned out, was also a dab hand at arson and police had managed, in several cases, to recover the matches he had used (below). But the killer himself supplied most of evidence, like the map (right) which he drew to show where he buried a victim.

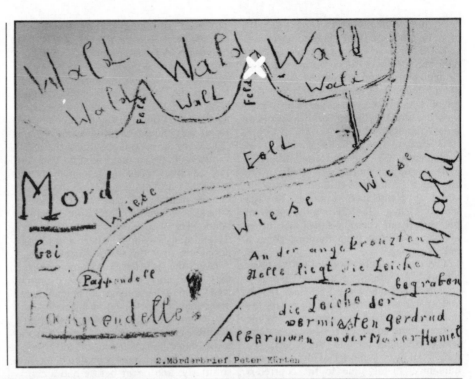

"I thought of myself causing accidents affecting thousands of people and invented a number of crazy fantasies such as smashing bridges and boring through bridge piers," he explained. "Then I spun a number of fantasies with regard to bacilli which I might be able to introduce into the drinking water and so cause a great calamity.

"I imagined myself using schools or orphanages for the purpose, where I could carry out murders by giving away chocolate samples containing arsenic which I could have obtained through housebreaking. I derived the sort of pleasure from these visions that other people would get from thinking about a naked woman."

The court was hypnotized by the revelations. To them, Kurten's narrative sounded like the voice of Satan. It was almost impossible to associate it with the mild figure in the wooden cage. While hysteria and demands for lynching—and worse—reigned outside the court, the trial itself was a model of decorum and humanity, mainly due to the courteous and civilized manner of the Presiding Judge, Dr. Rose. Quietly, he prompted Kurten to describe his bouts of arson and fire-raising . . .

"Yes. When my desire for injuring people awoke, the love of setting fire to things awoke as well. The sight of the flames delighted me, but above all it was the excitement of the attempts to extinguish the fire and the agitation of those who saw their property being destroyed."

The court was deathly quiet, sensing that the almost unspeakable had at last arrived. Gently, Dr. Rose asked, *"Now tell us about Christine Klein . . ."* Kurten pursed his lips for a second as if mentally organizing the details and then—in the unemotional tones of a man recalling a minor business transaction—described the horrible circumstances of his first sex-killing.

"It was on May 25, 1913. I had been stealing, specializing in public bars or inns where the owners lived on the floor above. In a room above an inn at Köln-Mülheim, I discovered a child of 13 asleep. Her head was facing the window. I seized it with my left hand and strangled her for about a minute and a half. The child woke up and struggled but lost consciousness.

"I had a small but sharp pocketknife with me and I held the child's head and cut her throat. I heard the blood spurt and drip on the mat beside the bed. It spurted in an arch, right over my hand. The whole thing lasted about three minutes. Then I locked the door again and went back home to Düsseldorf.

"Next day I went back to Mülheim. There is a cafe opposite the Kleins' place and I sat there and drank a glass of beer and read all about the murder in the papers. People were talking about it all round me. All this amount of indignation and horror did me good."

In the courtroom, the horrors were piling up like bodies in a charnel house. Describing his sexual aberrations, Kurten admitted that the sight of his victims' blood was enough to bring on an orgasm. On several occasions, he drank the blood—once gulping so much that he vomited. He admitted drinking blood from the throat of one victim and from the wound on the temple of another. In another attack, he licked the blood from a victim's hands. He also had an ejaculation after decapitating a swan in a park and placing his mouth over the severed neck.

Everyone in the courtroom realized they were not just attending a sensational trial, but experiencing a unique legal precedent. The prosecution hardly bothered to present any evidence. Kurten's detailed, almost fussy, confession was the most damning evidence of all. Never before had a prisoner convicted himself so utterly; and never before had a courtroom audience been given the opportunity to gaze so deeply into the mind of a maniac.

Bitter sting

Every tiny detail built up a picture of a soul twisted beyond all recognition. Kurten described with enthusiasm how he enjoyed reading *Jack the Ripper* as a child, how he had visited a waxwork Chamber of Horrors and boasted "I'll be in there one day!" The whole court shuddered when, in answer to one question, Kurten pointed to his heart and said: "Gentlemen, you must look in here!"

When the long, ghastly recital was over, Kurten's counsel, Dr. Wehner, had the hopeless task of trying to prove insanity in the face of unbreakable evidence by several distinguished psychiatrists. During Professor Sioli's testimony, Dr. Wehner pleaded:

"Kurten is the king of sexual delinquents because he unites nearly all perversions in one person. Can that not change your opinion about insanity? Is it possible for the Kurten case to persuade psychiatry to adopt another opinion?"

Professor Sioli: "No."

Dr. Wehner: "That is the dreadful thing! The man Kurten is a riddle to me. I cannot solve it. The criminal Haarman only killed men, Landru only women, Grossmann only women, but Kurten killed men, women, children, and animals, killed anything he found!"

Professor Sioli: "And was at the same time a clever man and quite a nice one."

Here was the final twist to the conundrum. The face peeping over the wooden cage was recognizably only too human. Witnesses had spoken of his courteous-ness and mild manners. Neighbours had refused flatly to believe he was the Vampire. Employers testified to his honesty and reliability. He could charm women to their deaths, indeed was regarded as a local Casanova. His wife had been completely unaware of his double life and had only betrayed him on his insistence, so she could share in the reward for his arrest. Right at the beginning of the Düsseldorf Terror, a former girlfriend who suggested he might be the Vampire was fined by the police for making a malicious accusation.

Some of the bourgeois puritanism which made Kurten so plausible burst out in his final statement before sentence was passed. Speaking hurriedly and gripping the rail, he said:

"My actions as I see them today are so terrible and so horrible that I do not even make an attempt to excuse them. But one bitter sting remains in my mind. When I think of Dr. Wolf and the woman doctor—the two Socialist doctors accused recently of abortions performed on working-class mothers who sought their advice—when I think of the 500 murders they have committed, then I cannot help feeling bitter.

"The real reason for my conviction is that there comes a time in the life of every criminal when he can go no further. And this spiritual collapse is what I experienced. But I do feel that I must make one statement: some of my victims made things very easy for me. Manhunting on the part of women today has taken on such forms that . . ."

At such self-righteousness, Dr. Rose's patience snapped. "Stop these remarks!" he ordered, banging his desk. The jury then took only 1½ hours to reach their verdict: Guilty on all counts. Dr. Rose sentenced him to death nine times.

On the evening of July 1, 1932, Peter Kurten was given the traditional *Henkers-Mahlzeit,* or condemned man's last meal. He asked for Wienerschnitzel, fried potatoes, and a bottle of white wine—which he enjoyed so much that he had it all over again. At six o'clock the following morning, the Vampire of Düsseldorf, a priest on either side, walked briskly to the guillotine erected in the yard of Klingelputz Prison. "Have you any last wish to express?" asked the Attorney-General. Without emotion, almost cheerfully, Kurten replied "No."

For in the few minutes before that walk, and the blow that separated his head from his body, he had already expressed his last, earthly desire. "Tell me," he asked the prison psychiatrist, "after my head has been chopped off, will I still be able to hear, at least for a moment, the sound of my own blood gushing from the stump of my neck?" He savoured the thought for a moment, then added: "That would be the pleasure to end all pleasures."

THE MAIDS OF LE MANS

The Papin Sisters

Everything appeared to be cut and dried. The brutally slaughtered bodies had been found, along with the murder weapons, and the two killers had immediately confessed to the crime. Yet something, surely, was wrong. These were not hardened criminals; they were not even psychopaths. They were two ordinary housemaids. What had driven them to hack their employers to death?

THE newspapers had called them "the monsters of Le Mans", "the diabolical sisters", and "the lambs who had become wolves". But as Christine Papin, 28, and her sister, Lea, 21, took their seats in the courtroom of the provincial French town of Le Mans on the morning of September 20, 1933, it was difficult to believe that these were the girls who had inspired those black headlines.

They were impassive. No emotion showed on their peasant-like, but not coarse, faces; they kept their heavy-lidded eyes on the floor. It was almost as if they were in a trance or under heavy sedation. On their way to the dock they moved like robots.

And yet they were charged with a double murder which has been described as "one of the most awesome recorded occurrences of motiveless ferocity"—a crime which "shocked France, baffled psychiatrists, and has yet to be satisfactorily explained".

The men and women in the public seats were hushed as they heard—from the principals this time, not from the columns of their daily newspaper—the macabre details of the crime committed in a middle-class home in Le Mans on a dark winter's evening nearly eight months earlier.

The date was February 2, 1933. Monsieur René Lancelin, an attorney who had been away on business all day, was due to

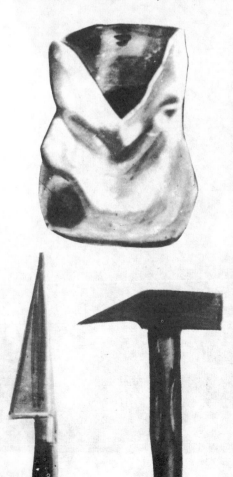

THE NARROW staircase (above) leading to the servants' room where Christine and sister Lea lay huddled together in a single bed. The landing is where the bodies of Madame and Mademoiselle Lancelin were left, horribly mutilated. The weapons used by the "monsters of Le Mans" were a knife, a hammer, and a severely battered pewter pot (left) and all three were found beside the lifeless bodies.

THE SCENE awaiting Monsieur Lancelin on arrival at his house (below). The front door was locked and the only light came from the maids' room. Inside, his wife and daughter lay hacked to pieces.

meet his wife and 27-year-old daughter Geneviève, for dinner at the home of a friend. "They were not there," he told the court. "After waiting for a while, I tried to telephone my home. There was no answer. I excused myself and went to the house.

"The front door was locked from the inside and the house was in darkness except for a faint glow from the upstairs room occupied by the two maids, Christine and Lea Papin. I was unable to get in so I called the police."

Deep wounds

The story was then taken up by the police inspector who arrived in response to M. Lancelin's call and forced his way into the house. The ground floor was deserted, but on the first-floor landing . . .

"The corpses of Madame and Mademoiselle Lancelin were lying stretched out on the floor and were frightfully mutilated. Mademoiselle Lancelin's corpse was lying face downward, head bare, coat pulled up and with her knickers down, revealing deep wounds in the buttocks and multiple cuts in the calves. Madame Lancelin's body was lying on its back. The eyes had disappeared, she seemed no longer to have a mouth and all the teeth had been knocked out.

"The walls and doors were covered with splashes of blood to a height of more than seven feet. On the floor we found fragments of bone and teeth, one eye, hair pins, a handbag, a key ring, an untied parcel, numerous bits of white, decorated porcelain and a coat button."

That was not all. There were more discoveries—a kitchen knife covered with blood, a damaged pewter pot and lid, a blood-stained hammer. But where were the maids? The police found them, naked and huddled together in a single bed, in their room. Christine, the elder, immediately confessed to the crime.

In the horror-struck courtroom, she kept her eyes downcast as her words —spoken in a sullen, dull monotone— were recalled.

"When Madame came back to the house, I informed her that the iron was broken again and that I had not been able to iron. She wanted to jump on me. My sister and I and our two mistresses were on the first-floor landing. When I saw that Madame Lancelin was going to jump on me, I leaped at her face and scratched out her eyes with my fingers.

"No, I made a mistake when I said that I leaped on Madame Lancelin. It was on Mademoiselle Lancelin that I leaped and it was her eyes that I scratched out. Meanwhile, my sister Lea had jumped on Madame Lancelin and scratched her eyes out in the same way.

"After we had done this, they lay and crouched down on the spot. I then rushed down to the kitchen to fetch a hammer and a knife. With these two instruments, my sister and I fell upon our two mistresses. We struck at the head with the knife, hacked at the bodies and legs, and also struck with a pewter pot, which was standing on a little table on the landing.

"We exchanged one instrument for another several times. By that I mean that I would pass the hammer over to my sister so that she could hit with it while she handed me the knife, and we did the same with the pewter pot. The victims began to cry out but I don't remember that they said anything.

"When we had done the job, I went to bolt the front door, and I also shut the vestibule door. I shut these doors because I wanted the police to find out our crime before our master. My sister and I then went and washed our hands in the kitchen because they were covered with blood.

"We then went to our room, took off all our clothes, which were stained with blood, put on a dressing-gown, shut the door of our room with a key and lay down on the same bed. That's where you found us when you broke the door down.

"I have no regrets or, rather, I can't tell you whether I have any or not. I'd rather have had the skin of my mistresses than that they should have had mine or my sister's. I did not plan my crime and I didn't feel any hatred towards them, but I don't put up with the sort of gesture that Madame Lancelin was making at me that evening."

No regrets

Lea Papin confirmed her sister's statement. "Like my sister," she said, "I affirm that we had not planned to kill our mistresses. The idea came suddenly when we heard Madame Lancelin scolding us. I don't have any more regrets for the criminal act we have committed than my sister does. Like her, I would rather have had my mistresses' skins than their having ours."

The murders had been triggered off by the iron mentioned in Christine's statement. Lea had damaged it at some time during January. On February 1, the day before the killings, Madame Lancelin had deducted five francs from her month's wages to pay for the repair. Then, while the maids were ironing in the otherwise empty house on February 2, the iron fused, putting out all the lights. "What will Madame do to us when she gets back?" Lea had asked anxiously.

It seemed certain that, on her return, Madame Lancelin had been irritated and might have raised her hand to one or both of the sisters. But how could such a trivial incident have led to such savagery —two healthy women having their eyes gouged out and then, blinded and in agony, battered almost beyond recognition with the hammer and pewter pot, and finally their bodies further mutilated with a knife?

Even the judge found it difficult to credit both the story and the lack of emotion of the two sisters as it was related. Lea, looking very much the younger of the two, her dark coat buttoned to the neck, her hands thrust deep into her pockets, gazed vacantly in front of her.

Christine still gazed rigidly at the ground. She might have been asleep but for a strange smile, almost of contentment, that strayed across her lips.

Barely audible

The judge, speaking quietly and calmly, as if to two children, went over the salient facts with them again, almost as if seeking reassurance that he had heard correctly the first time. He said to Christine:

"You knocked Madame Lancelin down with a blow from a pewter pot. As she cried out, your sister came running. What did you say to her?"

"I told Lea to tear her eyes out."

A murmur of horror ran through the listeners in the public seats. The judge then asked Lea: "When your sister saw that Madame Lancelin wanted to get up again, did she say to you: 'Tear her eyes out'?"

"Yes," replied Lea in a barely audible voice.

"You came rushing up. You knocked her out by banging her head against the floor and then you tore her eyes out. How?"

"With my fingers," Lea replied in a flat, matter-of-fact voice.

There was a renewed hubbub in the public seats. "Death to them!" someone shouted. "Death to them!" The judge threatened to clear the court if there was any further disturbance.

Drunkard father

As peace was restored, he resumed the interrogation. What, he wanted to know, had happened after Lea had torn out Madame Lancelin's eyes and helped to batter her to death?

"I slashed her body with the knife," she responded.

"Have you any excuses for your action, any explanation, any regrets?" asked the judge.

Lea made no reply. Nor did Christine when the same question was put to her.

Could there be anything like a deep-rooted resentment of their lives as maids to account for the ferocity of their sudden assault? That suggestion, too, led the court nowhere.

Christine had gone straight into domestic service on leaving her convent school. Lea had followed her after being brought up in an orphanage (their father was a drunkard). They had worked

A GENERAL VIEW of the court (above) during the trial and (left) the outside of the Palais de Justice at Le Mans. The courtroom was always packed with eager spectators fascinated by this bizarre story of monstrous murder. They were not disappointed by what they heard and saw: there were sensational and horrific confessions from both girls as well as a succession of gory exhibits. The verdict of guilty seemed inevitable.

together and changed jobs frequently before joining the Lancelins. Changing employers had been motivated by nothing more sinister than better wages, and all their references spoke of them as "willing, hard-working, and honest".

Both agreed that they had been well treated by the Lancelins. They were sufficiently well paid to have saved 24,000 francs; they ate the same food as the Lancelins; they even had electric heating in their room—considered something of a luxury for servants.

"What *did* you have against the Lancelin family?" the judge asked, sounding almost desperate in his anxiety to find some clue that would explain the sisters' violent action. "There has been mention of the social hatred of the employee for the employer. But this was not the case. You have said that you suffered from no feeling of inferiority, that 'a servant's profession is as good as any other'. Did you love your employers?"

Lea answered: "We served them and that was all. We never talked to them."

Totally indifferent

With that avenue of exploration apparently closed, the court turned to the personal relationship between the two sisters. Were they lesbians?

They spent nearly all their spare time together in their room, never going to the cinema or to dances. They had no friends of either sex. In fact, they seemed totally indifferent to everything except their work and each other.

Why had Madame Lancelin and her daughter gone home unexpectedly when they were due to meet M. Lancelin at a friend's? The parcel which the police found on the first floor had contained meat. Why had Madame Lancelin—or her daughter—taken the parcel upstairs instead of, as would have been normal, taking it straight to the kitchen?

Could it be that the mistress and her daughter suspected an illicit relationship, and had caught the maids in a compromising situation—and that this had sparked off the horror?

Evidence to support this theory came from Christine's behaviour during the seven months she and Lea had been in prison awaiting trial. She, like Lea, had ceased to menstruate. When they were separated and placed in separate cells, she at first wept, then screamed threats, and howled like a dog.

Once, like a distraught lover, she cried all night for her "darling Lea". Another time, she rolled on the ground, screaming obscenities. "It seemed she was tormented by sexual desires," said a warder.

She begged for Lea to be reunited with her. When they were kept apart, she went on hunger strike and became so violent that she had to be placed in a straitjacket. Finally, they were allowed to meet for a brief reunion. Witnesses gave two slightly differing accounts of the meeting, both bizarre and both suggesting there was more—at least from Christine's point of view—in their relationship than mere sisterly love.

One version claimed that, as soon as Lea entered the cell, Christine leaped upon her and hugged her so hard they had to be forcibly separated before the younger girl choked. Then, as they sat on a bed, Christine tried to tear Lea's blouse off and to kiss her on the mouth, pleading with her: "Say yes to me, Lea, say yes to me."

Hysteria

In the second version, Christine, in a fit of hysteria, pulled her skirts up above her thighs, and, apparently in a paroxysm of sexual desire, begged her sister: "Come to me, Lea, come to me." Both accounts agreed that, for her part, Lea had remained calm and passive.

The medical evidence for the prosecution discounted this behaviour. The director of the lunatic asylum at Le Mans, in a joint report with another doctor, declared: "Christine and Lea are in no way depraved. They are not suffering from any mental illness and are in no way

FLANKED by gendarmes, Lea Papin stares grimly at the judge while sister Christine, head bowed, stares stonily at the ground.

labouring under the burden of a defective heredity. From an intellectual, affective, and emotive point of view, they are completely normal."

Three other doctors appointed to examine the sisters came to the conclusion "there is no question of an attachment of a sexual nature".

The exact nature of the relationship between the two girls proved a point on which the judge was anxious to satisfy himself and the jury. Once again he spoke almost like a parent trying to coax the truth out of reluctant youngsters.

Sexual relationship?

There were, he pointed out—somewhat hesitantly as if choosing his words carefully—several strange aspects to the life they lived in the Lancelin household. They never indulged in the kind of social activities that most young people enjoyed. They had no boy friends, and on breaking down the door of their room, the police found them in the same bed.

"I am bound to ask you," he said, "whether there was anything sexual in your relationship?"

Christine answered that they had merely been sisters. "There was nothing else between us," she shrugged.

And that was basically that. They had committed two brutal murders which, for their ferocity, were virtually without parallel in modern times . . . they had confessed . . . they were, despite their grim crime, sane and normal girls according to all the medical opinion produced by the prosecution.

In prison, awaiting trial, Christine had often said stoically: "I shall be punished —my head cut off, even. *Tant pis!*" Now it looked as if her prediction would be fulfilled.

The slender basis of the defence plea of not guilty was that the two sisters were not, in fact, sane and normal girls. In support of that contention, however, the only witness of distinction they could produce to try to refute the overwhelming medical evidence amassed by the prosecution was a Dr. Logre, a well-known psychiatrist of the era.

LES DEUX SŒURS CRIMINELLES
PRÉCISENT DEVANT LE JUGE D'INSTRUCTION
LES CIRCONSTANCES DE LEUR FORFAIT

Hier soir dans les couloirs du Palais de
LÉA (à gauche) et **CHRISTINE**
(Photos

The prosecutor's case was simple. Christine and Lea Papin were fully responsible for their actions. They had committed a crime which he described, in a ringing phrase, as "the most horrible, and the most abominable, recorded in the annuls of justice." And nobody need look beyond sheer bad temper for a motive.

The defence restricted itself to the plea that psychiatry was a complicated and incompletely-understood science. The question of whether the sisters were of sound mind was still a matter of debate.

The argument carried little weight with the jury. At 1.25 a.m., after 100 minutes, they brought in their verdict. Both sisters were guilty. From the public benches came an audible sigh of relief and a ripple of applause.

Christine showed her first sign of emotion when the judge sentenced her to death. She slumped to her knees for a moment before her lawyer helped her back to her feet. Lea, for whom the jury had found extenuating circumstances in the way she was dominated by her sister, received a sentence of ten years' hard labour. Neither sister appealed.

Later, however, Christine's punishment was commuted to a life sentence of hard labour. But she served only four years, during which she refused to work and showed signs of insanity. She was finally transferred to a psychiatric hospital where she died in 1937. During that time she never once asked for Lea who, when her own term of punishment was over, was released to live in obscurity.

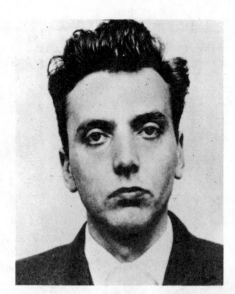

THE MURDERERS OF THE MOORS

Brady and Hindley

"All over the place . . . we have been practically all over the place," said Myra Hindley. With Ian Brady, she had haunted the bleak Pennine moorlands of Northern England. Their ghoulish journeys ended when shallow graves were discovered on the moors. For the dominant Brady and his worshipping mistress, the next journey was to the courtroom. Some called it "The Trial of the Century".

Brady and Hindley...
"I love him," she croaked
"And I still... I love him"

THE DOCK, surrounded on three sides by four-inch thick bulletproof glass, dominated the courtroom. It had been specially altered and strengthened at the request of the British police, who, weeks before the trial began, feared that an attempt might be made to assassinate the prisoners—28-year-old Ian Brady and his worshipping mistress, Myra Hindley. As they sat behind the glass—safe from any guns there might be in court, but exposed to the public's hostility—they sucked mints, passed copious notes to their counsels, and occasionally nudged one another—especially if an adjournment was due. Once, losing her composure for a moment, Hindley stuck her tongue out at a reporter who stared too nakedly at her. But Brady's impassiveness never faltered; he appeared to regard the proceedings as a tiresome formality, a charade to be enacted before he was found guilty and sent to prison for life. "They smell blood," he told a policeman stoically. "I'll be convicted whatever happens out there."

The trial of Brady and Hindley—an event which the judge, Mr. Justice Fenton Atkinson, said has been called "the trial of the century"—opened at Chester Assizes on Tuesday, April 19, 1966. In its own perverse and macabre way, it was just as impressive an occasion as a theatrical first night or a fashionable film première. Hundreds of journalists and television reporters from every part of the world descended on Chester Castle, and the Post Office installed a special cable and rows of telephones to handle their calls. Although only 60 seats were available to the public, scores of spectators—mainly middle-aged women in floral hats or silk headscarves—scrambled to get a place in the gallery of No. 2 Court. A corps of

VICTIM: Homosexual Edward Evans (far left). He was picked up at a railroad station snack bar by Ian Brady, and taken home. At the house Brady shared with Myra Hindley, Evans was battered to death with an axe (in room arrowed). Brady asked brother-in-law David Smith to help in the killing, but Smith was frozen by what he saw. He reported Brady to the police, and is pictured (right) going to court with his wife. Evidence given by Mr. and Mrs. David Smith helped send their brother-in-law to jail for life. Accomplice Myra Hindley also received a life sentence... a deadly partnership was finally broken by prison walls.

MURDERER'S HOME: Myra Hindley grew up in a city slum... a child of World War II, daughter of a paratrooper. Her lover's hero was Hitler.

five well-known authors was present, hoping to concoct bestsellers from the affair, and in the distinguished visitors' gallery another 23 people looked down on the crowded courtroom, or arena.

There were few citizens in Chester—or indeed in Britain—who did not know why Brady, a £12-a-week stock clerk, and Hindley, her hair dyed a startling shade of lilac, were in the reinforced dock. They were accused of murdering three young people—Edward Evans, a 17-year-old homosexual, Lesley Ann Downey, a child of 10, and John Kilbride, aged 12. It was common knowledge that the sexually-assaulted bodies of John and Lesley

had been discovered by the Lancashire police in shallow graves on Saddleworth Moor, near Manchester, and that Evans had been found in a bedroom of Hindley's council house home with his head smashed in by an axe. There appeared to be no rational explanation for the crimes and, in the 14 days that followed, those in the court listened to a twentieth-century horror story as Sir Elwyn Jones, the Attorney-General, submitted that, "In association with all these killings there was present not only a sexual element but an abnormal sexual element, a perverted sexual element."

Hushed courtroom

The main prosecution witness was Hindley's brother-in-law, David Smith, 18, a delinquent with an unenviable police record of violence for his age. Despite his conduct in the past, it was Smith who had informed the police the morning after he had seen Brady beat Edward Evans to death. The murder took place on the evening of October 6, 1965, after Brady had picked up the youth outside the buffet of Manchester Central Station and brought him to 16 Wardle Brook Avenue, Hattersley—the box-like house in which he shared a bedroom with Myra Hindley and living quarters with her grandmother. Wearing tight-fitting blue jeans, and with his dark brown hair falling over his forehead in the manner of the late James Dean, Smith told a hushed court how he had been summoned round to Hindley's house ostensibly to drink some miniature bottles of wine. A minute or so later he heard "a hell of a scream", followed by Hindley shouting "Dave, help him!" Clutching a stick he had brought with him, he ran from the kitchen and into the living room where he saw a scene that made him "freeze".

"My first thoughts were that Ian had hold of a life-sized rag doll and was just

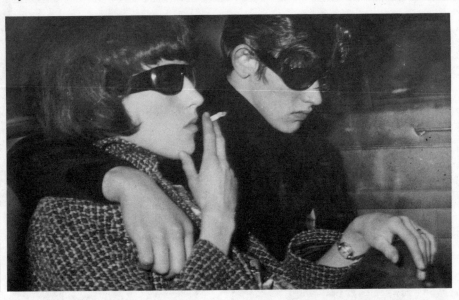

waving it about," he said tightly. "The arms were going all over. Then it dawned on me that it was not a rag doll. It fell against the couch not more than two feet away from me. My stomach turned over. It was half screaming and groaning. The lad was laid out on his front and Ian stood over him with his legs apart with an axe in his right hand. The lad groaned and Ian just lifted the axe over his head and brought it down upon the lad's head. There were a couple of seconds of silence and the lad groaned again, only very much lower. Ian lifted the axe way above his head again and brought it down. The lad stopped groaning then. He was making a gurgling noise like when you brush your teeth and gargle with water. Ian placed a cover over his head. He had a piece of electric wire, and he wrapped it round the lad's neck and began to pull it; and he was saying: 'You f . . . ing dirty bastard', over and over again. The lad just stopped making this noise, and Ian looked up and said to Myra: 'That's it. It is the messiest yet!' "

Supreme pleasure

As Smith left the witness stand—after admitting to Brady's counsel, Mr. Emlyn Hooson, Q.C., M.P. that he had written in a notebook that, "People are like maggots, small, blind, worthless, fish bait. Rape is not a crime. It is a state of mind. Murder is a hobby and a supreme pleasure"—the spectators in the court relaxed. Surely, they told themselves, they had heard the cruellest, the bloodiest, the most chilling details. But, unbelievably enough, there was worse, far worse, to come. Turning to the killing of Lesley Downey—who had disappeared after visiting a fairground at Hattersley on December 26, 1964—the judge had to decide whether or not to allow a tape recording to be played, a recording made by Brady and Hindley in which the terrified youngster pleaded for safety, for her mother, for her life.

Leaning gravely forward, Mr. Justice Atkinson said: "There is a question whether this piece of evidence should be heard in camera or not. There has been so much talk, that in my opinion we have no right to exclude the public. Anyone who wishes not to listen should leave now. During it I request complete silence. The Attorney-General will beforehand read out the transcript, at dictation speed."

It was at this stage, as the transcript

VICTIM: John Kilbride (left), aged 12, was sexually assaulted. His body was found in a shallow grave (arrowed) by police searchers on the moors. Brady denied all knowledge of his death, but the Attorney-General said that Kilbride was "killed by the same hands" as the other Moors victims.

POLICE CHIEF Joe Mounsey discovered the bodies. After arresting Brady and Hindley, police became their protectors against any assassination bid.

was read out and the tape played, that the assassination attempt—if there was to be one—would be made. Police closed in and formed a protective semicircle in front of the dock, their eyes roving from face to face as they scanned those in the press box, the well of the court, and the galleries. As the spool began to revolve—and the words and then the screams were heard—a number of women in the public gallery shuddered and closed their eyes. The all-male jurors (half of whom appeared to be under 30) lowered their heads, a man in the distinguished visitors' gallery put his hand over his face, and a policeman attended to another man who slumped forward in distress.

It was the screams punctuating the tape which turned most people's stomachs—and then there was Lesley's voice, shrill with panic and fear, as she begged, whispered, and sobbed. "Please God, help me!" she cried. " . . . Can I just tell you summat? I must tell you summat. Please take your hands off me a minute, please . . . I can't breathe . . . What are you going to do with me? . . . Don't undress me, will you? . . . It hurts me. I want to see mummy, honest to God . . . I have to get home before eight o'clock . . . Or I'll get killed if I don't. Honest to God . . . It hurts me neck . . ."

In a way the most appalling section of the tape came towards the end when a radio was turned on, bells rang out, and two Christmas-style songs were heard: *Jolly St. Nicholas,* and *The Little Drummer Boy.* Later, opening Brady's defence, Mr. Hooson was to say: "It is terribly, terribly important that you dispose from your minds all the natural revulsion one has in reading or hearing evidence connected with the death of children." But as, after 16 minutes and 21 seconds, the tape whirred to a close there was no one in the court—with the possible exception of the two accused—who did not sit stun-

ned and sickened, and who found it hard not to allow their "feelings to be aroused to the exclusion of dispassionate justice."

The evidence of the recording was more monstrous even than the photographs Brady had taken of Lesley, showing her naked and with a scarf over her mouth, posing obscenely in the shoddily furnished bedroom. It was not until the ninth day of the trial that Brady was escorted by two prison officers from the dock to the witness stand. People craned forward to look at him as, sallow-faced and lanky, he affirmed rather than take the oath on the *Bible*. In appearance he seemed neither better nor worse than any of the young men who lived in Hattersley—a drab estate which acted as an overspill for Manchester. He wore an ordinary grey suit, plain white shirt and had a neatly-folded handkerchief in his breast pocket. He might boast of worshipping Hitler, agree with the French writer the Marquis de Sade that inflicting pain upon others was the ultimate thrill, and believe in the Germanic philosophy of the superman who was "beyond good and evil" But none of this was apparent until the illegitimate son of a Glasgow waitress arrogantly answered questions put to him by Hooson.

Despite an accent that veered between a thick Scottish brogue and a Lancashire drawl, he spoke out firmly and loudly. Yes, he had spent the autumn of 1964 discussing a "perfect payroll robbery" with his disciple David Smith. As he spoke, his cold, pale eyes were as blank and lifeless as stones seen under water, and a ray of animosity seemed to stretch between him and the public. It was a two-way band of hatred and it broadened and intensified when he admitted to offering Lesley Downey ten shillings to pose for him and Hindley in the nude, and to unintentionally killing Evans as part of "a bit of practice".

Insolent contempt

During this stage, and throughout the cross-examination that followed, he showed his wholesale contempt for the trial and all its trappings, and displayed his insolence towards the judge and the Attorney-General (he never addressed them as "My Lord", or "Sir"). In contrast to this, Sir Elwyn Jones spoke to him in polite, restrained tones, as if interviewing a somewhat sullen and disinterested job applicant. "You never intended Evans to leave that room alive?" —"Yes," came the answer. "The right side of his skull was smashed to pieces and some of his brains were on the floor?" Brady nodded. "Yes—in fact Smith made a joke about it. He said, 'He was a brainy swine, wasn't he!'" And— how did he feel when he had heard Lesley Downey's screams filling the courtroom?

The answer was he found it "embarrassing".

Later on Brady demonstrated some of the reasoning power and misplaced "brilliance" which had dominated Smith and made Hindley his eager slave. The exchange came when Elwyn Jones asked him about his library: "This was the diet you were consuming. Pornographic books. books on violence and murder?" – "Not pornographic books. You can buy them at any bookstall . . ." "they are dirty books, Brady" – "It depends on the dirty mind. It depends on your mind . . . Let me give you the names of just two." (Here the judge intervened saying: "*Uses of the Torture Chamber, Sexual Anomalies and Perversions*.") Brady shrugged. "These are written by doctors. They are supposed to be social . . ." "Was your interest in them on a high social plane?" – "No, for erotic reasons . . ." "Of course. This is the atmosphere of your mind. A sink of pornography, was it not?" – "No. There are better collections than that in lords' manors all over the country."

Warped philosophy

Although Brady admitted that he had murdered Evans, he denied any knowledge as to how Lesley Downey had died, and said he knew nothing of the disappearance and death of young John Kilbride. Both the children were found in graves on the moors only 400 yards apart. Lesley had been stripped of her tartan skirt and pink cardigan, and John's trousers and underpants had been rolled down to the thighs, indicating sexual interference. After spending $8\frac{3}{4}$ hours in the box Brady was allowed to return to the dock, to sit next to Hindley – the typist who had worked for the same chemical distributing firm as himself, and who had adored him for a year before he spoke to her, writing in her red-bound diary:

MOTHERS: Mrs. Kilbride (left) and Mrs. Downey. Their children were victims. Friend Linda Clark (inset) was with Lesley Downey the day she vanished.

"Ian looked at me today . . . He smiled at me today . . . The pig . . . he didn't look at me . . . He ignored me today . . . I wonder if he'll ever take me out . . . I almost got a smile out of him today . . . Ian wore a black shirt and looked smashing . . . He is a loud-mouthed pig . . . I love him." Then, shortly before Christmas 1961, she was able to record: "Eureka! Today we have our first date. We are going to the cinema."

The movie Brady took her to see was *Trial at Nuremburg*, which dealt with Nazi war criminals and atrocities, and he chose this as an introduction to his warped and secondhand philosophy of "power over others". They were both children of the slums (she was a war baby, the daughter of a paratrooper), but there their early resemblance ended. Brady had been a boy who enjoyed torturing cats, flashing the flick-knife he habitually carried, and viewing as many horror movies as he could get into. His boyhood nickname in the Glasgow Gorbals had been "Dracula", whereas Hindley had been of slightly above average I.Q. as a schoolgirl, had always had religious tendencies and was later to return to the Roman Catholic church in which she had been raised.

Expressionless voice

Interrupted from her note-taking and the scowls she delivered across the court, she was led to the witness stand, leaving Brady to resume sketching the brutal looking thugs with fierce black eyes and low foreheads – which was his way of killing time during the long and repetitive hours of the trial. By then, the 11th day of the proceedings, Hindley's lilac hair

had undergone a bizarre change. It was now dyed a banana-yellow with tell-tale black zigzags at the roots. It looked as if she was wearing a grotesque raffia wig – a squat figure in a speckled tweed suit, pale blue blouse, a pair of white high-heeled shoes belonging to her mother, and giving every indication as to why she was called "square-arse" by the local youths.

Like Brady, she affirmed instead of taking the oath. With her hooked, parrot nose and thick lips there was nothing outwardly attractive about her, and this impression was heightened when she spoke. Her expressionless voice was low-pitched and hoarse as she answered her counsel, Mr. Godfrey Heilpern, as to her feelings towards Brady. "I loved him," she croaked, "and I still . . . I love him." She then explained that she was suffering from a sore throat, and told how she had passed her driving test in November 1963 – when she was aged 21 – and had driven Brady around the moors and countryside of Lancashire in an Austin Mini Traveller. "All over the place . . . we have been practically all over the place," she said.

Frightened, upset

Although she lacked Brady's surly self-confidence, she maintained her poise until Mr. Heilpern brought up the subject of the tape recording. She frowned and clenched her hands as he said: "You have heard that recording played and you have had a copy of the transcript? – Yes . . . What are your feelings about that?" – "I am ashamed." The lawyer nodded and went on to the night when Lesley Downey had been taken to the house in Wardle Brook Avenue. "What was the child like at the beginning?" he asked. "Willing or reluctant or what?" There was a pause, then Hindley replied that the little girl had been quiet at first, and then frightened and upset when she was taken upstairs.

She added: "As soon as she started crying I started to panic because I was worried. That is why I was so brusque and cruel in my attitude, because I wanted her to be quiet. I didn't expect her to start making such a noise . . . The front door was wide open. The bedroom door was open and the bedroom window was open. I was frightened that anyone would hear. I just wanted her to be quiet and I said, 'Be quiet until we get things sorted out.' The girl sat on the bed. I switched on the radio then because I was hoping she would remain quiet and that the radio would help to alleviate her fears."

After that, claimed Hindley, Lesley left the house with Smith and she and Brady did not see the child again. In answer to Mr. Heilpern she also said she had nothing at all to do with the

VICTIM: Lesley Ann Downey, aged 10 (top). She went to a Christmas fair . . . and vanished. Brady and Hindley taped her screams for mercy before murdering her. Lesley's body was also found in a shallow grave (arrowed) on the moors. At the trial, the horrifying tape was played back to a stunned court, and obscene photographs of Lesley taken by Brady and Hindley were shown. "Dispose from your minds all natural revulsion," said the defence Queen's Counsel.

killing and burying of John Kilbride, and it was not until she was cross-examined by the Attorney-General that her role in the two other murders became more apparent. Hardening his voice, Sir Elwyn asked her how she had reacted to the scream made by Edward Evans as he was attacked by Brady: "You could not stand the scream?" "The noise was so loud I put my hands over my ears." "This Court has heard of another scream, more than one, in a room where you were?" "Yes." "The screams of a little child of ten, of your sex, madam?" "Yes." "Did you put your hands over your ears when you heard the screams of Lesley Ann Downey?" "No." "Why not?" "I wanted her to be quiet." "Or get the child out and see that she was treated as a woman should treat a female child, or any child?" "I should have done and I didn't. I have no defence for that. No defence. It was indefensible. I was cruel." "Cruel and pitiless?" "I was cruel." "And pitiless?" "I was cruel."

Depraved killers

Finally, after 5 hours and 46 minutes, she came to the end of her evidence and rejoined Brady—who pointedly looked away from her—in the dock. The trial of

A MOTHER'S FAREWELL to a child whose last cries for help had been in vain. "I was cruel," Myra Hindley told the court. "I am ashamed."

the century was now in its closing stages and in winding-up his final address the Attorney-General said dramatically: "My submission is that the same hands killed all three of these victims, Evans, Downey, and Kilbride—and these are the hands of the two accused in the dock." The two defence counsel followed by asserting that—although Brady was patently guilty of murdering Evans—there was no evidence to show that he, or Hindley, had been responsible for the deaths of the other two victims. And, although nothing had been openly stated, there was a feeling in the court that the accused were not normal, not balanced, not sane. Aware of this, Mr. Justice Atkinson warned the jury: "I suppose that hearing and reading about these allegations, the first reaction of kindly, charitable people is to say this is so terrible that anyone doing anything like that might be mentally afflicted. You must put that aside at once . . . It is a presumption of our law that anyone who comes into the dock is sane. There has not been the smallest suggestion that either of these two are mentally abnormal or not fully and completely responsible for their actions. If, and I underline it, the prosecution is right, you are dealing with two sadistic killers of the utmost depravity . . ."

The jurors listened attentively to the careful summing-up. Then, at 2.40 p.m. on Friday, May 6, they retired to consider their verdict. They were out until five o'clock, when they returned and pronounced Brady guilty of all three murders, and Hindley guilty of the murders of Edward Evans and Lesley Ann Downey; she was found not guilty of the murder of John Kilbride, but guilty of harbouring Brady knowing that he had committed the crime.

Equally horrible

Once the judge heard that, the trial came to an abrupt, almost anticlimactic end. "Ian Brady," he said coldly, "these were three calculated, cruel, cold-blooded murders. I pass the only sentence which the law now allows, which is three concurrent sentences of life imprisonment." Brady did not flinch and the judge said dismissively to the prison officer in the dock, "Put him down." Hindley now stood alone as Brady left her without a glance. She nervously thrust another mint into her mouth and chewed on it as the judge said: "In your case, Hindley, you have been found guilty of two equally horrible murders and in the third as an accessory after the fact. On the two murders the sentence is two concurrent sentences of life imprisonment. On the accessory charge a concurrent sentence of seven years' imprisonment."

She passed to prison, where, eight years later, a woman prison officer formed so close a relationship with her that she assisted her in a bungled attempt at escape.

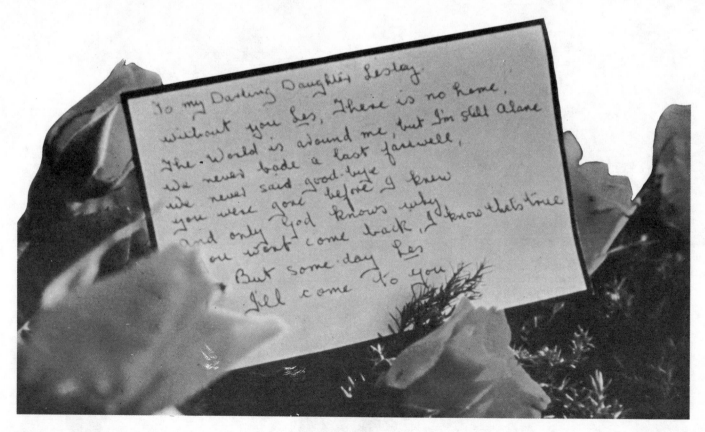

THE SHARON TATE MURDER

The Manson Family

Beautiful actress and film star Sharon Tate and six others had been savagely murdered during two nights of terror in Hollywood in the summer of 1969. Now three young girls and a 35-year-old man were on trial. But Manson and his "harem" behaved as if they were on a Sunday picnic!

PHOTO 5780

PHOTO 5755

PHOTO 5758

VAN HOUTEN, Leslie
AKA:

FLYNN, Susan Denise
AKA: GLUTZ, Sadie Mae

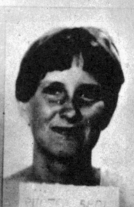
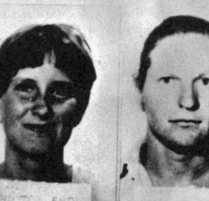

PHOTO 5807

PHOTO 5806

PHOTO 5801

HARMON, David Brian

JONES, Larry
AKA:

GRAVES, Larry Eugene
AKA: "Little Larry" Jones

WHEN Charles Manson entered the Los Angeles courtroom for the first time his presence seemed to evoke, among the waiting newsmen and spectators, a strange mixture of misgiving and complete revulsion. Charged, along with three female members of his "family", with the savage murder of Hollywood actress Sharon Tate and six others in August 1969, it was the revulsion which held sway in people's minds. But the disquiet was there too, as the memory of Manson's weird outbursts to the press invaded the courtroom. "I'm at the other end of your society," he had asserted.

Now, as the audience stared at this curious figure of horror and tragedy their fascination was not untinged with fear. When he turned to face them, a gasp of shocked astonishment went round the court. For 35-year-old Manson, pale but composed in blue prison denim, his dark hair flowing like a prophet's round his intense, wiry face, had branded in blood on his forehead the symbol of the outcast: an X, put there because "I have X-ed myself from your world".

Even before the 9½-month trial began Manson provided reporters with plenty of headline copy. He clearly intended to be the star of the proceedings, and made an early attempt to be allowed to conduct his own defence so that no "interfering" lawyer could come between him and his "public". Judge Charles Older, however, decided otherwise. Manson, it was argued, was incapable of safeguarding his own procedural rights and must, therefore, be represented by a defence team.

With stubborn perversity the defendant then proceeded to interview more than 60 hopeful attorneys before settling on three. It would be difficult to imagine a group of lawyers less likely to work well together than this strange, ill-matched trio.

First, there was Ronald Hughes, 35, a onetime conservative turned hippie who had flunked the bar exam three times be-

MURDER SCENE . . . Police (top right) watch over the house where the murder of Sharon Tate and friends took place. Two of the victims were Polish writer and director Frykowski (top left) and his girlfriend Abigail Folger (above). Panel (opposite) shows Manson with his family.

fore passing and had never taken a case in his life. In his favour was that he had met Manson previously—and, at the latter's insistence, he agreed to appear in court wearing a beard.

Hughes did not see the end of the trial through. He disappeared suddenly while on a short camping trip in north California and was later found drowned. The trial had to be adjourned for 2 weeks while a replacement—Maxwell Keith—familiarized himself with the case.

Then there was Irving Kanarek, 52, whom Manson brought in. Kanarek was a well known attorney in Los Angeles and he hoped that his legal skills would be able to reduce Manson's infamy in the eyes of the court and the general public. Not many people shared his optimism and even Manson himself must have had many doubts

and uncertainties about the outcome of the case.

The third member of Manson's team was Daye Shinn, 53, a former used-car salesman, who sometimes earned his living by arranging immigration papers for wealthy clients seeking to employ foreign maids.

To Manson's fury, the public defender's office assigned a fourth defence lawyer to the case—in a necessary effort to ensure a modicum of sanity and competence in dealing with the complexities of what was obviously going to be a gruelling and lengthy legal ordeal. This was the young but highly skilled Paul Fitzgerald who, at 33, was soon to reveal how much better than his older colleagues he had mastered the art and science of courtroom crossfire.

Fitzgerald soon became the unofficial defence leader. But he often found himself aligned not only against the prosecution case—admirably led by Vincent Bugliosi—but also against Hughes, Kanarek, and Shinn—whose courtroom techniques frequently undercut his own efforts. Kanarek, in particular, sometimes seemed actually to assist incompetent prosecution witnesses, leaving them more confident and impressive than when they started.

"It's like living in a concentration camp," Fitzgerald remarked. Even Prosecutor Bugliosi was dismayed by some of the defence "tactics". "This isn't a trial," he blurted at one point, "this is a laugh-in comedy!"

There was nothing amusing, however, about the prosecutor's opening remarks on the first day of the trial, in which he referred to the full horror of the Tate murders. The quiet tone in which he outlined the case against Manson—and the three young members of his harem accused with him—belied the savage story

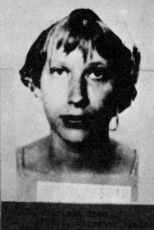

COTTAGE, Madaline
AKA: BALDWIN, Linda Lou
"Little Patty"

DRUM, Kenneth Richard
AKA: "Grebs"

BARTELL, Susan Phyllis

PHILLIPS, Thomas Anthony

LUKASHEVSKY, Bryn Lesue
AKA: LUKAS

DAMION, Mark Bloodworth

BAILEY, Ella Jo
AKA: SINDER, Ella Bell

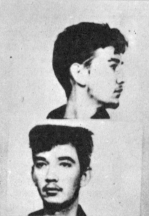
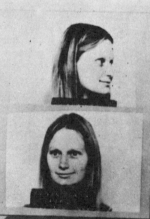

BLUESTEIN, Johnny
AKA: HALL, Bruce Vern.

ALDEN, Thomas
AKA: "T.J."

DE CARLO, Daniel
AKA: SMITH, Richard Allan
Danny

SPRINGER, Alan LeRoy

TRUE, HAROLD E.

of hatred and blood lust to which the jury of seven men and five women listened in awestruck silence.

Patiently and with commendable clarity, Bugliosi explained that two of the girls on trial—Susan Atkins, 22, and Patricia Krenwinkel, also 22—had been involved both in the murder of Sharon Tate and house guests on the night of August 9, 1969, and in the murder of Mr. and Mrs. Leno LaBianca in Los Angeles on the following night. The third girl, Leslie Van Houten, 20, was on trial only for the LaBianca murders.

Violent death

Two others, said Bugliosi, were involved. One of these, Charles Watson, was in a Texas jail fighting extradition and would be tried later. The second, 21-year-old Mrs. Linda Kasabian, was the only defector from the Manson "family" and would, later, give a detailed account of the events on the two murder nights.

First, however, Bugliosi wanted to implant in the minds of the jury his own version of what happened to the victims. He began with a brief account of what he called "Manson's mind". He told of the defendant's passion for violent death and his bitter hatred for the "establishment". Son of a prostitute, Manson seemed destined for some kind of career in crime. As a young boy, he was frequently in court for juvenile delinquencies and later he graduated first to car theft and then to pimping—which culminated in a ten-year jail sentence.

Armed, continued the prosecutor, with a grudge against society and a fanatical interest and belief in hypnotism and the occult, Manson began to see himself as a kind of messiah. A messiah who, just as in the Bible, was the creator of a new

way of life. The poor and the dispossessed —particularly if they were young girls— were offered a place where they could feel accepted.

But, Bugliosi added, Manson's messianic ravings were not about love but about hate, violence, lust, sexual depravity, and ritual murder.

Bugliosi talked briefly about the Manson "family" and the quasi-hypnotic effect which he exercised over its members so that they would, apparently, obey his every wish with unquestioning devotion. Then he mentioned one of the most absurd—and for that reason frightening —of the influences which had motivated Manson's behaviour: his devotion to the Beatles, who spoke to him "across the ocean". One song in particular, called *Helter Skelter,* whose lyrics seemed unexceptional to the normal ear, had been given a weird interpretation by the defendant.

According to him, Bugliosi asserted, the words signified a black uprising against the whites. Manson would escape from it by leading his followers into the California desert—where they did have a hideout—and then recreate a paradise of sex and drugs. First, however, the family would precipitate helter-skelter by fostering the idea that it had already arrived. That is why they scrawled the words PIG and WAR in blood on the walls of their victims' homes.

The murders themselves, the jury were

HOME ON THE RANGE . . . The Manson family home was an abandoned cabin once used as a movie set. Described at his trial as a "human vegetable", Charles Watson (right) was chosen to lead the band sent to attack Tate household. There were many helpers (opposite) to choose from.

told, had not been directly conducted by Manson. Like some demoniac general he had sent out his troops to kill the pigs, the "enemies". To a tense courtroom Bugliosi spelt out the murderous happenings. He told of the approach to Sharon Tate's rented house in Hollywood and how Charles Watson, armed with a .22 calibre rifle, had led Susan Atkins and Patricia Krenwinkel into the house, leaving prosecution witness Linda Kasabian on watch outside.

In the temporary absence of her husband, film director Roman *Rosemary's Baby* Polanski, eight-months pregnant Miss Tate had invited round former boyfriend Jay Sebring, writer Voityck Frykowski and his lover, coffee heiress Abigail Folger. It was, said Bugliosi, a quiet, intimate evening of drinks and talk. The arrival of the Manson family signified not merely an end to the get-together, but an end to their lives. One by one the guests were brutally hacked to death.

Frykowski alone was shot twice, hit at least 13 times on the head with a blunt instrument, and stabbed no less than

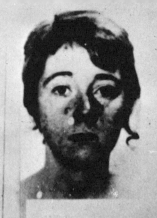

AKA: Irene

IARR, Diane Elizabeth
AKA: BLUESTEIN, Diane E.
"Snake"

PROSER, Lynette Aline
AKA: WASHINGTON, Elisabeth E.
"Squeeky"

MINETTE, Manon
AKA: WRIGHT, Kathleen May
"Gypsy"

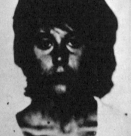

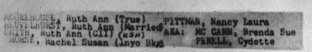
MOORLHOUSE, Ruth Ann (True)
HEUVELHURST, Ruth Ann (Married)
SMITH, Ruth Ann (G11) (WSN)
MORSE, Rachel Susan (Inyo Bkg)

PITTMAN, Nancy Laura
AKA: MC CANN, Brenda Sue
PERELL, Cydette

PUGH, Sandra Collins
AKA: GOOD, Sandra Collins
"Squeeky"

MYERS, Catherine Rene
AKA: GILLIS, Catherine Irene

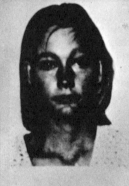

HEUVELHURST, Ruth Ann
(I.D. Unknown - above name is
married name of MOORLHOUSE)

ANDREWS, Sherri
AKA: "Colleen"

SMITH, Barbara

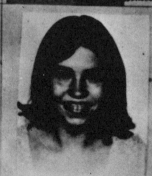

SWARTZ, John Harold
AKA: SCHWARTZ, John

NIKALAS, Colleen Ann
AKA: SHEPPARD, Collie
Lynn, Nancy

SCHARM, Mary Ann
AKA: VON AUN, Diane Marie

SHEPPARD, Laura
AKA: NOGANTP, Julie

CHAINED and manacled, Manson is led away to San Quentin's death row. He had had no trouble persuading unhappy youngsters to join him. Susan Atkins, Linda Kasabian and Leslie Van Houten (right) were just three of them. Others are shown in police photographs opposite.

Los Angeles Times

51 times. Sharon Tate, the jury heard, heavy with her unborn child, was left until last. Then, to the "music" of her pleas— as one of the murderers later described it—her frantic pleas to save the child, she too was stabbed repeatedly in her neck, breast, back—and womb.

The murder of Mr. and Mrs. LaBianca on August 10, in which Leslie Van Houten also took part, was of similar brutal savagery, said the prosecutor. Only Linda Kasabian, he stated, had balked. She, as a relative newcomer to the Manson family, was the only one who was unaware of the purpose of the August 9 mission—and only fear had led her to accompany the murderers on the second night's outing.

For Prosecutor Bugliosi, this was the crucial point of his case. Only if he could establish that Mrs. Kasabian—who was originally indicted but later promised immunity in return for her testimony— was not legally an accomplice to the murders, could this key witness be considered reliable and trustworthy. Otherwise his case would be seriously weakened. For it would undoubtedly be argued by the defence that Kasabian was merely trying to save her own skin and was as guilty as the rest.

Girlish figure

Thus her story would be seen as presenting tailored evidence designed merely to convince the jury of her own innocence. Ultimately Judge Older would decide the issue. Much depended on the young mother's performance in court, and it was a tense moment when, in July 1970, she stepped for the first time into the witness box.

She was a girlish figure in her simple blue and white dress and blonde pigtails. It was difficult to believe that someone who looked so unremarkable could have been involved at all in crimes whose bloodiness and cruelty had horrified the world. As Bugliosi approached her, she glanced nervously round the packed courtroom. For a moment her eyes rested on the three accused girls, each of whose foreheads now bore the X mark of the outcast. They grinned at her with a kind of unconcerned maliciousness. Then she turned to Manson, her lips set firm in determination as if trying to prove to herself that he no longer had control over her actions.

For seconds she held his fierce stare and only turned away when, in an obvious

attempt to frighten her, Manson drew a thin forefinger across his throat. But Linda Kasabian did not falter, and her composure drew a quick smile of relief from Bugliosi. He knew from that moment that she would adhere to her evidence.

Under the prosecutor's questioning, Kasabian told how she had first joined the Manson clan shortly before the murders. "I felt like I was a blind little girl in a forest. I took the first path," she said. It was not a surprising statement from a girl who had run away from a broken home as a young teenager and by the age of 20 had had two husbands, two children, and lived in at least 11 drug-orientated communes. To her, Manson was the bountiful giver of life and happiness; she loved him and believed "he was the Messiah come again".

Then, as she began to reveal details of the Tate murders—which had been inspired by Manson's jealousy of the rich and famous—the courtroom grew silent. Audience and jury strained forward to hear every word of her narrative, and held their breath at peak moments as if

in the presence of a great dramatic performance. She related how, left on guard outside the Tate home, she suddenly became aware of what was happening inside: "Then all of a sudden I heard people screaming saying 'No, please, no!' "

"What kind of screams?" snapped Bugliosi.

"Loud, loud."

"How long did they last?"

"Oh, it seemed like forever, infinite. I don't know."

She went on to describe how the dying Frykowski had crawled out of the house towards her: "He had blood all over his face . . . and we looked into each other's eyes for a minute—I don't know however long—and I said, 'Oh, God, I am so sorry. Please make it stop.' And then he just fell to the ground into the bushes."

Upraised knife

Entering the house, the witness continued, she saw Watson beating one of the victims on the head. "And then I saw Katie—Patricia Krenwinkel—in the background with the girl, chasing after her with an upraised knife . . ." Watson, she said, was screaming: "I'm the Devil. I'm here to do the Devil's work!"

By the time Linda Kasabian had finished her testimony several members of the audience were in tears, and the jury looked suddenly fatigued and pale. Even Judge Older was visibly moved, and Bugliosi, whose probing, intelligent questions— continuously interrupted by literally hundreds of objections from the defence —had provided a framework for her story, was trembling with emotion and fury.

Mrs. Kasabian herself stood up well to the harrowing ordeal, though at the end of her testimony she, too, was clearly exhausted. The pressure on her had been enormous. For, apart from the

131

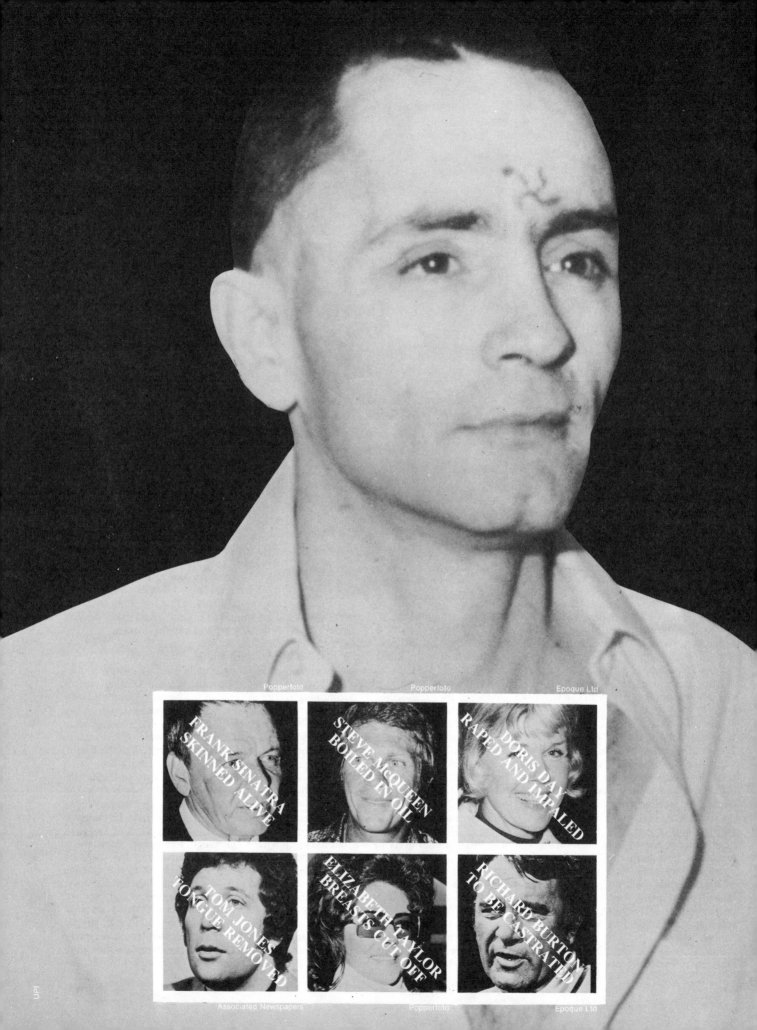

FRANK SINATRA
SKINNED ALIVE

STEVE McQUEEN
BOILED IN OIL

DORIS DAY
RAPED AND IMPALED

TOM JONES
TONGUE REMOVED

ELIZABETH TAYLOR
BREASTS CUT OFF

RICHARD BURTON
TO BE CASTRATED

extraordinary obstructionist antics of the defence, she also had to face continuous pressure from the four accused. Once, Susan Atkins fixed her eyes upon Linda's. "You are killing us," she breathed. "I am not killing you," came the reply. "You are killing yourselves."

Undaunted, Mrs. Kasabian continued, for ten days, to pour out her narrative and face the barrage of often absurd questions flung at her by the defence.

The latter's tactics were simple. Their whole method lay in attempting, by any means possible, to discredit Mrs. Kasabian as a reliable witness. Kanarek, in particular, was persistently belligerent. He made the witness go through her story detail by detail in a vain effort to secure an admission from her that she was involved in the killings—thus rendering her whole testimony suspect. When this failed he tried a new tack.

"Have you ever taken hallucinogenic drugs?"

"Yes."

"LSD, for example?"

"Yes."

How many trips had she made on LSD?

"Oh, about 50, I guess."

At the time this looked like a rewarding line of questioning, and Kanarek followed it up by delving into her sexual life with the Manson family. Mrs. Kasabian admitted that drug-induced orgies were frequent—and pleasurable. What happened during an orgy? Kanarek wanted to know.

"Everybody made love to everybody else. We all shed our clothes and we were lying on the floor, and it was like it didn't make any difference who was next to you."

Did she know who was the father of her second child—the one conceived during her time with the Manson family?

"No," she replied, "I couldn't be sure."

It was more sensational material for newsmen, and exciting entertainment for the spectators—many of whom had come, no doubt, in anticipation of hearing just such confessions as these. But, in the end, Kanarek's probings and innuendos were in vain. Judge Older stuck to his ruling that Linda Kasabian's testimony was in order and acceptable as evidence.

Even so, Bugliosi had never intended to rely entirely on Mrs. Kasabian. He then

CHARLIE'S HATE LIST. It was rumoured that Manson kept a secret list of future targets with graphic details of how he was going to "deal" with them. He is seen here, clean shaven and with hair cropped close, but with his forehead marked with the X of an outcast from society, as he appeared at his trial. Most of the hatred seemed to be directed at the rich and famous (left) for whom Charlie invented a wide range of crude tortures.

called a further 84 witnesses, and presented some 300 exhibits, in his effort to prove that Manson—in spite of the fact that he was not personally present at the killings—was "as guilty as sin"; and he took four months to present the prosecution case. At the end of this marathon there came another unusual twist.

The four beleaguered and bickering defence lawyers finally managed to reach some kind of uniform agreement between themselves. Before a stunned court they promptly announced that the defence rested. In short, there would be no defence at all. The reasons for this curious procedure—or lack of it—were not, on examination, difficult to understand.

Manson had devised a curious and almost satanic means to escape the law. He had persuaded—the word seems totally inadequate—the three girls to take the stand, "confess" that they were responsible for the murders, and declare their "master" innocent. Manson would then confirm their story and would subsequently proceed to tell the world about his divine "mission".

Life story

Appalled, the lawyers refused to let them do it. When the girls insisted—backed by the judge, who ruled that they had a right to testify—the legal team declined to ask any questions. The girls countered by demanding to tell their stories verbatim, whereupon the jury was removed so that they could later be presented with a written version with the inadmissible portions edited out. Then the girls objected once more, and refused to testify unless the jury was present. It looked like stalemate—and a difficult decision for the judge.

Unbelievably, the situation was rescued by Manson himself. He suddenly sprang up, asked to take the stand, and talked for fully 90 minutes about his origins, his "family", and his beliefs. It was, possibly, the most remarkable testimony ever heard in a United States court. And though it did nothing to allay the horror of his actions, it did much to explain them. Occasionally in tears, but more often restrained and seemingly sincere, Manson began with the story of his life, and ran it through to the "end".

"I have stayed in jail," he stated, "and I have stayed stupid and I have stayed a child while I have watched your world grow up. And then I look at the things you do and I don't understand. Most of the people you call the family were just people that you did not want, people that were alongside the road; I took them up on my garbage dump and I told them this: that in love there is no wrong.

"I have done my best to get along in your world, and now you want to kill me. I say to myself, 'Ha, I'm already dead,

have been all my life . . .' What you want is a fiend. You want a sadistic fiend because that is what you are. You only reflect on me what you are inside of yourselves, because I don't care anything about any of you. If I could I would jerk this microphone off and beat your brains out with it, because that is what you deserve. You kill things better than you.

"I don't care what you do with me. I have always been in your cell. When you were out riding your bicycle, I was sitting in your cell looking out the window and looking at pictures in magazines and wishing I could go to high school and go to the prom. My peace is in the desert or in the jail cell, and had I not seen the sunshine in the desert, I would be satisfied with the jail cell much more over your society."

There was an almost tangible silence as everyone hung on Manson's words. For the next few seconds the weird, merciless killer held the whole court under his fanatical spell. Then as nothing more came from him, Bugliosi stepped into the gap determined to normalize the strained atmosphere with a blast of ridicule:

"You say you're already dead, don't you, Charlie?"

"As anyone will tell you," Manson retorted, "you are dead when you are no more."

"You think you've been dead for close on 2000 years, don't you?"

This was an allusion to Manson's expressed belief that he was Christ incarnate, and the defence promptly objected. Judge Older sustained the objection, but Bugliosi pressed on.

"Just who are your children, Charlie?" he demanded.

"Anyone who will love me," Manson replied quietly, and then stared fixedly at the judge for several seconds.

Finally he stepped down, shuffled over to the accused girls and whispered: "Don't testify."

They didn't. And neither did Manson when offered the chance to repeat his story before the jury. "I've relieved all my pressure," he told the judge.

In his summation, Bugliosi called Manson "one of the most evil, satanic men who ever walked the face of the earth". The jury agreed, and all four defendants were found guilty and later sentenced to death—which, in the legal situation of the time, meant they would be kept alive and waiting in Death Row.

As a murderous family unit they were no more. Whether they were eventually executed or not, the essential thing was that they were kept apart from each other. And that Manson—so named, he said, because he was the "son of man" —was no longer the all-powerful, all-vengeful patriarch.

MURDER WITH A HATCHET

Lizzie Borden

Lizzie Borden was not a violent woman and, even though she hated her stepmother, she adored her father. Yet who else had the opportunity to murder them both . . . ?

LEGEND and folklore are the marginal notes of a good historical story, but the consummate enemies of historical truth. Lizzie Borden would testify to that. The actual charge against her was that she gave her stepmother—not her mother—20 blows with a sharp instrument, and her father 10. And, since she was acquitted, she even stands unjustly accused in the popular doggerel quoted below.

For all that, Lizzie deserves her place in folk-song. Her life-style, her mute, brooding family and the tight little community of Fall River, Massachusetts— in which she lived—were like the perfect setting for a play by Eugene O'Neill or Tennessee Williams.

At 32, she did not rank among the beauties of Fall River. Her large, pale eyes protruded from a sallow complexion framed by curly red hair. She had few friends, although those few thought highly of her. Perhaps that was because Lizzie did not choose them for their social positions, for she was no snob, although she liked money. Unlike her father, she was generous and charitable, and her supporters were quick to point out all the good works with which she was associated as a Congregationalist.

Among the 50,000 New Englanders who lived in Fall River, the family of Borden was as celebrated as were the Medicis in Florence. No street was without its Borden. Andrew Borden, Lizzie's 70-year-old father, was among the most prosperous of the line; he had started his career as the town's undertaker, next turned property speculator, then invested his quick profits in the textile industry—whose mills provided Fall River folk with most of their work. By the time Lizzie was in her teens, Andrew Borden was worth half a million dollars,

Lizzie Borden took an axe
  And gave her mother forty whacks.
When she saw what she had done,
  She gave her father forty-one.

and was soon to be worth a lot more.

His meanness with money was a local legend. He took his own hens' eggs in a basket to market, and lived in a shabby, three-bedroom house at No. 92 Second Street that had hardly changed since the days of the Civil War. Curiously, he had two weaknesses that invariably caused his purse strings to open; they were his two daughters Emma, the elder, and Lizzie.

The reason for this was Andrew Borden's desperate anxiety to buy peace within his family. Lizzie had given him many troubled moments—particularly when she had her "funny spells", which caused her to act totally unpredictably.

One of her turns

Once, during one of these turns, she had reported to her father upon his return from an outing that the bedroom of her stepmother Abby had been entered by a thief, who had ransacked the room and stolen a watch and trinkets. Mr. Borden called the police at once, and then dismissed them half-way through their investigations. His knowledge of the geography of the house, and the circumstances of the theft, had rightly convinced him that the burglary could only have been committed by Lizzie.

Then there was Lizzie's relationship with her stepmother. Whenever the two women were in the house, which was frequently, for Abby Borden rarely went out, the atmosphere was electric. It was obvious to all who knew them that Lizzie hated her stepmother, whom she called "Mrs. Borden". She never ate at table when Abby Borden was present, and spoke to her stepmother only when it was absolutely necessary to do so.

The breach between them had begun over a trifling incident—a decision by Andrew Borden to buy the house his wife's sister lived in and to put it in the name of his wife. It was an act which saved his sister-in-law from possible eviction. But in it Lizzie Borden saw a move on her stepmother's part to usurp her father's fortune.

In a small town like Fall River—where the affluent Bordens could afford to spend long, lacklustre summer days brooding in boredom over supposed injustices—the episode of the house was enlarged beyond all reason. And because the eye of envy distorts most vision, Lizzie Borden never forgave her stepmother for it.

Poor Abby Borden scarcely merited such fierce attention. She was a pathetic figure covered in rolls of fat, and had difficulty in moving her colossal boneless flesh around even her own house. Without friends, without ambition, and without avarice, Abby Borden was one of life's non-starters . . . only her husband had seen warmth and sympathy in her, and had married her because of it.

The year of 1892 provided a rare 12 months of total summer; a period when New England sweated and suffocated. As the hot sharp sun cut the symmetrical streets, and made stiff shadows from the whitewood houses, several strange happenings disturbed the tedious routine of the Bordens' lives in Fall River.

Twice intruders broke into the outbuilding at the bottom of the Borden garden, where Lizzie, an animal fanatic, kept her pigeons. "They're after those birds," Andrew Borden said shortly. His remedy against the intruders was effectively simple: as if by some clairvoyant symbolism, he took an axe and decapitated the pigeons.

Small doses

Lizzie Borden's reaction to this extraordinary act was never recorded. Perhaps she said nothing, brooding on it beside the window in her bedroom. Perhaps she made a scene. Perhaps she simply stored up all the emotion it generated for the day of its total release, three months later, on the hottest day of the year and the most momentous one ever in the town's history.

It was then, as summer scorched on, the local drugstore owners began to notice that Lizzie was asking regularly for small doses of prussic acid; a lethal poison. In fact, they noticed it so acutely that Lizzie was obliged to cut down on her drugstore shopping trips, and to make her inquiries more discreetly.

As none of the drugstores would sell the poison without a prescription, Lizzie's attempts to buy it cannot be related to the stomach sickness which afflicted the entire Borden household at the end of July in that year. But oddly, Abby Borden was convinced that she *had* been poisoned after a long bout of vomiting. She made one of her rare outings—to the doctor's house across the road—and was afterwards soundly reproached by her husband for her "nonsensical" behaviour.

Andrew's view of it was supported by the doctor, who pointed out that the whole family seemed to be retching,

136

including Bridget the maid. As July gave way to August the summer's events had already established the Borden attitudes: there was hate in Lizzie's heart, fear in Abby's, and a feeling of growing irritation in Andrew's.

August 4 was the hottest day of all that hot summer; at first light Fall River already simmered. It was also the last day that Andrew and Abby Borden were to spend alive on earth.

Borden malady

Fortunately for her, sister Emma was out of town. Uncle John Morse, a guest in the house for the past few days, was up early. The Irish maid, Bridget Sullivan, followed him down and as she busied herself with her early morning chores she had to stop to be sick — the Borden malady still lay heavily upon her.

By 7.30 a.m. Abby and Andrew had dressed and were sitting at breakfast with

THE BLOODSTAINED bodies of Andrew Borden (below) and his wife Abby Borden (below left) were photographed by police. Left: the family house at Fall River.

Uncle John. Just over an hour later Uncle John left to go into town. Lizzie then came downstairs for a light breakfast, and Bridget went outside to clean the windows while Abby got on with the dusting and housework.

At about 9 am a young man walked up to the Bordens' front door, rang the bell, and delivered a message. The message, it was later assumed, was addressed to Abby, and indicated that she should leave the house to visit a sick friend. Either shortly before or shortly after this event, Andrew Borden set off for downtown. He waited outside the bank and then made up his mind to return home — where he arrived about 10.30.

While he was away, the arrival of another young man had been noticed by the neighbours. He was said to have hung about outside the Bordens' house, sometimes looking agitated. Then he disappeared, and was never identified.

Inside No. 92 Second Street horrific things had begun to happen. Someone crept up behind Abby Borden while she was dusting the guests' bedroom and, with a mighty, crushing blow, brought a

hatchet down upon her head — a blow that killed her instantly. Abby's barrel-like body collapsed on the bed, where more blows were rained upon it. When the murderer had finished this frenzied work, the room was awash with Abby's blood.

No noise had occurred to bring anyone running, and, if Lizzie, who was alone in the house, is to be believed, no one knew of the bloodsoaked corpse in the bedroom. Then, at half-past ten, the key turned in the front door lock and Andrew, hot and tired by his walk back from downtown, entered the house.

Stark horror

Again, Lizzie is the authority for what happened next. She helped her father settle himself for a rest on the sofa in the sitting room and then went outside to the outbuilding. She was away for 20 minutes; when she returned a scene of stark horror confronted her.

On the sofa lay the crumpled body of her father. Half his head had been cleaved away by blows from an axe and his blood, still piping from the hideous wounds, covered the floor and walls.

During the next few hours Lizzie was to summon up some remarkable resources of self-control, which could not fail to be missed when the day's events were later recounted in a hushed courtroom. She went first to a neighbour, who quoted her as saying, "Oh, Mrs. Churchill, do come. Someone has killed Father!"

Lizzie stated then that her mother had received a note asking her to go out and visit a sick person—she said, therefore, that she did not know where Mrs. Borden was. Even when the police and a doctor arrived, the corpse of Abby still lay unrevealed in the bedroom. It was found only after Lizzie had suddenly "remembered that she thought she had heard Abby come back from town", and an inquisitive neighbour went to look . . .

Double murder

Even with the hottest day of the year to constrain their movements, the people of Fall River flocked in droves down Second Street to the scene of the town's first ever double murder. While they gaped from a reverent distance at the hard wooden rectangle of the Bordens' front door, a man came up the street.

It was Uncle John, whose behaviour, like Lizzie's, was now remarkable. Instead of hurrying forward at the sight of the crowd surrounding his brother-in-law's front garden, he slackened to a loitering pace. When at last he reached the house he went first into the back garden, picked some fruit from a tree and munched it. With all the visible evidence of a disaster about him, Uncle John was in no hurry.

Once inside the house, however, his story gushed out like jackpot coins from a one-armed bandit. Uncle John remembered everything he had seen and done that morning. No detail, however insignificant, had escaped his suddenly prodigious memory. So perfect was his alibi that he became a leading suspect.

The swelling crowd around No. 92 Second Street, which had brought the town's traffic and work at the local mills to a standstill, had no doubts about Uncle John. When he ventured out a few nights later a thousand outraged citizens chased him back inside. After that, the police advised the family to stay indoors until they had decided whom to arrest.

Their deliberations were long and earnest before they plumped for Lizzie. For five days District Attorney Hosea Knowlton had resisted police requests for Lizzie's apprehension. "You don't have any evidence against her," he told the senior police officers. When he finally gave in the situation wasn't much better —it simply seemed more than ever evident that Lizzie was the only one who could have done the "bloody deed".

If the murders had been committed by someone outside the household, they reasoned, the murderer had relied upon an extraordinary set of coincidences to enable him to enter the house and get away twice. There was the unplanned absence of sister Emma; Uncle John's excursion into town; Bridget's morning spent washing the outside windows, and Lizzie's disappearance to the outbuilding long enough for murder to be done twice.

And where was this bloodstained axeman, if he existed? There was a large reward out for information leading to the arrest of a man who had presumably vanished into the shopping crowds of the closed Fall River community while stained red with blood from head to foot. No one came forward with even a hint of his existence.

Of the three connected with the household, Uncle John had an alibi which checked out, and Bridget had been seen by so many people while cleaning the windows that her every movement was accounted for. Lizzie had no corroboration as to how she had spent that morning.

"Why had she gone to the outbuilding?" she was asked. "To look for a piece of metal with which to mend a window screen", she replied; also to get some lead suitable for fishing weights (Lizzie was a keen angler). But detectives searching No. 92 found no broken screens, and no lead that could be used for fishing.

Where exactly did she go in the outbuilding? "Into its loft," she replied. But a policeman searching the loft afterwards thought it unlikely that the dust on the floor had been disturbed.

How long was she in the loft? "About 20 minutes," even though it must have been stifling hot. And, although she had a queasy stomach from the Borden sickness, she remembered eating three pears while she was there.

No fingerprinting

There was still plenty in Lizzie's favour to disquiet the District Attorney. In Fall River, although Lizzie had made no secret of her hate for her stepmother, her deep love for her father was well known. Of all the people who lived in that town, Lizzie Borden would have been the last to be suspected of parricide.

Then there was the murder weapon. A newly-broken axe handle had been found in the house, and, on a high shelf, its blade—rubbed with wood ash which bore no resemblance to the dust in the box in which it lay—suggested that there was no need to look further. But fingerprinting wasn't allowed in Fall River in the 1890s, so that the only thing which could connect Lizzie with the axe was that they both happened to be in the house.

Most puzzling of all was the absence of any bloodstained garment. If Lizzie killed her parents, she would have been soaked

"Why had she gone to the outbuilding?" she was asked. "To look for a piece of metal with which to mend a window screen," she replied; also to get some lead suitable for fishing weights . . .

in their blood, not once, but twice, at an interval of 90 minutes. Yet when the house was searched, all Lizzie's clothes were seen to be clean and spotless.

Later, when a friend of the Bordens, Miss Alice Russell, had moved into No. 92 Second Street to keep Lizzie and Emma company, it was announced that there would be another search, for the police were now convinced Lizzie was hiding something from them.

Was she, in fact? At Lizzie's trial nine months later, Alice Russell and Emma told an extraordinary story. They revealed how, before the second search was held, Lizzie began to tear up an old dress and burn it in the kitchen stove—"Because it was all faded and paint-stained".

But, Alice Russell testified later, she saw no paint on that condemned dress. Possibly with a deeper reason in mind for its destruction, she had declared, "I wouldn't let anybody see me do that, Lizzie, if I were you."

Innocence wronged

In the right hands that was a story which might have demolished the case for Lizzie Borden. But when Alice Russell spoke at the trial, there had been a dramatic volte-face in public opinion on the Borden case. Instead of the mob howling for her blood—as it had been in the murder week—all America was now loving Lizzie Borden. From every part of the country flowers poured in for her. Suddenly, she was innocence wronged, a maiden cruelly mistreated, a demure and heartbroken girl racked by the State on a charge that tried to make her a fiend.

The burnt dress? It couldn't possibly have been stained with blood, snorted her supporters, because no two people could agree what dress Lizzie wore on the day of the tragedy. The dress that *she* said she wore was unstained and unmarked.

By now Lizzie had a lot more going for her. The considerable fortune she had inherited from her dead father enabled her to brief the best lawyer in Massachusetts. He was George Robinson, a former Governor of the State. One of the three judges, Judge Dewey, was a man whom Robinson had elevated to the bench when he was Governor; Dewey, therefore, owed the defence lawyer a

LIZZIE'S STORY relied a great deal on her whereabouts at the time of the killings. Right: the exact location of the house and (inset) the Borden barn.

138

debt and he was aware of it.

It was certainly lucky for Lizzie that Judge Dewey refused to hear evidence about her attempts to buy prussic acid before the murders, citing it as irrelevant. And when, with a nice sense of timing, Lizzie fainted half-way through her trial, the emotional newspaper-reading public cried hysterically for an end to her torture.

They got their wish. The court shook with applause when, after a ten-day trial, Lizzie was found not guilty. That night she was guest of honour at a celebration party and laughed joyfully over the newspaper cuttings of the trial that friends had kept for her.

If Lizzie was innocent, then who was the guilty party? No one else was ever arrested for the Borden murders; indeed, no one else was ever seriously suspected. Was there ever such a person who, in the words of one of Lizzie's lawyers, had "a heart that was as black as hell"?

Peculiar turns

Who was the agitated young man seen outside the house? Did he, or someone else, dart in from the street that morning, kill Abby, strike again and make off undetected?

The idea of an intruder stumbles and collapses under a mass of facts. The front door was double locked and bolted all that morning. Even if the intruder had overcome that obstacle, it would have been impossible, in the small house, for him to have gone unnoticed by Lizzie.

Overwhelmingly the evidence points to the crime having been committed by someone who was alone in the house that morning – someone who could have only been Lizzie. What could have happened on the murder morning, says a modern American writer, Victoria Lincoln, was that Lizzie could have had an attack of temporal epilepsy – the medical term for what her family called her "peculiar turns".

They occurred in Lizzie, asserts Miss Lincoln in her book *A Private Disgrace*, about four times a year and were accompanied by menstruation. She goes on: "During a seizure, there are periods of automatic action which the patient in some cases forgets completely and in others remembers only dimly."

There was, suggests Miss Lincoln, a catalyst for the double tragedy of August 4. It was the note delivered to 92 Second Street just before Abby died. Uncle John Morse had come to stay at the Borden house to help arrange the transfer of another property to Abby at the bank on the morning of the murder. Naturally enough, the last person anyone wanted to tell about the transfer was temperamental Lizzie.

If Lizzie killed twice that day in an epileptic fit and believed that she did not

LIZZIE BORDEN.   EMMA BORDEN.   REV. MR. BUCK.   MRS. C. J. HOLMES.   MR. C. J. HOLMES.
THE PRISONER AND HER FRIENDS IN COURT.

THE TRIAL . . . Lizzie was lucky to have George Robinson, seen at work (below and right), as her defence attorney. He was both a good lawyer and a friend of Judge Dewey.

kill, it would be one way of explaining her peculiar post-trial conduct. For although she then had wealth enough to keep several permanent servants, and enjoyed travelling, she went right on living in Fall River until the day she died.

But it was a different Lizzie Borden. She gave up church-going and quickly lost all the local popularity she had won during her ordeal. At first Emma lived with her; then, as the years passed, they became incompatible and Emma left.

Lizzie lived on alone except for her servants in a big, old-fashioned house she had bought in a better part of the textile town—a lonely, elderly woman about whom other elderly folk still whispered to the new, unknowing generation, when she passed in the street.

There, in 1927, she died; and there, in the town's graveyard, she was laid to rest. Her body lies in the family lot—along with Andrew and Abby. The family which made violent and lethal war within itself is now together in peace.

PRESERVED for all time, the murder exhibits can be seen by the public and include the two battered skulls of Andrew and Abby Borden and also the axe.

POSITIVELY NO PHOTOGRAPHS

A MYSTERIOUS TELEPHONE CALL

William Wallace

The ringing telephone shatters the studious evening silence of the club. The captain takes a message for Mr. Wallace from a mysterious Manxman. The call turns out to be historic . . . and deadly.

THE TELEPHONE call that was to end Julia Wallace's life was made to the Liverpool Central Chess Club at 7.20 on a cold, rainy evening in January 1931. The caller—a man whose voice was later described as "gruff but ordinary"—asked if he could speak to one of the club members—William Herbert Wallace, a quiet, nervous, short-sighted person who worked for the Prudential Assurance Company.

Although Wallace had put his name down to play in the Second Class Championship that night, he hadn't yet reached the club—which met twice a week at the City Café in North John Street. The club captain, Samuel Beattie, spoke to the caller, and so took part in what was to become one of the most controversial conversations in British legal history.

After stating who he was, Beattie told the stranger that Wallace would be arriving shortly. "I suggest you ring back later," he said helpfully. There was a pause, followed by the caller's agitated rejection of the idea.

"Oh, no, I couldn't do that," he protested. "I'm too busy. I have my girl's twenty-first birthday on, and I want to do something for her in the way of business. I want to see Mr. Wallace on a matter of business. Will you ask him to come round to my place tomorrow evening at 7.30?"

Beattie agreed to pass the message on, and asked for the man's name and address. "The name's Qualtrough," the caller replied, "and I live at 25 Menlove Gardens East, Mossley Hill."

Although an unusual name in other parts of England, Qualtrough was fairly common in Liverpool and the nearby Isle of Man. It was, in fact, a Manx name, but even so Beattie asked the man to spell it out for him. He wrote it on the back of a used envelope, and gave this to Wallace when the insurance agent entered the club half-an-hour later.

"I belong to Liverpool"

At first the 52-year-old Wallace denied knowing anyone called Qualtrough. He also appeared doubtful as to the exact location of Menlove Gardens East—but imagined it must be somewhere in the vicinity of Menlove Avenue. Beattie advised him to look the street up in a directory, but Wallace scoffed at the idea. "I belong to Liverpool," he said airily. "Besides I've a perfectly good tongue in my head. I can make inquiries once I get to the district."

After that the subject of Qualtrough, his daughter's party, and the business he apparently intended putting Wallace's way was forgotten about. Chess ruled the remainder of the evening, and Wallace—who was considered a sound but uninspired player—won his round against a fellow member named McCartney.

He left for his home at 29 Wolverton Street, Anfield in what for him were high spirits. Slow to anger and difficult to please, Wallace was regarded as something of a mystery man. With his steel-rimmed glasses, sparse grey hair, and ragged moustache, he looked like a typical insurance salesman.

But despite his conventional appearance—bowler hat, high white collar, dun-coloured mackintosh—he did not fit in or mingle well with other people. Perhaps his height (he was a slender six feet two inches) had something to do with it; he always seemed anxious, awkward, willing to please yet pathetically failing to do so.

Added to this, he thought himself to be a cut or two above the men and women whom he visited in his job (he earned £260 per annum) and from whom he collected insurance contributions.

As a young man he had spent some years working as a clerk and then an advertising manager in India and Shanghai. He was interested in the violin, in chemistry, and was something of an amateur philosopher. He had studied the works of the Roman emperor Marcus Aurelius, and tried to conduct his life on the principles of the Stoics.

Because of this he believed that misfortunes happened only to the wicked. And no one—despite the misfortune that was to strike her the following evening—could have seemed less wicked than Wallace's shy, music-loving wife, Julia.

A childless couple, the Wallaces were noted for their utter devotion to each other. Their neighbours in the terraced cul-de-sac in which they lived had never known them to quarrel or even raise their voices. They played musical duets together, went on weekend rambles in the Cheshire and Lancashire countryside, and shared a deep, but mainly uncreative interest in the arts.

If the Wallaces had a common fault, it was that they were *too* loving, *too* placid, *too* ultra-respectable. At nights when her husband was called out on business, 50-year-old Julia contented herself with daubing one of her somewhat insipid water-colours, or playing nocturnes on the piano.

A not unattractive woman with greying auburn hair, she was not unduly put out when Wallace left the house at a quarter-to-seven on the evening of Tuesday, January 20. He had eaten his usual substantial high tea, and looked as well—or as ill—as he ever did.

A sallow complexion

His years in what he sometimes called the "Mysterious Orient" had left him with a sallow complexion which was not improved by a chronic kidney ailment. He was prone to headaches and severe colds, and Julia told him to wrap up well as the night was wet and chilly.

He did as she counselled, pecked her goodbye on the cheek, and promised to be home as soon as his business with Qualtrough was concluded. Julia returned to her domestic chores—she always kept their two-storey, red-brick house spotless—and Wallace proceeded by tram and foot through the drizzle that blanketed Anfield and Mossley Hill.

Up until that time the worst that could be said about Wallace was that he had been born middle-aged. But before the night was out suspicion of murder was to be raised against him, and within a fortnight he was to be arrested and charged with the brutal slaying of his wife.

Yet to the people he encountered on that rainy night, he was no more than a shabby rather forlorn figure looking for a man and a street which just didn't seem to exist. There was no one called Qualtrough living in the district, and although there was a Menlove Gardens West (and

GRUFF BUT ORDINARY, the voice from the call box leaves a name, Qualtrough – and a non-existent address – with the Liverpool Central Chess Club. For Julia Wallace, the telephone call signals a violent death.

Jonathan Goodman

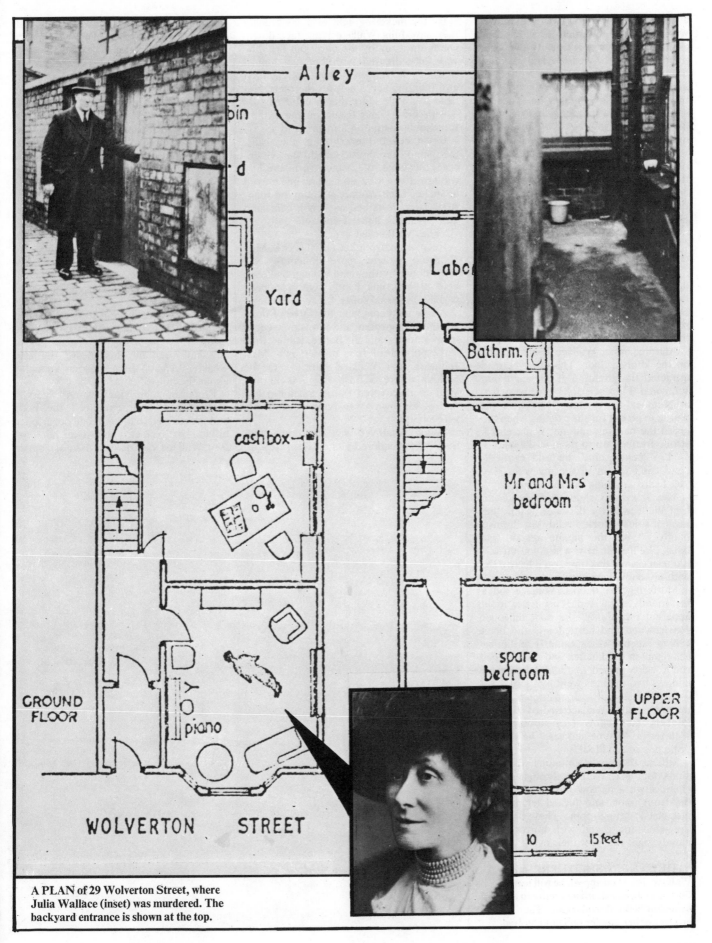

Alley

bin

d

Yard

Labo

Bathrm.

cash box →

Mr and Mrs'
bedroom

B Y

piano

spare
bedroom

GROUND
FLOOR

UPPER
FLOOR

WOLVERTON   STREET

10   15 feet

A PLAN of 29 Wolverton Street, where
Julia Wallace (inset) was murdered. The
backyard entrance is shown at the top.

a house in it numbered twenty-five) there was no Menlove Gardens East.

In all, Wallace spent nearly two hours roaming through Mossley Hill, asking a tram conductor, a policeman, and the manageress of a newsagent's shop where the "missing" street might be. Those he spoke to—and who later gave evidence at his trial—were impressed by his earnestness, his bewilderment, his persistence.

Finally, frustrated and depressed, he returned to the drab concrete corridor that was Wolverton Street. It was shortly before nine o'clock when, shivering from the cold, he hurried up to his front door. He was eager to be inside, take his damp clothes off, and relax by the fire.

Around to the back lane

He took out his key and fitted it into the maroon-painted front door. He tried to turn the key but the door wouldn't open. Surprised rather than worried, he walked round to the back lane where the door there also refused to budge.

Alarmed now, Wallace began to bang on the kitchen door. The noise he made attracted the attention of his neighbours, John and Florence Johnston, who lived at Number Thirty-One. They were preparing to go out for the evening when they heard the banging and met Wallace as he strode fretfully up to them in the lane.

"I'm locked out," he said excitedly, "and can't get in to see my wife. Have you heard anything unusual tonight?"

The Johnstons shook their heads and told Wallace to try the door again. "Perhaps it's just stuck," said Mr. Johnson bluffly. "Give the handle a good hard twist. We'll wait here while you do it. If it doesn't work this time, we'll have a shot with my back door key."

Muttering his thanks, Wallace did as his friends suggested. This time, to his apparent incredulity, the door did open. He frowned and hurried into the house calling out his wife's name. The dimmed gas-lights in the kitchen and upstairs bedroom were turned up, and a seemingly endless two minutes went by.

Then, just as the Johnstons were becoming uneasy, Wallace rushed out of the kitchen, his yellow face turning white with terror. "Come and see," he shouted. "She has been killed!"

Stifling their own emotions, the Johnstons followed Wallace through the kitchen, down a narrow passage leading to the front door, and turned left into the little-used sitting-room. They halted in the jamb and gazed with horror at the bloody sight that met their eyes.

"THEY'VE FINISHED HER!" cries Wallace. Freed on appeal, he will leave the site of Julia's death and retire to a bungalow in the Wirral (right). The mystery of her murder remains unsolved.

By the flickering light of a gas bracket they saw Julia Wallace lying face downwards on a rug by the burnt-out fire. She was fully dressed with her feet almost touching the fender, her outstretched left arm pointing accusingly to the door. Her head was little more than a battered pulp—with brains and tissue oozing from a three-inch wound on her forehead.

Blood covered everything: the walls, the piano, the music-stand, the violin-case, the table, the aspidistra in the bay window. For a long moment no one moved or spoke. Then Wallace—whom the Johnstons later described as "cool, calm and quiet"—shook himself and said dully:

"They've finished her."

Recovering from her initial shock, Mrs. Johnston showed more humanity. She knelt down by the dead woman and took hold of her rigid hand. "Oh, you poor darling," she said softly. "You poor dear."

A few moments later the three of them left the sitting-room, and Johnston went to fetch a doctor and the police. Rather than leave poor dead Julia on her own, Mrs. Johnston and Wallace returned to the parlour where a fresh fire was lit and Wallace discovered that a mackintosh—one of his own—was lying beneath his wife's body.

"Why, whatever was she doing with that?" he wondered aloud. Then, resuming his earlier lament, he intoned: "They've finished her. They've finished her. Look at the brains!"

Within half-an-hour of this, 29 Wolverton Street had more visitors inside its walls than the Wallaces had invited in all the sixteen years they had lived there. Police scoured the building from coal-house to back bedroom. No evidence was found that directly incriminated Wallace, although an iron bar used for poking the fire was noted to be missing.

Hypnotized by blood

It was obvious that the residence had not been broken into or burgled, and that whoever had slain Julia Wallace that night had been on friendly terms with her. No woman of her temperament and disposition would have allowed a stranger into the house, let alone the hallowed front sitting-room.

Wallace, looking on in stunned dismay, seemed to be hypnotized by the blood and disorder. "Julia would have gone mad if she had seen all this mess," he said weakly. "And all these strangers knocking about the house."

Professor John MacFall, an expert in forensic medicine, examined the body and proclaimed that death had occurred at around six o'clock—almost an hour before Wallace had said he had set out in

146

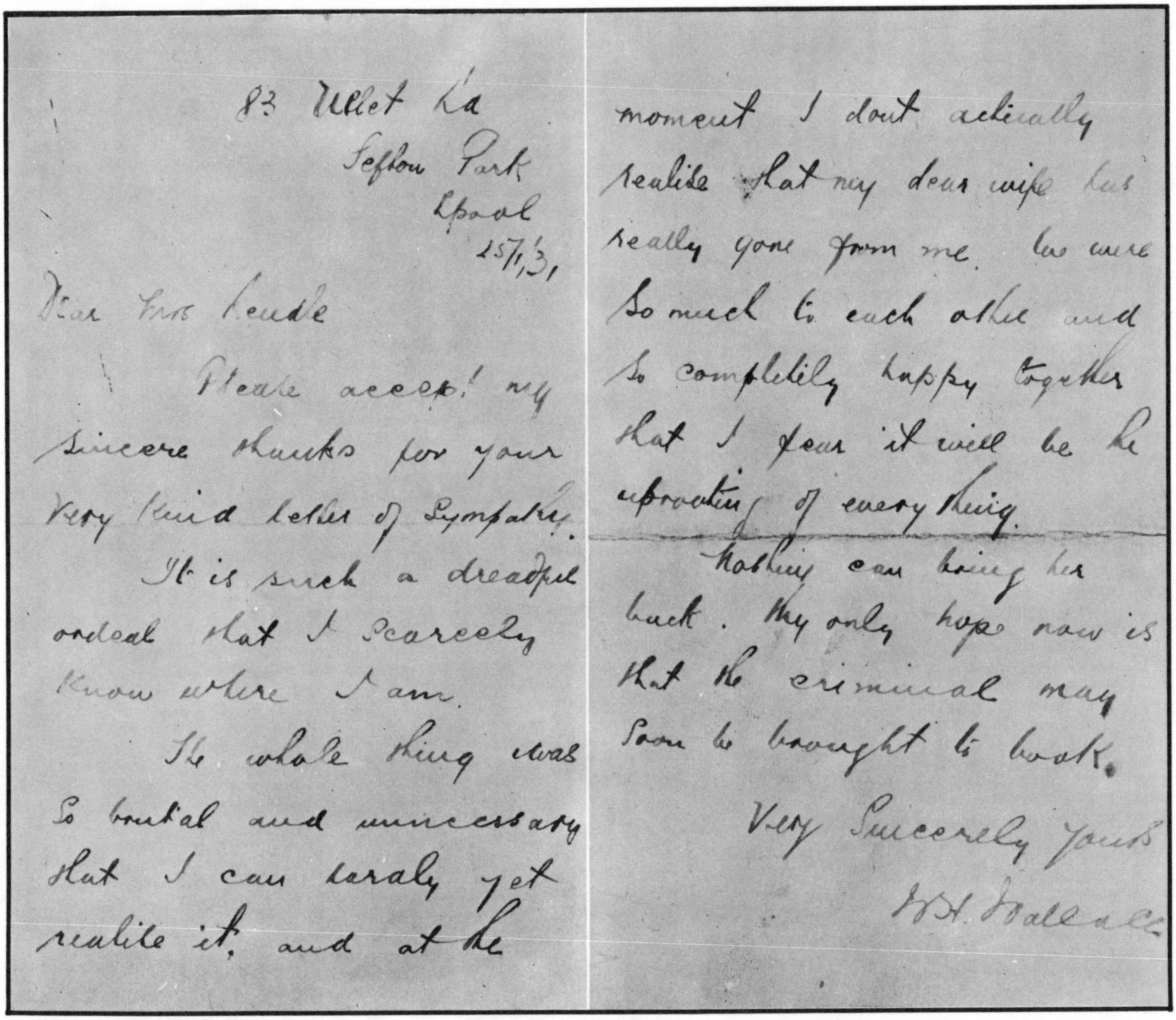

83 Ullet La
Sefton Park
Lpool
25/1/31

Dear Mrs Peudle

Please accept my sincere thanks for your very kind letter of Sympathy.

It is such a dreadful ordeal that I scarcely know where I am.

The whole thing was so brutal and unnecessary that I can scarcely yet realise it, and at the moment I dont actually realise that my dear wife has really gone from me. We were so much to each other and so completely happy together that I fear it will be the uprooting of everything.

Nothing can bring her back. My only hope now is that the criminal may soon be brought to book.

Very Sincerely Yours
W.H. Wallace

---

search of Qualtrough. MacFall was also suspicious of the way Wallace behaved while the police ransacked the rooms.

"He was too quiet, too collected, for a person whose wife had been killed in the way described," said the professor later. "He was not nearly so affected as I was myself. . . . He was smoking cigarettes most of the time.

"Whilst I was in the room, examining the body and the blood, he came in smoking a cigarette, and he leant over in front of the sideboard and flipped the ash into a bowl upon the sideboard. It struck me at the time as being unnatural."

For the next few days the police under Detective-Inspector Herbert Gold, of Liverpool City Police, made their way down one blind alley after another. Each time their feet were re-directed towards Wallace – who at least was flesh and blood, and not a mere spectre like the elusive and presumably non-existent Qualtrough.

SINCERE GRIEF for his wife was shown by Wallace in letters to friends.

Although there was no evidence against him, though some local suspicion, Wallace was charged with the murder of his wife. "What can I say," he answered, "except that I am absolutely innocent?"

Not a single spot of blood

Wallace's trial was held at Liverpool Spring Assizes on April 22, 1931. Witnesses recalled and repeated his now celebrated alibi concerning Qualtrough, and much was made of the fact that Wallace – if indeed he had committed the crime – had done so without getting a single spot of blood on his clothing.

To the defence this seemed a clear sign of his innocence, but the prosecuting attorney, Edward Hemmerde, K.C., took this as proof of Wallace's guilt. "One of the most famous criminal trials," he asserted, "was of a man who committed a crime when he was naked.

"A man might perfectly well commit a crime wearing a raincoat . . . and come down, when he is just going to do this, wearing nothing on which blood could fasten, and . . . he might get away, leaving the raincoat there, and go and perform the necessary thorough washing."

Despite a favourable summing-up by the judge, Mr. Justice Wright, the jury of ten men and two women brought in a verdict of "guilty". Wallace, still protesting his innocence, was condemned to death, and then went on to make startling legal history.

An appeal was lodged before the Court of Criminal Appeal, which, after deliberating from May 18-19, quashed the verdict and made Wallace a free man again. This was the first time since the Court had been established in 1907 that the Appeal Judges had decided that a British jury had made a grave – but not irrevocable – mistake.

HIS COLLEAGUES at the Prudential rallied to Wallace's support. He is seen here, with his brother, being congratulated after his acquital.

Wallace — who died in February 1933 of his long-standing kidney complaint — returned to Wolverton Street and to an office job with the head Liverpool office of the Prudential. Scandalmongers and his rapidly decreasing health, however, forced him to retire to the Wirral countryside, where he fitted an electric switch and lamp on the porch of his house.

"The position of the switch is known only to myself," he declared, "and before I open my door I touch it, so that the house, outside and inside, and every recess where an assailant may be lurking, is lit up.

"The figure which one day I fully expect to see crouching and ready to strike will be that of Qualtrough, the man who murdered my wife."

JOHN BULL
THE MAN THEY
DID NOT HANG

THE BLACK DAHLIA

Elizabeth Short

From the top of her raven-tressed head to the tip of her black patent shoes, her sombre sexiness was indelibly blazoned on the soul of any man who knew her. Miss Elizabeth Short knew a lot of men. At least one man too many.

UPI

ON the chill, blustery morning of January 15, 1947, a sobbing, hysterical woman frantically flagged down a passing police patrol car in a suburb of Los Angeles, California, and screeched out an incoherent stream of words. When the patrol car crew had managed to calm her a little she pointed with shaking fingers to a nearby, garbage-strewn vacant lot. The police car leapt forward, turned on to the lot, and there the officers immediately understood the woman's behaviour.

What she had seen, and what the policemen now saw for themselves, were the nude halves of the corpse of a young woman. The body had been crudely cut in two at the waist, and each half tied with ropes. Deep into one thigh the killer had carved the initials "BD".

It was a sickening sight, but the repulsion which the hardened police officers felt was deepened when pathologists examined the body in detail and found that it had been revoltingly mutilated. What was even more hideous was the fact that most of the injuries had been

A SICKENING SIGHT met the horrified gaze of the police: Elizabeth Short's hideously mutilated body. Her injuries had obviously been inflicted while she was still alive. Her mother (below) had often been unable to cope with her young family. . . .

inflicted before death—probably while the victim was suspended, head down, by ropes or wires. She might, indeed, have been still living when her murderer began the incisions to sever her body.

It was clear that the girl had not been long dead when the passing woman came across the dismembered corpse. The immediate theory was that she had been killed somewhere nearby, and the remains tipped on to the lot from a car. The police were puzzled by the incised initials "BD", and there were no obvious clues to identification. But, as a matter of routine, the police took fingerprints from the few fingers that had escaped mutilation. These were sent to the Federal Bureau of Investigation in Washington, D.C., for checking against the millions on file.

The Los Angeles police knew only too well that the print check was an outside chance. To their satisfaction, a message came back from the F.B.I. within hours stating that the prints matched those on file for 22-year-old Elizabeth Short, born in the small town of Medford, Massachusetts, who had a police record as a juvenile delinquent.

Her mother, Mrs. Phoebe Short—who was separated from her husband—was then traced. She had the task of trying to identify the body. So thoroughly had the killer carried out his work that she was

151

La Times

unable positively to say that what she looked upon had once been her daughter. But she *was* able to produce a letter which Elizabeth had written to her a few weeks before from San Diego. Detectives went immediately to the address and learnt that Elizabeth Short had left there six days before the discovery of her body. Since she had taken no luggage with her, it seemed as though she had intended to return, and had gone to Los Angeles for no more than a brief visit.

Slowly the police built up a picture of Elizabeth Short, her life and her background. One fact is beyond any doubt and dominated all others: she had been tall, graceful, and exceedingly beautiful, with milk-white skin and a mass of raven hair. She was the kind of girl upon whom all men's eyes focused when she walked into a room; if ever any girl was instantly desirable, that girl was Elizabeth.

Great Depression

However, there was little of beauty in her background. She had grown up in an unhappy home and was only six when, in 1931, her parents separated and her father moved to California. He took one child of the family with him, and left his wife to look after Elizabeth and their other three children.

It was the period of the Great Depression, and Phoebe Short often found herself unequal to both making a living and bringing up the youngsters.

Often alone and miserable, without much close contact with her mother, Elizabeth's one main ambition began to grow into an obsession: the moment she was old enough she would leave home

THE TIDE TURNED in Elizabeth Short's life when she met Army Air Force Major Matt M. Gordon Jr. (above). But he was killed in action . . . and the Black Dahlia was born. Many men felt driven to confess to the spectacular murder: six of them are shown opposite; one (bottom right) was arrested but later released.

and make a new and independent life for herself.

The opportunity came in 1942, when she was not yet 17. With the United States engulfed by world war there were plenty of job opportunities for young women. Elizabeth decided to seize one of those opportunities for herself—but as far away and as different from Medford as she could make it. She chose Miami.

It seemed to her that the "sun city" was tailor-made for her ambitions. She was already well aware of her physical appeal; there was an air base near Miami, and at week-ends there was no shortage of young servicemen enjoying their brief leaves on the Florida beaches.

The only information the police could obtain about her life in Miami was sketchy—but it was enough to show that it had finally added to her unhappiness and loneliness. She had taken a job as a waitress. For a time it seemed that she had found her hoped-for young lover. But the romance languished when the man went off to the war. Then, while she worked and counted the days to his return, he died on a distant battlefield.

It was a blow from which Elizabeth Short did not recover. She took to drink, and she took to men—any men. She became so promiscuous that word of her

readiness to go to bed with anyone who would buy her drinks and a meal swiftly spread around the Miami bars.

Eventually, almost inevitably, the police caught up with her, and, found drinking with soldiers in a café, she was arrested as a juvenile delinquent. The authorities decided that, since she was in need of care and protection, she should be sent home to her mother. They gave her a rail ticket to Medford and a small amount of subsistence money and put her on a train.

She stayed aboard the train as far as Santa Barbara, and there she got off and found herself another job as a waitress. In the distraction of war no one had checked to see if she had reached home and the custody of her mother, and Elizabeth stayed in Santa Barbara until 1944. But once more, as though she were singled out to be one of nature's chosen victims, the fates were unmerciful to her.

Having got over her first sad love affair, she formed an attachment for an Army Air Force major. It seemed like the turning of the disastrous tide of her life, and, as though to confirm her own good intentions, she returned, in 1944, to her mother in Medford, to await the major's homecoming from the Far East and the marriage which was to follow.

Home was no happier than it had been in the past, but this time, at least, she could look forward to settling down to a new life with a husband to whom she could devote herself. On the morning of August 22, 1946, when it seemed so certain that her major would soon be back from the war, the front-door bell rang and Elizabeth answered it. A taciturn postal messenger handed her a telegram addressed to herself. Excitedly she tore it open. The message inside was from the mother of the major. Cryptically it said: "Have received notification from War Department my son, Matt, killed in air crash."

Zombie-like trance

In a zombie-like trance, Elizabeth screwed the telegram into a tight-knit ball of paper, tossed it aside and went straight to the nearest bar. There she drank until her lovely grey-green eyes were cloudy with alcohol and her tall, elegant frame sagged over the edge of the bar. The barman became embarrassed by her tipsy monologue in which she declared: "Some people have a hex on them, y'know what I mean? Some people can't never get the breaks, and nuthin' they can do will give 'em the breaks. Y'listenin' me, now? Why'd things happen to me, this way?"

The next day she decided that there was nothing to keep her in Medford any longer, and she set out for California, this time to the place for which her

outpoise and stunning looks seemed so perfectly fitted: Hollywood. The major studios had not yet been overtaken by the TV revolution, and the feeling in the movie capital was that business would be as it always had been, booming. Every day there were calls for "extras", and Elizabeth Short joined the casting lines successfully. For her there was regular and reasonably well-paid work.

She had heard that there were producers and casting directors who were prepared to give a photogenic girl a chance in pictures, for "a consideration". Elizabeth was only too ready to oblige, especially when she was sufficiently anaesthetized with liquor, and she devoted her spare time to going to bed with almost all men who invited her, even though most had no more than tenuous associations with the studios.

Black stockings

She had learned that in Hollywood it was as well to establish some kind of particular identity. Her method was to match her raven hair by dressing totally in black: black sheath dresses, black stockings and underwear, black shoes, even a jet black ring. In its own strange way the ploy worked, and someone named her the "Black Dahlia". The title stuck, she used it herself, and few men who passed in and out of her life were unaware of it.

She took, and discarded, lovers the way most women accept and discard clothing fashions. Some of them she lived with for brief periods. With one man she formed something more than a passing attachment, for in the few effects found after her death was a note addressed to her which read: "I might be gone before you arrive. You say in your letter that you want us to be good friends. But from your wire you seemed to want more than that. Are you really sure what you want? Why not pause and consider just what your

coming out here would amount to? You've got to be more practical these days."

No one would ever discover where "out here" was, and certainly one thing that the Black Dahlia seemed incapable of achieving was practical behaviour. In any case, as the Hollywood movie empire declined into an era of uncertainty it was clear that stardom was not waiting around the corner for Elizabeth Short, and, no longer earning anything like a regular income, she drifted south to San Diego and resumed her career as a waitress.

Her drinking continued unabated, and men pursued her as readily as ever. One man with whom she established a brief liaison was tall and red-haired and reported as having been seen with the Black Dahlia in a San Diego bus station a few days before her dismembered body was discovered. The man was traced by the police and admitted that he had been with the girl. He declared that he went on a drunken binge with her, took her afterwards to a motel and then drove her to the Biltmore Hotel in Los Angeles.

"She said she was going to meet her sister at the hotel," the man told detectives. "I left her there. That was the last time I saw her, and I have no idea what happened to her afterwards or where she went." The police accepted his story; in any case, the man was able to prove that, at the time when the Black Dahlia must have been murdered, he and his wife were visiting friends.

For the authorities the trail set by Elizabeth Short ended at the front entrance to the Biltmore Hotel. She had become lost in the city sprawl; somewhere she met the man who was to so brutally slay her. Her clothing had totally disappeared, and extensive searches—including examinations of drains and sewers—failed to produce any garment that could be traced to her.

From the moment that the news of the severed corpse discovery appeared in the newspapers the police were overwhelmed by supposed "confessions" and reports of suspects. The anxiety of so many men to "confess" to such a deed said a great deal about individual mental states, but told the police nothing that was relevant to their inquiries. One man, at least, had an unusual motive for presenting himself as the killer. His wife, he said, had deserted him. He hoped that if he could make himself notorious, and have his picture in the papers, she might return.

Hysterical cases

One person sent the police a message, composed of pasted-up letters cut from a magazine, offering to meet them and provide them with information. He signed himself "Black Dahlia Avenger". Detectives waited at the proposed rendezvous but no one turned up. One woman walked into a police station and announced: "The Black Dahlia stole my man, so I killed her and cut her up."

Tired-eyed but patient officers chatted to the eager woman, and discreetly mentioned one or two facts about the murdered girl's corpse that could only have been known to the killer. From the woman's response, it was clear that she was no more than another hysterical case.

In the midst of such confessions there was one curious and baffling event. A Los Angeles newspaper received a note which read: "Here are Dahlia's belongings. Letter will follow." Enclosed with the note were Elizabeth Short's birth certificate, address book, and social security card. No letter followed and fingerprints, clearly visible on the envelope and note, were forwarded to the F.B.I.—but they matched none on file. Detectives spent long days searching out men named in the address book, but none of the interviews produced a positive murder lead.

Calls promising information were made to the Los Angeles police from all parts of the United States, and some of the

CURIOUS AND BAFFLING, this note came with Elizabeth's address book, but one page was missing. No letter ever followed.

UPI

callers were asked to appear in person. But officers discovered nothing of value.

One development, however, looked promising. U.S. army investigators arrested a 29-year-old corporal, just back from 42 days' leave, who had talked loudly and convincingly about having known the Black Dahlia, and having been with her a few days before her body was found. There were bloodstains on his clothing and, in his locker, newspaper clippings about the murder. He seemed to possess a lot of circumstantial evidence about some of the injuries to the body, and he insisted: "When I get drunk I get rough with women." However, on closer examination, he, too, was found to be an unbalanced personality and recommended for psychiatric treatment.

The gory facts

Despite all the time and energy that the police spent on such confessions, they were helped by one important factor in the case: some of the mutilations of the body were so foul that no newspaper had written about them in any detail. This served in eliminating false confessions, since it was clear that none of the would-be "murderers" knew the full, gory facts.

As a variation on the theme of most of the confessions, one man later came forward and announced that, although he

THE MYSTERY surrounding her death has helped keep alive the memory of the Black Dahlia: this beautiful young victim who seemed so destined for suffering.

had not murdered the girl, he *had* helped to dismember her body. The murderer, he said, was a friend of his. He did not, or could not, identify him—and, as in other offers of "information", his statements did not conform to the facts known only to the police.

Almost certainly someone, somewhere in Los Angeles, knew the identity of the killer. The police considered it hardly credible that he could have committed such an atrocious crime without leaving some clues behind. The killing and mutilation might have taken place in a deserted warehouse, or some remote building—and yet there was no evidence of the girl being seen with a man just before her death. It seemed unlikely that she might have gone to meet her end, in a place conveniently designed for it, without even being observed by a passer by.

In fact two bartenders reported having served her with drinks, two or three days before her death, when she was in the company of a woman. These reports gave rise to rumours that she had been murdered by a lesbian acquaintance. But there was neither direct evidence nor

even remote indications to suggest that she was homosexual.

Then there were those who claimed that the murder was the work of a madman driven by motives similar to those of Jack the Ripper—the unidentified nineteenth-century killer who disposed of prostitutes in the East End of London. Perhaps, they argued, the Black Dahlia murder was a case of a man wishing to rid the world of a woman of easy virtue.

The bald fact was that the killer was never found, and his motives, therefore, remain undisclosed. For some time the police inquiries continued and—for a long time after—the "confessions" flowed in.

These—and the nickname she was given—have kept alive the memory of the young victim who seemed so destined for suffering. The most important is that her murderer knew her, and had probably been out with her several times before.

From the address book, sent anonymously to the local newspaper, one page was missing. It had apparently been removed because it contained the name and address of the Black Dahlia's "friend", who turned out to be her murderer. Was the person who posted that book to the newspaper the killer himself? The odds are that it was. And that, having made his "gesture", he turned his attention to other women—and perhaps other victims.

Index

Abbreviations: p=photograph or illustration

Acknowledgments

Front of jacket: Syndication International/Popperfoto/Radio Times Hulton Picture Library
Back of jacket: AP/Quartet, Syndication International, Radio Times Hulton Picture Library

Q

Qualtrough 144, 147, 148
quicklime: disposal of body in 80

R

radio: first use in catching
    murderer 79
Randle, Deputy-Sheriff Clarence
    70
Reese, Marilyn, *see* Sheppard,
    Marilyn
Relf, Ivor 18
religious upbringing: leading to
    murder 66–8
Remy, Madame 52
Reuter, Ida 102p
    murder of 103
revolver: .38 Webley 62p
Roberts, G. D. 23, 24, 26, 29
Robinson, George 138, 141p
Robinson, John Philip (alias) 79
Robinson, Master (alias) 79
Rose, Dr 108
Russell, Miss Alice 138

S

sacrifice: victim left like 9
Saddleworth Moor, near
    Manchester 119, 120p
sadism:
    early signs of 55
    factors fostering 106–8
Sagan, Françoise: *Landru* 54
Savage, Joseph 99
schizophrenic 34, 38
Schottke, Sergeant Robert 90–1
Schoub, Dr Ina 28p, 30
Schulte, Gertrude 103p, 103
Scrutton, Mr Justice 40, 44, 46
Seabrook, Martha, *see* Beck, Mrs
    Martha
Seabrook, William 75
Sebring, Jay: murder of 129
Segret, Fernande 53–4
Selway, Captain, M.C. (alias) 16
Shaw, George Bernard 9
Shawcross, Sir Hartley 66
Sheppard, Ariane 90, 92p, 92
Sheppard, Marilyn (née Reese)
    86p, 87
    murder of 87–9, 88p
Sheppard, Dr Richard (Jr) 86,
    87, 89
Sheppard, Dr Richard Allen 86,
    87, 90p
Sheppard, Dr Samuel 85–92, 85p,
    86p, 89p, 90p, 92p
Sheppard, Stephen 86
Sherman, Russ 90, 91

Shinn, Daye 127
Short, Elizabeth 150p, 152p
    murder of 149–56
Short, Mrs Phoebe 151–2, 151p
Simpson, Dr Keith 15
Sing Sing Prison 76
Sioli, Professor 108
skulls: as exhibits 106, 142p
Slesers, Anna 32p
    murder of 33–4, 38
Slesers, Juris 33
Smith, David 119p, 119, 121, 122
Smith, F. E. 84
Smith, George Joseph 39p, 40–6,
    41p, 42p, 45p
Smith, Major Henry 11
Spellacy, Leo 90, 91
Spilsbury, Sir Bernard 44, 46, 46p
Star:
    letter to 9
    report in 8
Steadman, Mrs Marguerite 34
Steer, Frederick 26
Stone, Miss 80p
strangulation: features of 28, 30
Stride, Elizabeth: murder of
    8, 10
surgical instrument: as murder
    weapon 89, 91
suicide: resulting from trial verdict
    86
Sullivan, Bridget 137, 138
Sullivan, Mary: murder of 38
Sventonski, Charles 28
Symes, Detective-Inspector Shelley
    65
Symonds, Yvonne 15p, 16

T

Talty, Judge Francis 90, 91
tape recording: used in court 121
Tate, Sharon 125p
    murder of 125–33
Teare, Dr Donald 28
terminal act: in strangulation 28,
    30
Thompson, Mrs Jane: murder of
    70
Thornhill, Caroline Beatrice 40,
    41p
Thornton, Roy 56
Times, The: reports in 8, 9
torture: causing orgasm 106
'trademarks': left by murderer 34
Turner, Martha: murder of 8

U

urine: presence in cases of
    strangulation 28, 30

V

Vampire of Düsseldorf 101–8
vampire practice 62, 65, 66, 108
Van Houten, Leslie 129, 131p, 131
Versailles, Palais de Justice:
    trial 48
Victoria, Queen 8

W

Wallace, Julia: murder of 144–8
Wallace, William Herbert 143–8,
    148p
Walpole State Prison 38
Wardle Brook Avenue, No. 16,
    Hattersley: murder at 119,
    121, 122
Warren, Sir Charles 8, 9–10, 11
Watkins, Police Constable 10, 11
Watson, Charles 129, 129p, 131
weapons, murder 62p, 102p, 110p,
    112, 134–5p
Webley .38 revolver 62p
Webster, Professor James 30
Wehner, Dr 108
White, Dr William A. 98
Whitechapel Vigilance Committee
    10
Williams, Henry (alias) 40
Winchester Assize Court: trial at
    23–30
Wolverton Street, No. 29, Anfield:
    murder at 144–7
Wright, Mr Justice 147
Wyatt, Mrs Alice 15

Y

Young, Myrtle: murder of 70,
    73p